Attachment and Family Systems

THE FAMILY THERAPY AND COUNSELING SERIES

Consulting Editor

Jon Carlson, Psy.D., Ed.D.

Erdman and Caffery   *Attachment and Family Systems: Conceptual, Empirical, and Therapeutic Relatedness*

Attachment and Family Systems

Conceptual, Empirical, and Therapeutic Relatedness

Edited by

PHYLLIS ERDMAN
TOM CAFFERY

Brunner-Routledge
New York and Hove

Published in 2003 by
Brunner-Routledge
29 West 35th Street
New York, NY 10001
www.brunner-routledge.com

Published in Great Britain by
Brunner-Routledge
27 Church Road
Hove, East Sussex
BN3 2FA
www.brunner-routledge.co.uk

Brunner-Routledge is an imprint of the Taylor & Francis Group.
Printed in the United States of America on acid-free paper.

Cover Design: Daniel Sierra
Cover Photo: Corbis

10 9 8 7 6 5 4 3 2

Library of Congress Cataloging-in-Publication Data

Attachment and family systems : conceptual, empirical, and therapeutic relatedness /
Phyllis Erdman, Tom Caffery, (editors).
    p. cm.
    ISBN 1–58391–351–3
    1. Family psychotherapy. 2. Attachment behavior.   I. Erdman, Phyllis, 1949–
II. Caffery, Tom.
    RC488.5 .A885 2002
    616.89′156—dc21

                                                              2002005300

TO MY HUSBAND:
HOWARD, WHO IS MY SECURE BASE

TO MY FRIEND AND COLLEAGUE:
DR. RICHARD WATTS, WHO ALWAYS STANDS BY ME

—PHYLLIS ERDMAN

TO MY FAMILY:
CHRISTINE, TJ, AND SEAN, FOR THEIR LOVE AND SUPPORT

TO MY FRIENDS AND COLLEAGUES:
MARK, BOB, ANNA, JANE, ROBBY, AND JAN

AND TO MY MENTORS:
RICHARD MATHIS AND RON CRAWFORD, FOR THEIR SUPPORT AND
GUIDANCE

—TOM CAFFERY

SPECIAL THANKS TO THE AUTHORS OF THESE CHAPTERS:
THEY ARE TRULY THE LEADERS IN THE FIELD OF ATTACHMENT AND
FAMILY SYSTEMS

—PHYLLIS ERDMAN AND TOM CAFFERY

Contents

Contributors

Editors

Phyllis Erdman, Ph.D., Department of Counseling, Texas A&M University-Commerce, Commerce, Texas

Thomas Caffery Ed.D., Department of Human Services, Stephen F. Austin State University, Nacogdoches, Texas

Chapter Authors

Pamela C. Alexander, Ph.D., Department of Psychology, University of Maryland, College Park, Maryland

Marlene Best, University of Ottawa, Ontario, Canada

Ann Carns, Ed.D., Education Administration in Psychological Services, Southwest Texas State University, San Marcos, Texas (Retired)

Michael R. Carns, Ph.D., Education Administration in Psychological Services, Southwest Texas State University, San Marcos, Texas

Stacy Cretzmeyer, Ph.D., Women's Advocacy Center Counseling Services, Coastal Carolina University, Conway, South Carolina

Robin English, Round Rock ISD

Judith A. Feeney, Ph.D., School of Psychology, University of Queensland, Brisbane, Australia

Claire Worrell Haslam, Ph.D., Director of Counseling Services, Family Haven Crisis and Resource Center, Paris, Texas

Leslie L. Huling, Ph.D., Assistant Dean of Education, College of Education, Southwest Texas State University, San Marcos, Texas

Susan M. Johnson, Ph.D., Center for Psychological Services, University of Ottawa, Ontario, Canada, and Ottawa Couple and Family Institute

Susan K. Mackey, Ph.D., The Family Institute at Northwestern University, Evanston, Illinois

Sylvia A. Marotta, Ph.D., Department of Counseling/Human and Organizational Studies, The George Washington University, Washington, D.C.

Robert S. Marvin, Ph.D., Child-Parent Attachment Clinic, Department of Psychiatric Medicine, The University of Virginia, Charlottesville, Virginia

James McHale, Frances L. Hiatt School of Psychology, Clark University, Worcester, Massachusetts

Mary Carole Pistole, Ph.D., Department of Education Studies, Purdue University, West Lafayette, Indiana

Jean Talbot, Ph.D., Department of Psychiatry, Strong Behavioral Health Center, University of Rochester Medical Center, Rochester, New York

Stephanie Warner, M.A., University of Maryland

Foreword

If there is everything we wish to change in the child, we should first examine it and see whether it is not something that could better be changed in ourselves.

—Carl G. Jung

Those of us who work in daily clinical practice find no mystery in the merging of attachment and family systems theories. Of course we were taught that they are totally incompatible theories and we had to decide if we were a contemporary systems thinker or an outdated classical therapist. We began to see the world of our clients as if there was only one valid explanation. This became our method–of–origin (MOO). Although we acted as if what we saw was true, we really knew that there were many gaps and unexplainable phenomenon with our approach.

We all can see the importance of the context or system but we also understand the power of attachments to early caregivers. Most of us have realized that in order to help our clients it is necessary for us to merge these theories on our own.

Attachment theory appears to be at the root of all relationships. How we got along with our early caregivers tends to be the script we follow throughout our lives. Think of how you got along with your early caregivers. Was it safe? Was it smothering? Was it inconsistent? Was it unfair? Was it unpredictable and so forth? These early relationships probably are still present in your relationship with your partner as well as those with your children and other loved ones.

Family systems theory, on the other hand, describes the structures in which we live. The family system is certainly closely connected to the styles of attachment. By learning both theories and how they interrelate with one another, practitioners are armed with a new perspective and tools to make efficient yet positive interventions in the lives of the family members.

A book on attachment theory and family systems theory has been long overdue. In this volume both theories are explained along with their historical roots. The editors also provide opportunities to see these theories applied in a variety of settings.

In the fields of social and emotional development, attachment theory is the most widely accepted and researched. According to clinical literature and the affects of early parent child relations including troubled and abusive relationships, it seems to be well accepted. I am hopeful that armed with this knowledge, those with systems emphasis will become effective practitioners. I am delighted that Erdman and Caffery have taken the time to develop such a useful text.

JON CARLSON

Preface

Two thoughts occurred to us as we were developing the initial idea for this book, and those two thoughts remained with us throughout the process of publishing it. The first thought is that systems theory and attachment theory are so obviously conceptually linked. The second thought is that if this is so obvious, why are there not already books in print linking the clinical application of the two approaches? This book is a seminal work linking these two conceptually complementary theories—systems theory and attachment theory. Although Bowlby alluded to the systemic nature of attachment theory in his original work, the ongoing development of attachment theory has followed an individually oriented focus. The authors of the following chapters have written extensively in the fields of family therapy and attachment theory, and in their previous writings they have presented both conceptually based and empirically based research to support the complementary nature of these two theories; however, no one until now has combined the clinical and conceptual work of these authors into a single volume.

As you read the chapters in this book, it will become clear how the authors apply attachment theory within a systemic framework to a variety of life cycle transitional tasks and clinical issues. In chapter 1, Robert Marvin illustrates a view of attachment theory and research from the perspective of a family researcher and family therapist and presents his thoughts about future directions. In chapter 2, Jean Talbot and James McHale explore how family theory and research can broaden the way we conceptualize, within an attachment framework, how individuals develop their styles of affective coping.

Conceptualizing various life cycle transitions from an attachment–systemic perspective is important, and Stacy Cretzmeyer, Susan Mackey, Carole Pistole, Judy Feeney, and Susan Johnson and Marlene Best explore this idea in chapters 3 through 7. Chapters 3 and 4 illustrate the application of attachment theory in family counseling work with adolescents and how a secure attachment can provide the basis for developing differentiation in adolescence. Chapters 5, 6, and 7 focus on attachment-related issues in the context of adulthood, including intimate love relationships as well as those developed in the work place. In the last four chapters, Claire Haslam and Phyllis Erdman, Mike Carns, Sylvia Marotta, and Pamela Alexander and Stephanie Warner describe specific clinical applications of attachment theory, involving such issues as trauma and family violence.

We hope that after reading this book, both researchers and clinicians will be enlightened about the therapeutic value of applying attachment theory within a systemic framework, hence validating one of Bowlby's original propositions of attachment theory—that it is, indeed, systemic in nature.

PHYLLIS ERDMAN
TOM CAFFERY

PART 1

Theoretical Overview

CHAPTER 1

Implications of Attachment Research for the Field of Family Therapy

ROBERT S. MARVIN

A central feature of my concept of parenting [is] the provision by both parents of a secure base from which a child or and adolescent can make sorties into the outside world and to which he can return knowing for sure that he will be welcomed when he gets there, nourished physically and emotionally, comforted if distressed, reassured if frightened. In essence this role is one of being available, ready to respond when called upon to encourage and perhaps assist, but to intervene only when clearly necessary.
—John Bowlby, MD, *A Secure Base: Parent–Child Attachment and Healthy Human Development*

Over the past 15 years, there has been increasing interest in integrating the field of attachment theory and research with clinical assessment and intervention (e.g., Fonagy, 1999; Marvin, 1992; Marvin, Cooper, Hoffman, & Powell, 2000; Van den Boom, 1995; Lieberman & Zeanah, 1999). The two areas of clinical intervention most focused on are object relations therapy (Fonagy, 1999) and family rherapy (Marvin & Stewart, 1990; Byng-Hall, 1999). Both of these movements are in their preliminary stages, and both offer much promise. In the case of attachment research and family therapy, the excitement and motivation seem to be coming primarily from the family therapists.

In writing this chapter I have three main goals. First, I want to present a view of attachment theory and research from the perspective of a family researcher and family therapist. This will be a very personal view, somewhat different in focus from the work of most current attachment researchers. This personal view stems primarily from (a) my longstanding interest in the systemic nature of attachment theory, (b) the fact that my clinical orientation has always been a family systems model, and (c) my active involvement in developing attachment-based interventions for at-risk children and their families. My impression is that most practicing clinicians have an understanding of attachment theory and research that is limited to the individual child, or at most the child–parent dyad, rather than to the child or dyad as a subsystem of the larger family system. This limitation is understandable because most current research on attachment is focused on the child, or at most the child–parent dyad.

My second goal is to present examples, from the research and clinical work of my colleagues and myself, of interventions that do integrate these two fields. Third, I will end the chapter with some thoughts about future directions. As will become obvious, I do think an integration of attachment and family systems is both possible and promising. I also think, however, that the integration will require specialized tools and specialized training or collaboration. Although the school of family therapy I will focus on here is structural family therapy, I think the integration applies equally well to others, such as the "constructivist" and "psychoanalytic" schools of family therapy.

ATTACHMENT THEORY AND FAMILY SYSTEMS THEORY: POINTS OF CONVERGENCE AND DIVERGENCE

Interestingly, the founder of attachment theory himself, John Bowlby, always espoused a family systems perspective. From early in his career, Bowlby was struck with the fact that children develop within an extended family system and that our understanding of relationship problems and our interventions should be viewed from that perspective. In fact, Bowlby (1949) wrote one of the first papers on family therapy. In it he suggested that the problems child guidance clinics faced actually reflected tensions with the overall family, that even very dysfunctional families have a strong drive to live together in a healthy way, and that working jointly with all family members was a procedure that held considerable hopes for successful intervention.

What turns out to be Bowlby's most important contribution was his desire to study these relationship problems within a truly scientific, empirical framework. In the late 1940s and early 1950s, Bowlby thought that family systems were too complex to study with the scientific methods then available, and he decided to take just the first step in this process (i.e., the study of parent–child dyadic relationships as a subset of larger family systems). Bowlby went on to develop the theory, and the Robinsons, H. R. Schaffer, Mary Ainsworth, and others provided the initial empirical validation for the theory.

Although Bowlby did not highly develop that part of his theory that would apply to family systems, systems theory was one of the two primary theories Bowlby used in developing attachment theory—the other being the field of ethology. In fact, he drew heavily from general systems theory, information theory, and cybernetics in developing what he eventually called his "Control Systems Theory of Attachment." Finally, toward the end of his life, Bowlby (1988) again placed strong emphasis on the child as developing within the family system and called for research on that topic.

To my knowledge, it was Patricia Minuchin (1985) and Marvin and Stewart (1990) who first argued that the two fields could benefit by an integration. A quick review of these papers suggests points of similarity and of difference. What has always been intriguing to me is that the two frameworks do not appear to have contradictory basic theoretical assumptions. To the extent this is true, it implies that an integration that does not violate the tenets of either theory is possible.

Systemic Similarities

From P. Minuchin (1985) and Marvin and Stewart (1990), both theories share the following basic ideas:

1. Any system is an organized whole, and elements within the system are necessarily interdependent. This applies equally, and in the same manner, to triadic mother–father–child roles within the family, to the reciprocal behaviors of caregiver and child, and to components of the child himself[1] (e.g., its attachment and its exploratory behavior systems).
2. Complex systems are composed of systems and subsystems. This nested set of systems is equally applicable to the child-as-system or to the family-as-system. The subsystems within a larger system are separated by boundaries, and the interactions across boundaries are governed by implicit rules and patterns. Dysfunction within the system is often the result of the breakdown in the adaptive rules governing those boundaries.
3. Behavior patterns in a system are circular rather than linear. This forces us to assume a much more complex model of the factors that activate and terminate different behavior patterns. Attachment theory (Bowlby, 1969) and family systems theory (P. Minuchin, 1985) have similar frameworks for conceptualizing these factors—both based largely on information theory, broadly defined.

---

1. To avoid confusion, throughout this chapter the child will be referred to in the masculine form and the caregiver in the feminine form.

4. Systems have homeostatic, or self-regulatory, features that maintain the stability of certain invariant patterns or outcomes. This is true whether we are speaking of a dysfunctional pattern of boundary violation within a family system or the basic operation of the young child's use of the attachment figure as a secure base for exploration.
5. Evolution and "developmental" self-(re)organization are inherent to open systems. Children's attachment behaviors, as well as family structures, undergo developmental changes according to many of the same underlying developmental processes.

The systemic similarities between the two frameworks also include the fact that interactions between and among individuals are as much a focus of observation and conceptualization as the behaviors of the individuals themselves. They also include a focus on lifespan developmental changes in the overall family system coinciding with developmental changes in the child or sibling subsystem. Finally, they include the recognition of the child's role in organizing family interaction patterns, as well as the child himself being organized by family patterns.

Systemic Differences

Although there are differences in the two frameworks, I maintain that these differences are more those of focus and emphasis rather than of substance. For example, attachment research has focused primarily on the structure and functioning of affectional bonds. Family systems work has focused primarily on family subsystems, boundaries, roles, hierarchical relations, communication and conflict-resolution, and homeostasis and change. Certainly, both fields acknowledge the importance of the other's focus, both are increasingly moving in the other's direction, and both would profit from more integration. Fifteen years ago, the two frameworks had markedly different focuses: Attachment research started with the individual child and caregiver and worked toward the dyad-as-system. Family therapy and research, conversely, started with a focus on triads or larger systems and subsystems (see Bowen's work). In recent years, however, there is as much movement in family systems thinking toward a focus on individual family members as there is in attachment research toward a focus on triads.

ATTACHMENT THEORY FROM THE PERSPECTIVE OF A FAMILY SYSTEMS THERAPIST

Bowlby (e.g., 1969) and Ainsworth (e.g., 1990) thought of attachment behavior as belonging to a coherent system of behaviors that have the predictable outcome of bringing the youngster and caregiver into proximity and contact with one another. The attachment behavior system has an internal organization of thoughts, feelings, plans, and goals (*internal working models*) and has the biological function of protecting children from a wide range of dangers while they are developing the skills to protect themselves. Attachment researchers are especially interested in three additional behavior systems that operate in a dynamic equilibrium with the attachment system (e.g., Ainsworth, 1969, 1990; Cassidy & Shaver, 1999). These other systems are the exploratory system, the wary–fear system, and the affiliative, or sociable, system. In a self-regulatory manner family systems therapists can immediately appreciate, these four behavior systems activate and terminate each other in a way that protects the child by inhibiting the exploratory and sociable systems and activating the attachment system when distressed or afraid, and then facilitates the child's developing competence by activating its exploratory and sociable systems when its wary or attachment systems are not activated (see Figure 1.1).

Ainsworth (e.g., Ainsworth, 1967; Ainsworth, Blehar, Waters, & Wall, 1978) identified this complex, cyclical pattern of behavior as using the attachment figure as a secure base for exploration. When it is functioning properly, this attachment provides the child with a sense of emotional comfort and security in knowing that he can move off from the attachment figure to explore and that the attachment figure will be available for protection and assistance if necessary. This is the "basic trust" that Erik Erikson spoke

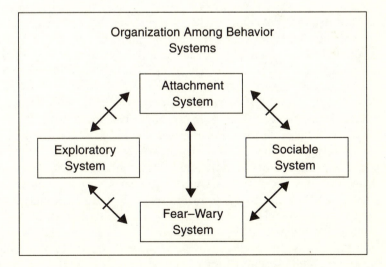

FIGURE 1.1. Organization among behavior systems.

of so many years ago, and it provides the youngster with an internal, developmental foundation of seeing others as loving, and seeing himself as lovable.

An attachment is part of one form of "affectional bond." An affectional bond is a relatively long-enduring tie in which the partners are important to one another as unique individuals who are not interchangeable with others. As the term implies, these bonds are partially governed by strong affect and have the tendency to bring the partners together—either physically or in some form of communication—with regularity. In the case of the attachment bond, this is especially true when one partner or the other senses some danger. Some other affectional bonds include the caregiving bond (the other side of an attachment), sibling bonds, sexual pair bonds, peer or friendship bonds, and mentor or teacher bonds.

The Attachment–Caregiving Systemic "Dance"

What really brings attachment theory and family systems theory together is this notion of a bond, which itself conceptually demands the interactions of at least two partners. From the beginning of his work, Bowlby insisted that an attachment cannot exist, or be understood, outside of the interactions and relationship with the partner who has a reciprocal caregiving bond with the child. Like the child's attachment behavior system, the parent's caregiving behavioral system also has an internal and external organization, with the biological function of protecting the infant or child (e.g., Marvin & Britner, 1995; Solomon & George, 1999). To me the most exciting aspect of Bowlby's (1969) first volume in his trilogy on attachment is his detailed, clear, and wonderfully systemic descriptions of how the young child's attachment behavior system and the parent's caregiving system activate and terminate each other in an intricate "dance" on a minute-to-minute basis over the course of a day, and how this "dance" changes and adapts over time as the child develops or as the circumstances (e.g., risk conditions) in which the family lives change. As so aptly described by family systems theorists, it is often difficult to tell who is "leading" the dance, and who is "following."

Ainsworth observed this "dance" taking place naturalistically in her observational studies of parent–infant interaction in Uganda (e.g., Ainsworth, 1967), in Baltimore (e.g., Stayton, Ainsworth, & Main, 1973), and under standardized, laboratory conditions in the "Strange Situation" (e.g., Ainsworth et al., 1978). The descriptive framework for which she is so renowned focused on the child's contribution to the pattern of attachment–caregiving interaction. Most of her published statements on the caregiver's contribution to the patterns were in the form of rating scales. Her students' and her written descriptions of the caregiver behavior that led to those ratings, however, are rich descriptions for understanding the complex patterns of interaction. Along with Bowlby's theory, these descriptions have led some attachment researchers to describe the caregiver's contribution to the inter- action and the caregiver's internal working models (IWMs) of the relationship in a manner that really begins to describe systemic (at least at a dyadic level) patterns of interaction (Marvin & Britner, 1995; George & Solomon, 1996).

Because it is so widely used, and especially because it is so standard- ized across the infancy and preschool years, describing the attachment– caregiving behaviors in the Strange Situation offers an excellent opportu- nity to illustrate this systemic interaction. A mother carries her two-year-old son, Jochen, into a 15' x 15' room with some chairs, toys on the floor, and a one-way window through which the situation is being videotaped. She puts the toddler down among the toys, and she sits in one of the chairs. Jochen watches closely as his mother sits and smiles at her when he realizes she is not going to move off. His attachment behavior then terminates and his exploratory behavior becomes activated as he turns and begins exploring the toys, using her as a secure base for exploration. Mother watches as he plays, occasionally smiling with mild but obvious delight at his activity. Her caregiving system is "on," but she sees no reason to intervene and therefore merely monitors Jochen's play, available to him should he need her. For three minutes (the length of this first episode) Jochen plays, occasionally looking at his mother, showing her the toy with which he is currently play- ing, and naming the toy or making some other brief comment.

After three minutes a friendly adult enters the room, introduces her- self, sits quietly for a few moments, and then begins a conversation with the mother. As the stranger enters the room and sits, Jochen's wary system is activated. As represented in Figure 1, this automatically terminates his ex- ploration and mildly activates his attachment behavior system. Out of the corner of her eye, his mother realizes that he is looking rather wide-eyed at the stranger, has stood up and stopped playing, and is slowly moving to- ward her. While she finishes introducing herself to the stranger, her caregiving system is activated in response to his attachment behavior, and she holds her hand out toward Jochen as he approaches her. He stands behind her knee as he continues staring at the stranger with interest. His mother rubs his back gently. As his feeling of security returns, Jochen actually smiles sociably at the stranger and then returns to playing, although closer to his mother's feet. When the stranger slowly joins him on the floor, Jochen looks once more at his mother—who smiles at him as a signal that it's safe—and he plays happily with this new person.

The next episode begins with the mother responding to a signal and leaving the room. Jochen looks up as she walks out the door, his exploratory and sociable behavior stops, and his attachment behavior is activated strongly as he moves immediately to the door. He reaches up for the doorknob, calls his mother twice, and then starts fussing. He looks briefly at the stranger as she attempts to distract him with a toy, then begins to cry, and again calls his mother as he attempts unsuccessfully to open the door.

At this point his mother, who, along with the clinicians behind the one-way mirror, has been experiencing an increasing urgency to go back into the room, calls Jochen's name outside the door and reenters the room. Her caregiving system is highly activated as she focuses completely on her son rather than the stranger. Jochen immediately looks up at her, holds his arms out to be picked up, clings to her for a few moments when picked up, stops crying, and then sniffles once or twice as he watches the stranger leave the room. Still holding him, his mother looks directly at him, snuggles him for another moment, notices he has stopped sniffling, leans over toward the toys and asks him if he wants to play again. Immediately, Jochen clings to her again and says "no" in a fussy tone. His mother says, "Not ready yet, huh? . . . that's OK." She moves to and sits in her chair, holding Jochen in her lap. After another moment, Jochen again feels secure and moves to get down, his mother accommodates to his movement, and he again sits at the toys, playing just as he did in the first episode. His mother again monitors his play, responding to his vocalizations about the toys, helping him briefly with a toy when he requests it, and delighting in his enjoyment of the toys.

Attachment–Caregiving Interactions Within Larger Family Systems

Throughout the Strange Situation, one can observe the attachment system of the child and the caregiving system of the parent activating and terminating each other's behavior in intricate patterns as each anticipates and responds to the other's behavior and to changing conditions in the room. And the patterns become even more intricate when another family member is added to the system being observed. For example, Stewart (1977) and Stewart and Marvin (1984) have studied attachment–caregiving patterns in Strange Situations in which not only mothers and children are present, but also either fathers or slightly older siblings. Stewart (1977) found that in "traditional" families, when the stranger enters the room in which mother, father, and toddler are present, the normative tendency is for the toddler to display attachment behavior toward his mother. When the mother then exits the room, leaving the toddler with his father, the toddler tends to stop playing and use the father as a haven of safety, followed soon by a return to the toys. Although not very distressed at his mother's absence, the toddler nonetheless tends to seek contact with her when she returns.

Stewart and Marvin (1984) observed toddlers and their older preschool siblings in the Strange Situation. They found that if the older sibling was four years or older, that older sibling tended to play a protective role toward his or her younger sibling, that the younger sibling actively used the older sibling as a haven of safety, and that the mothers of those sibling dyads tended to ask the older sibling to help out when she left the room. If the older sibling was approximately 3½ years or younger, however, both children tended to become upset when left by their mother, and neither depended on the other or protected the other. These more complex patterns of attachment–caregiving interactions within larger family systems are familiar to most of us from our own family experiences. They point to the importance of studying these bonds within whole familes. And they suggest that the procedures developed to study attachment–caregiving interactions in parent–child dyads might be adaptable to studying these more complex family systems patterns. After all, the parent–child dyad is nested within the larger family system. Stewart and Marvin are convinced that expanding the unit of observation from dyad to larger family systems and subsystems in this progressive, nested manner is both possible and promising.

Individual Differences in Attachment–Caregiving Bonds

The idea of using current procedures and findings within larger family systems can also be applied to the study of individual differences. This work, in fact, will make the greatest contribution to clinical intervention and the integration of attachment theory and family systems theory.

Attachment researchers have found three basic patterns, or classifications, of children's attachment behavior (e.g., Ainsworth et al., 1978; Cassidy & Marvin, 1992; Main & Cassidy, 1988), and three corresponding patterns of caregiver behavior and caregiver IWM (e.g., George & Solomon, 1996; Main & Goldwyn, 1994; Marvin & Britner, 1995). In addition, a number of patterns are best considered as disorganized, or *disordered*, versions of the three basic patterns. The three basic, or *ordered,* patterns can be considered "within normal limits," whereas the disordered versions of these patterns are associated with past or current unresolved loss or trauma to the caregiver and with high risk for current and future negative child development outcomes (e.g., Solomon & George, 1999). Although much more research is certainly needed, it is becoming increasingly apparent that these patterns are classifiable from standardized observational and interview procedures and are applicable not only to infants and preschool children but also to older children, adolescents, and adults. Furthermore, the patterns tend to be passed from one generation to the next through specific relationships (see Cassidy & Shaver, 1999). Brief descriptions of the patterns, as they occur in the Strange Situation, are as follows:

Ordered: Secure Child–Autonomous Parent

This pattern is the theoretical norm and comprises one-half to two-thirds of low-risk populations.

- The child plays happily when not distressed and easily asks for help when it is needed. The child easily "updates" the parent on his play activity, with shared eye contact and expanded conversations. The conversations can be about the play or about more personal topics. The parent is watchful of the child without being either intrusive or overly pressuring for the child to achieve in exploration.
- Both partners easily approach and interact with one another when the child is distressed.
- If the dyad experiences a moment of emotional or structural disequilibrium (usually coincidental), they are both willing and able to "repair" that disequilibrium. The parent is clearly "in charge" of this process, although she allows or encourages the child to participate and contribute in an age-appropriate manner.
- Physical or conversational contact, or both, predictably terminates the child's attachment behavior and emotional distress.
- Physical or conversational contact predictably leads to resumption of the child's exploration and developmental competence.

Ordered: Anxious, Avoidant Child–Dismissing Parent

This pattern comprises approximately 20% of low-risk populations.

- The child plays happily when not distressed. There is little or no shared eye contact or conversation or joint attention to personal topics. Conversations and joint attention tend to be focused on the child's competent performance rather than personal topics.
- The parent tends to be either disengaged from the child's play or at least mildly intrusive in pressuring the child toward competence.
- Both partners tend to minimize the more intimate attachment–caregiving interactions. If the child is mildly distressed, both partners work to dismiss the distress rather than directing their attention toward it and resolving it.
- Both partners tend to "distract" themselves from attachment–caregiving interactions through overactivation of the child's exploration.
- The parent tends to be clearly in charge and may in fact have (overly) high expectations for the child's behavior.

Ordered: Anxious, Ambivalent Child–Preoccupied Parent

This pattern comprises approximately 10% of low-risk populations.

- Both partners tend to overemphasize the child's dependence on the parent and relative inability to explore in a competent, independent manner. The parent tends to overinvolve herself in the child's activities, whether in exploration or management of the child's affect. As a result, both play and attachment–caregiving interactions are characterized by conflict and ambivalence as they intrude into each other's activities, conversations, and even thoughts!
- Even mild conflicts tend not to be resolved. Rather, attempts to resolve conflicts themselves lead to more conflict, and conflict tends to be terminated by eventually attending to some other topic rather than by addressing the conflict directly and resolving it.
- The child's distress and attachment behavior is very easily activated, and in fact this is encouraged by the parent, who feels better about herself when she is needed.
- The child tends to be overly distressed by separation, even late in the preschool years. When reunited, the proximity to one another and any ensuing conversation tend not to terminate the child's attachment behavior. The child is likely to "hang on" the parent rather than return to exploration.

It is intriguing that the three primary attachment patterns and the reciprocal caregiving patterns are so similar to S. Minuchin's (1974) three major patterns of family structure: adaptive, disengaged, and enmeshed (see Figure 1.2). Given this similarity, one contribution that attachment research

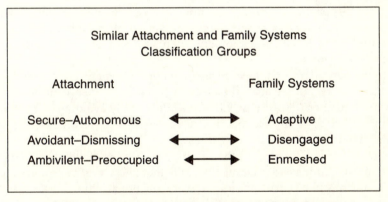

FIGURE 1.2. Classifications of Attachment and Family Patterns.

can quickly and easily make to the field of family therapy is the recognition that these patterns, which should probably be considered as within normal limits from both theoretical perspectives, become disordered and significantly dysfunctional under certain conditions. Specifically, attachment researchers have repeatedly found that unresolved loss or trauma in a parent's own history is strongly associated with disorganized attachment–caregiving bonds. The mechanism for this linkage is complex (see, e.g., Main & Hesse, 1990; Solomon & George, 1999), and a thorough discussion is beyond the scope of this chapter. The basic idea, however, is that unresolved loss or trauma in the caregiver's history (and apparently in her current life as well) is associated with conscious or unconscious fear on the caregiver's part when her child's attachment behavior activates her own caregiving system. This fear results in her behaving toward her child in a frightened or frightening manner at the very time he needs her as a secure, protective haven. As a result, the caregiver abdicates her "executive" caregiving role, at least in the area of attachment–caregiving interactions, if not in other areas or types of interactions as well. We thus have the following, fourth, attachment–caregiving pattern.

Disordered: Role-Reversed Child–Abdicating Parent

This pattern appears in 5–10% of low-risk populations and in percentages well above 50% across a wide range of high-risk populations.

- Child and parent are both frequently anxious when interacting with one another in low-distress contexts not usually associated with anxiety.
- When the child's attachment behavior is activated, the parent behaves in a frightened or frightening way. With training, an observer can reliably observe this parent abdicating her protective, organizing role. For example, when her child is distressed on reunion, this mother might briefly exhibit a frightened facial expression and then sit down, stare into space, and appear depressed.
- In the case of an infant (younger than approximately 2–2½ years), this caregiver reaction causes the child to behave in a disorganized–disoriented manner (e.g., crying silently while actively avoiding contact with the caregiver or approaching the caregiver while covering his eyes with his hands in a clearly fearful expression).
- Once the child has reached the age of 2½ or 3 years, he has developed the social–cognitive and relationship skills that allow him to develop an attachment strategy that appears to be very functional in the short run within this relationship but is a high-risk strategy in the long run (Main & Hesse, 1990). This child becomes keenly aware of his caregiver's mood, moni-

tors her behavior carefully, and reverses the roles in their attachment–caregiving interactions—and more generally in interactions involving strong emotions. The child, rather than the caregiver, tries to soothe the other's distress and organize the other's behavior. And the adult, rather than the child, encourages, or at least continues to allow, the other to carry out that role. In the short run this behavior is adaptive because it increases the likelihood that the caregiver will be available and responsive should anything *really* dangerous happen. In the long run it is dysfunctional and a very high-risk pattern for a large number of individual, developmental, dyadic, and family reasons. There is also compelling evidence that this pattern, unless resolved, has a high likelihood of being passed on to the next generation by the child when he grows up.

This pattern is very familiar to family therapists and has long been associated with many severe psychosomatic and other family problems. Attachment research can make a number of contributions to family therapists' understanding of role-reversed relationships. First, it is now clear that the pattern occurs, and has serious negative implications, at much younger ages than usually thought. Second, it is clear that these role-reversed, abdicating relationships have major emotion regulation and structural components. Third, we now have a more differentiated model for the etiology of this emotional–structural problem. Fourth, the standardized coding systems used in attachment research offer the family therapist a powerful set of observational tools for identifying the problem. And finally, the additional knowledge about the etiology of this structural problem should lead to new and possibly improved approaches to treatment of the problem across a range of referral questions.

It should be noted that we can use attachment-based procedures, as well as classifications, to help construct a "family map" of the sort that family therapists find useful. For example, Figure 1.3 shows two different three-person families for whom hypothetical Strange Situations have been conducted for each child–parent dyad and for whom the spouses have been interviewed about their relationship. On the left is a high-functioning, "adaptive" family. The attachment–caregiving patterns between each parent and the child are secure–autonomous, the spouse relationship is appropriately intimate and without undue conflict, and there are appropriate boundaries between the spouse relationship and each of the child–parent relationships. On the right is a dysfunctional family with a "classic" enmeshed mother–child relationship and disengaged relationships between the father and both the mother and the child. The spouse boundary is inappropriately permeable with spouse conflict. Finally, the relationship between the child and mother is role-reversed.

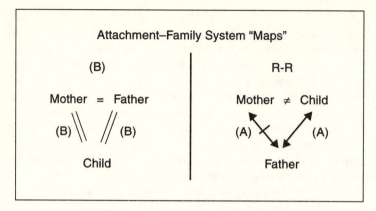

FIGURE 1.3. Attachment–family system maps.
B = Secure. A = Avoidant. RR = Role reversed.

THREE EXAMPLES OF INTERVENTIONS BASED ON AN INTEGRATION OF ATTACHMENT AND FAMILY SYSTEMS

With this review of attachment research as background, I would now like briefly to present three cases from my own clinical practice—cases that I think illustrate some of the potential contributions of attachment research to the practice of family therapy. It certainly has contributed to my own family work. Each example will be drawn from a different age-range for the child involved, and each will illustrate different but overlapping contributions from attachment research.

Case 1: 18-Month-Old Boy With a Reactive Attachment Disorder

Michael is an 18-month-old boy, referred by his adoptive parents because of a combination of symptoms, including indiscriminate friendliness toward adult strangers and a nearly complete lack of seeking contact with and comfort from his adoptive parents when hurt or distressed. His history was one of chronic neglect in his birth home, followed by a series of placements with three different foster families between the ages of 6 and 13 months. At about 14 months, he was adopted by the referring parents, who appeared to be very loving and sensitive caregivers. Despite their loving care, Michael continued displaying these symptoms, and his adoptive parents were distressed and very worried about his "recovery." The intervention took place in four phases.

Assessment

The family was initially observed in the therapeutic "playroom" through the one-way window. Although the father was not as frequently and actively involved as the mother, both parents monitored and delighted in Michael's play, played with him in a manner that supported, rather than interfered with his exploration, and easily talked with one another about Michael and his behavior. In a manner similar to the design of the Strange Situation, I entered the room after a few minutes. As the parents had described, Michael immediately approached me and made physical contact with me. Also as described, some minutes later he tripped over a toy, fell, and obviously hurt himself. He neither cried nor looked at or approached either of his parents. Yet he had happily approached them during his exploration and clearly preferred them to me despite his indiscriminate friendliness.

When Michael tripped, I noticed that both parents immediately leaned forward as if to go to him, paused, and then sat back with concerned and uncertain expressions on their faces once they realized he was not going to cry. In the course of discussing his behavior and their reaction to it, they described their uncertainty and their fear of responding in a manner that could make Michael's condition even worse. In effect, their uncertainty about what to do had led them to be too "respectful" of Michael's own inappropriate and disordered attachment pattern. Although not completely role-reversed, this family system had largely abdicated appropriate attachment–caregiving family roles, and the family patterns were contributing to the maintenance of Michael's disordered attachment. The parents easily recognized and acknowledged this confusion, "respect," and abdication.

Parent Education

As parents, much of our appropriate caregiving behavior toward our toddlers is based on scripts that are activated and terminated somewhat automatically rather than being carefully thought out. Our child falls, cries, and we automatically go to him and pick him up. Unexpected, seemingly contradictory, or incoherent behavior on the child's part can leave us confused and without a plan of behavior of our own. In this situation, merely understanding the "logic" of the child's disordered behavior, making explicit the expectable patterns of attachment–caregiving behavior, and experimenting with alternative plans for responding to the child's behavior is often sufficient to trigger change toward a more appropriate family pattern.

The next step was to make explicit the parents' knowledge of normal, ordered patterns of attachment–caregiving interaction and to help them understand the etiology and logic of Michael's disordered behavior. Making explicit that toddlers should be wary around completely unfamiliar adults and when hurt or distressed should become upset and quickly move toward their attachment figures was a "no-brainer." What was very helpful to Michael's parents was making explicit that because of his earlier history and attachment disorder, Michael was not taking the usual toddler role in seeking proximity and contact with them under either of those conditions: He was not carrying out *his* role in attachment–caregiving interactions. They were also relieved and empowered when reassured that actively intervening in their son's disordered behavior patterns would not do further harm.

Experimenting with Changing the Patterns

The third step in the intervention was to coach the parents in experimenting with ways to bring about the appropriate outcome, whether or not Michael enacted his role in the interaction. For example, if Michael were approached by an unfamiliar adult and exhibited no wariness, one of his parents were to move quickly to him, pick him up, and briefly talk with him about not going to strangers. From the safety of his parent's arms, Michael could then be introduced to the stranger and after a few minutes allowed to interact with that new person. If Michael fell and hurt himself or was distressed about something and failed to go to his parent(s), again one of them would move quickly to him, pick him up, and hold and soothe him even if he did not signal any desire for that. The explicit hope was that if the parents could, on their own, make happen what should have been partly *Michael's* responsibility, then Michael might gradually adapt to the appropriate family system outcome and eventually assume a more ordered role in the pattern.

Follow-up

Periodic follow-up was maintained over the next few months. Michael's parents reported a gradual shift in his behavior toward taking increasing responsibility in seeking proximity and contact under those conditions that normally elicit attachment behavior in toddlers. Approaching his parents when hurt or otherwise distressed was the first of the two major areas in which Michael assumed increased responsibility. Wary inhibition or retreat to his parents when confronted with an unfamiliar adult gradually improved as well, but was slower in doing so. As Michael assumed more responsibility in these situations, his parents gradually backed off to the point of assuming the usual parental role. Needless to say, the parents quickly gained increased confidence in their executive roles as parents and reported feeling much better themselves.

Two brief comments seem important about this case. First, we did not think about Michael's attachment disorder either as residing in him or as being the result of his adoptive parents' patterns of behavior. By focusing at the level of dyadic or family interactions and the outcomes expected at that level of "analysis," we were easily able to envision an outcome—or an equilibrium—that the parents could work toward and that they could easily keep in mind as they backed off in a manner consistent with Michael's assumption of responsibility.

Second, these parents were intact, secure, and effective enough in their parenting and in their relationships with each other to be able to profit from a model that can be thought of as family systems–based parent education. Had they exhibited more problematic patterns of interactions or more problematic patterns of internal working models about themselves or their relationship with Michael, the work would have had to take on a much stronger, individual or family psychotherapeutic component.

Case 2: Six-Year-Old Girl With Chronic Aggression Toward Her Mother

An otherwise healthy and normal six-year-old girl was referred by her pediatrician because of chronic aggressive and controlling behavior toward her mother. At first, the father was reluctant to participate in the intervention but did so when it was emphasized that he would have to play a crucial role in the solution to this problem.

Assessment

In this case, we began by conducting a family interview and then a complete attachment–caregiving evaluation of both child–parent dyads. This included a Strange Situation separately with each parent–child dyad, Adult Attachment Interviews (AAIs) with each parent, and the Doll Story Completion Task (Bretherton, Ridgeway, & Cassidy, 1990) with the child.

The results of the family evaluation were as follows: Mother and daughter were enmeshed. Father and daughter were disengaged. Father and mother were disengaged and in much conflict regarding mother's handling of the child's misbehavior. The typical pattern was that the child misbehaved, mother tried to manage the behavior and then gave up, father intervened firmly, mother then "protected" the child from father, father became angry toward mother and daughter and retreated in anger, and then child remained controlling toward mother.

The results of the attachment evaluation were as follows: The mother–daughter attachment–caregiving bond was disorganized, controlling, and role-reversed. The father–daughter attachment–caregiving bond was avoidant. Mother's classification on the AAI was unresolved regarding early loss (of her own mother), with a primary classification of preoccupied–enmeshed with respect to intimate relationships. Father's classification on the AAI was dismissing with respect to intimate relationships. Daughter's classification on the Doll Story Completion Task was disorganized.

Intervention

In this case the results of the components of the evaluation were highly consistent with one another. Given that the format of the intervention was to be family therapy, the primary advantage of the attachment–caregiving evaluations was in identifying the personal-historical factors (from the AAI), in combination with the immediate family interaction patterns, that were related both to the mother's fear and abdication toward her daughter and the father's tendency to feel rejected and retreat. This particular intervention took approximately one year of weekly meetings. Rather than presenting details, I will present an outline of the sequence of therapeutic steps that were involved.

1. Tracking the family pattern and helping the parents recognize and reflect on that pattern. Sometimes the entire family was present in the room and at other times only the parents.
2. Moving the discussion from behavior management to mother's experience of fear of her daughter's aggressive and controlling behavior (without child present).
3. Discussion of mother's loss of her own mother and of her father's and extended family's reaction to that loss.
4. Discussion of her old fear regarding the loss.
5. Discussion of how father's parents rejected his attachment behavior and emotional expression and how he learned as a young boy to withdraw when distressed or hurt.
6. Bringing her husband into the discussion to understand and soothe mother's loss.
7. Bringing the discussion back to the fear mother experiences around her child's behavior and her husband's attempts to intervene firmly.
8. Mother's recognition that she feels in a one-down, role-reversed position with her daughter during those times of misbehavior.
9. Discussion of how father replicates his old pattern as part of his current family pattern.
10. Development of a plan whereby the therapist would support father and keep him from withdrawing, while father soothes mother's fear and supports her in her attempts to take a stronger position with her daughter.

11. Many repetitions of this plan during therapy sessions. Ancillary, short-term grief work with mother.

12. Supporting and coaching mother in recognizing, staying with, and soothing her daughter's distress as the role-reversed pattern between mother and daughter was corrected. This further corrected the role-reversed pattern by appropriately placing mother in the position of terminating her daughter's distress and attachment behavior, rather than the other way around.

13. Supporting mother in occasionally taking a watching position while father managed the daughter's behavior. Exploring and reinforcing mother's relief that she no longer had to "protect" her daughter from her husband.

14. Planning for regular "dates" between husband and wife.

15. Discussion about future individual or couples therapy for the parents.

I think there are two especially important points to be made about this case. First, as mentioned earlier, the attachment evaluation allowed us to add the component of the parents' own attachment histories to the more traditional family systems evaluation of current patterns of interaction. These combined assessments, coming from theoretical frameworks that are highly complementary to one another, provided us with many additional therapeutic choices. Second, the attachment orientation was able to shift the therapeutic focus from one primarily of power, authority, and boundary violations to the additional and strong focus on intimacy and the effects that unresolved fear and loss have on intimacy and parenting.

Case 3: 15-Year-Old Girl With "Psychogenic" Pain

This third case is the most complex of the three and is such a classic case both from a family systems perspective and an attachment perspective that it becomes difficult to differentiate between the two. A 15-year-old girl was referred by her orthopedic physician for chronic "psychogenic" pain in her ankle (reflex sympathetic dystrophy). The pain had originally begun when she mildly sprained her ankle. The pain resolved normally, only to reappear within a matter of days, increase in intensity, and remain extremely resistant to a wide variety of medical interventions. The condition was extremely debilitating to the child and to her entire family. This family agreed to enter a program we had developed that consisted of a very specific and detailed protocol (Marvin, 1992). The 4-day protocol combines hypnosis with specific attachment–family systems interventions and can be conducted on an inpatient or an outpatient basis. Again, I will present only an outline of the protocol.

The protocol is based on the recognition that the following four family patterns are highly likely and completely normal, even in otherwise healthy and highly functioning families, when a child becomes ill:

1. There is increased activation of attachment–caregiving interactions between the child and one or both parents.
2. In the role of the sick family member, the child is relieved from some or all age-appropriate responsibilities and privileges. In this sense, the ill family member is typically treated as younger and/or less competent than usual.
3. There is a decrease in spouse interactions associated with the increase in concern and caregiving interactions with the child.
4. If the illness is resistant to intervention, there is an increased probability of a loss of "executive power" of the parenting subsystem associated with the increase in *medical* management.

Perhaps the most important thing about these four patterns is the ease with which they can stabilize and become chronic and resistant to change if the illness is not quickly resolved.

Assessment

The protocol begins with an extended family interview, during which the family is questioned for the purpose of eliciting very detailed and episodic descriptions of the four patterns listed above as they apply to this particular family. Typically, families are at first unaware of any changes that the illness has caused in patterns of family interaction. With persistent questioning, however, they begin to appreciate the changes they have experienced and often elaborate enthusiastically. A detailed interview is also conducted regarding real or anticipated losses for the family (e.g., death of an extended family member, anticipated loss or divorce, etc.). In the case of this family, what emerged was an anticipated separation between the parents.

Intervention

The actual intervention protocol consists of the following 5 steps, carried out over a period of 4 days:

Step 1. Presentation of the "frame" to the family. This frame is designed to help the family shift from seeking a medical solution to seeking an hypnosis and relationship-based solution. One crucial component of the frame is (in close consultation with the physician) to categorize this specific pain as an anomaly of the child's sympathetic nervous system, as non-life-threatening, and as "unnecessary." As such, the family can ignore the condition, as long as the child's experienced pain can be minimized.

Step 2. Hypnosis with the child, focused on pain reduction. Training in self-hypnosis quickly follows, so the child can continue this part of the work after this brief program has been completed.

Step 3. An extensive family interview is held with the goal of detailing very specific and concrete plans for how this family is going to return their family patterns to normal. A way is found for the family to begin practicing these changes during the protocol, with appropriate follow-up if the practice periods are not successful.

Step 4. An extensive family interview is then held with the goal of detailing very specific and concrete plans for how this family is going to "elevate" the child developmentally.

Step 5. On the final day of the program, the parents, in a meeting without the child, are presented with an *invariant prescription* (parents contract to go on "dates" or other activities with strong spouse boundaries). Not surprisingly to family therapists, this fifth step is often the most difficult step for the family to complete and is the step most likely to sabotage the entire protocol.

Actually, there is a sixth step. In consultation with the therapist, the parents make a decision about whether or not they will enter family, couples, or individual therapy, or some combination thereof, to work further on not-yet-resolved concerns.

This family was part of a clinical study of 19 families in which the young adolescent was experiencing chronic, psychogenic pain. As in all 19 families, an important loss was real or impending (feared parental separation in this case), and the chronic return of the child's pain was both an attachment strategy on the girl's part and a symptom "chosen" by the family system to maintain the current family equilibrium. As in 16 of the 19 families, the girl's symptoms were almost completely resolved by discharge. The family had returned many of its daily routines and patterns to normal. The parents returned to discussions about the future of their own relationship and entered couples therapy. On 6-month follow-up, the child remained symptom-free. The parents were still in a therapeutic trial period regarding their own spouse relationship.

CONCLUSIONS

Clearly there is much opportunity for cross-fertilization between family research and therapy and attachment research and therapy. For a number of reasons, this process has not taken place to any significant degree. First, attachment-research and attachment-based clinical work is so specialized and it takes so much training to become certified that it approximates an additional graduate training career. A second reason is purely historical. Attachment research has been almost exclusively focused, for the past 20 years, on individual differences, internal working models, and, with some notable exceptions, the mother–child dyad. This is due to the nature of American developmental psychology, with which attachment theory is primarily identified. But the theory, as developed by Bowlby and Ainsworth, is completely consistent with the field of family therapy. Third, methods have been developed for use in studying individuals and dyads. But as Stewart (1977) and Stewart and Marvin (1984) have shown in their work, even the Strange Situation itself can be used to study family subsystems larger than the dyad. Fourth, with a few notable exceptions, family systems research has largely been limited to clinical observation and self-report measures rather than to standardized observational procedures.

I see a number of future directions for action, based on two things I have focused on in my own attempts to integrate the two areas. First, there is an obvious need to further integrate research and intervention work on family *affectional* systems with work on family *structure*. Second, there is so much similarity in the classification systems that already exist across the two disciplines.

One direction is movement within the family systems area toward observational, descriptive studies of family interaction rather than pencil–paper measures. Paper-and-pencil measures are just too superficial and are subject to self-idealizing and other distortions, unless they are based on thorough description.

A second is the development of relevant measurement and data reduction tools. Given the proliferation of attachment-related procedures presently being developed, I am confident that this is possible. My hope is that family researchers will begin carefully to examine not only the final classifications that emerge from attachment research, but more importantly the observed patterns of interaction that are the basis for those classifications. The real-time descriptions of interactions contributed by Ainsworth back in the 1960s and 1970s, those developed by Mary Main for classifying disorganized infant attachment and adult representational models of intimate relationships, and those developed by such researchers as Solomon and George (1999) and Marvin and Britner (1995) to classify caregivers' bonds with their children, are couched in language that is completely accessible to family systems researchers and therapists and provide a wonderfully sensitive and elaborate set of lenses through which to view intimate interactions within families.

Because of budget constraints and because of the specialization required, there is a strong need for the development of specific protocols for the treatment of specific patterns. I am especially excited by the work currently being conducted in a few laboratories around the world on developing clinical assessment and intervention procedures based on those that have been developed and validated in basic and clinical attachment research (e.g., Cassidy, in progress; Dozier, Higley, Albus, & Nutter, in press; Marvin, Cooper, Hoffman, & Powell, 2000). Although this approach is clearly productive, it is also costly and time consuming, especially in terms of the necessary training.

Until more protocols are developed and successfully field tested, I think at least two useful approaches are available to family therapists who are interested in integrating attachment work into their practice. One is to establish a collaborative relationship between an attachment researcher or clinician and a family therapist. The second is for family therapists to learn as much as practical about attachment theory and procedures and to carefully apply them as part of their overall clinical practice—taking special care to make the attachment component a subset of their careful clinical activities. As clinicians, we should remain acutely aware that some of our interventions may carry some potentially harmful side effects. As is the case with any health care intervention, we must be alert to these possible effects and work continuously to minimize them.

REFERENCES

Ainsworth, M. D. S. (1967). *Infancy in Uganda: Infant care and the growth of love.* Baltimore: Johns Hopkins University Press.

Ainsworth, M. D. S. (1969). Object relations, dependency, and attachment: A theoretical review of the infant–mother relationship. *Child Development, 40,* 969–1025.

Ainsworth, M. D. S. (1990). Some considerations regarding theory and assessment relevant to attachments beyond infancy. In M. T. Greenberg, D. Cicchetti, & E. M. Cummings (Eds.), *Attachment in the preschool years: Theory, research, and intervention* (pp. 463–488). Chicago: University of Chicago Press.

Ainsworth, M., Blehar, M., Waters, E., & Wall, S. (1978). *Patterns of attachment: A psychological study of the Strange Situation.* Hillsdale, NJ: Erlbaum.

Bowlby, J. (1949). The study and reduction of group tensions in the family. *Human Relations, 2,* 123-128.

Bowlby, J. (1969). *Attachment and loss: Vol. 1. Attachment.* New York: Basic Books.

Bowlby, J. (1988). *A secure base: Parent-child attachment and healthy human development.* New York: Basic Books.

Bretherton, I., Ridgeway, D., & Cassidy, J. (1990). Assessing internal working models of attachment relationships: An attachment story completion task for 3-year-olds. In M. T. Greenberg, D. Cicchetti, & E. M. Cummings (Eds.), *Attachment in the preschool years: Theory, research, and intervention* (pp. 273–308). Chicago: University of Chicago Press.

Byng-Hall, J. (1999). Family and couple therapy: Toward greater security. In J. Cassidy & P. Shaver (Eds.), *Handbook of Attachment.* New York: Guilford Press.

Cassidy, J. (in progress). *The hand-in-hand infant-mother program.* Manuscript in preparation. The University of Maryland.

Cassidy, J., & Marvin, R. S., with the MacArthur Working Group. (1992). *Attachment organization in preschool children: Procedures and coding manual.* Unpublished manuscript, University of Virginia, Charlottsville.

Cassidy, J., & Shaver, P. (1999). *Handbook of Attachment.* New York: Guilford Press.

Dozier, M., Higley, E., Albus, K. E., & Nutter, A. (in press). Intervening with foster infants' caregivers: Targeting three critical needs. *Infant Mental Health Journal.*

Fonagy, P. (1999). Psychoanalytic theory from the viewpoint of attachment theory and research. In J. Cassidy & P. Shaver (Eds.), *Handbook of Attachment* (pp. 595–624). New York: Guilford Press.

George, C., & Solomon, J. (1996). Representational models of relationships: Links between caregiving and attachment. *Infant Mental Health Journal, 17,* 198–216.

Lieberman, A. F., & Zeanah, C. H. (1999). Contributions of attachment theory to infant-parent psychotherapy and other interventions with infants and young children. In J. Cassidy & P. Shaver (Eds.), *Handbook of Attachment.* New York: Guilford Press.

Main, M., & Cassidy, J. (1988). Categories of response to reunion with the parent at age six: Predictable from infant attachment classifications and stable over a one-month period. *Developmental Psychology, 24,* 415–426.

Main, M., & Goldwyn, R. (1994). Adult attachment classification and rating system. Unpublished manuscript, University of California, Berkeley.

Main, M., & Hesse, E. (1990). Parent's unresolved traumatic experiences are related to infant disorganized attachment status. In M. Greenberg, & D. Cicchetti (Eds.), *Attachment in the pre-school years.* Chicago: University of Chicago Press.

Marvin, R. S. (1992). Attachment- and family systems-based intervention in developmental psychopathology. *Development and Psychopathology, 4,* 697–711.

Marvin, R. S., & Britner, P. A. (1995). *Classification system for parental caregiving patterns in the preschool strange situation.* Unpublished coding manual, University of Virginia. (Available on request.)

Marvin, R., Cooper, G., Hoffman, K., & Powell, B. (2000, June). *Attachment-based interventions with at-risk Head Start child–parent dyads.* National Head Start Research Meetings, Washington, DC.

Marvin, R. S., & Stewart, R. B. (1990). A family systems framework for the study of attachment. In M. T. Greenberg, D. Cicchetti, & E. M. Cummings (Eds.), *At-*

tachment in the preschool years: Theory, research, and intervention (pp. 51–86). Chicago: University of Chicago Press.

Minuchin, P. (1985). Families and individual development: Provocations from the field of family therapy. *Child Development, 56,* 289–302.

Minuchin, S. (1974). *Families and family therapy.* Cambridge, MA: Harvard University Press.

Solomon, J., & George, C. (1999). *Attachment disorganization.* New York: Guilford Press.

Stayton, D. J., Ainsworth, M. D. S., & Main, M. (1973). The development of separation behavior in the first year of life: Protest, following and greeting. *Developmental Psychology, 9,* 213–225.

Stewart, R. B. (1977). Parent-child interactions in a quasi-naturalistic setting. Unpublished Master's thesis, Pennsylvania State University, University Park.

Stewart, R. B., & Marvin, R. S. (1984). Sibling relations: The role of conceptual perspective taking in the ontogeny of sibling caregiving. *Child Development, 55,* 1322–1332.

van den Boom, D. C. (1995). Do first-year intervention effects endure? Follow-up during toddlerhood of a sample of Dutch irritable infants. *Child Development, 66,* 1798–1816.

PART II

Family Perspective

Family-Level Emotional Climate and Its Impact on the Flexibility of Relationship Representations

JEAN TALBOT
JAMES McHALE

In endeavoring to define individual psychological health in terms that would distill its essence, Jack and Jeanne Block (Block & Block, 1980; Block & Kremen, 1996) focused on the ideal of flexibility. In their view, no fixed constellation of desirable traits could in itself be taken as an index of psychological robustness; indeed, if an individual manifested an unvarying approach to challenges posed by the environment, she would be able to remain free of stress and symptoms only if she found a compatible and equally unvarying "niche in which to abide" (Block & Kremen, 1996, p. 350). Because static niches of this kind are in short supply, and because the rewards they offer are necessarily limited, the Blocks concluded that true psychological well-being must entail a propensity for ongoing growth—an ability to alter one's behavior and modes of interpreting the world so as to keep pace with changing environmental demands while still maintaining a sense of affective equilibrium and personal integrity. According to the Blocks, this capacity for smooth, continual adaptation would facilitate optimal functioning across many domains of human endeavor.

In many ways, attachment theory's concept of security epitomizes this understanding of psychological health as it applies to socioemotional adjustment, for the central identifying characteristic of securely attached individuals is their skill and interest in constructing complex, flexible internal working models of self and other in relation, continually integrating new observations of their social world as they do so. Attachment theorists see this representational flexibility as the product of more basic interpersonal attitudes and self-regulation skills. These attitudes and skills have traditionally been viewed as emerging, in turn, from aspects of the individual's early relationship with his or her primary caregiver.

Increasingly, however, attachment scholars of the present generation have argued that other relational dynamics, including multiperson interaction patterns occurring within the family of origin, should also be studied as potential influences on the psychological processes underlying representational flexibility and secure attachment. This position is gaining proponents within the field of attachment at a time when developmental research based on family systems principles is beginning to receive greater recognition and attention. Workers in the realm of empirical family studies can now point to an extensive body of findings to make their case that the functioning of family subsystems beyond the parent–child dyad contributes significantly to dimensions of children's socioemotional adjustment.

These convergent advances within and beyond the discipline of attachment provide the premise for the current chapter. Its first aim is to describe how whole-family and family subsystem dynamics might affect the complex of attitudes and abilities that give rise to representational flexibility as conceptualized by attachment theory. The second goal of the chapter is to consider how characteristics of the larger family system may influence the specific ways in which representational flexibility manifests itself within an individual's whole-family or polyadic relationship representations. These two issues will be addressed using evidence from the marital conflict and coparenting literatures, as well as from attachment research.

The first part of this chapter reviews the attachment field's theoretical arguments and empirical findings relating to the internal working model construct and outlines the position of attachment scholars who advocate studying the effect of family context on attachment processes. The second part briefly presents the overall case for greater holism in the study of child development, using illustrative material from the past 20 years of research on family process and children's adjustment. The third and fourth parts examine findings on marital and coparenting quality as they relate specifically to this chapter's questions about representational flexibility. In the concluding part, we will attempt to integrate attachment principles and conclusions from the previous two sections into an expanded model for the development of representational flexibility in the family context. We will also advance suggestions for future research.

THE CONCEPT OF RELATIONSHIP REPRESENTATION IN ATTACHMENT THEORY AND RESEARCH

The Construct of the Internal Working Model as Described in Attachment Theory

Psychoanalytically oriented approaches to development, such as object relations theory (e.g., Fairbairn, 1952; Sandler & Rosenblatt, 1962), have long maintained that individuals build enduring social-cognitive structures based on their participation in early childhood relationships and that these structures influence people's interpretations of interpersonal situations encountered in later life. Bowlby's (1958, 1959, 1960, 1969, 1973, 1980, 1988) formulation of the attachment perspective, which synthesized object relations principles with ethological concepts concerning such phenomena as instinctive imprinting behavior in animals (e.g., Lorenz, 1957), will be familiar to most readers of this volume.

Bowlby's formulations, attachment-related affects, such as for distress, are thought to activate an instinctually based set of organized behaviors, the function of which is to help infants maintain proximity to their caregiver and elicit that person's nurturance. As babies grow, they repeatedly encounter situations evoking attachment-related affects and so participate in many interactions in which they are motivated to seek their caregiver's protection and soothing. Over time, the infant comes to organize the recurring features of such interactions into generalized cognitive–affective representations of self and other in relation. According to Bowlby, these representations, or internal working models of attachment, structure the child's accumulated learning as to which affective displays evoke positive attention and which lead to caregiver withdrawal. Thus, internal working models serve an immediate adaptive function in that they permit infants to anticipate caregiver responses and to adjust their behaviors to maximize benign engagement by caregivers. Because caregivers vary with respect to their modes of perceiving and responding to their infants' manifestations of affect, it follows that infants' working models of attachment, being based on their experiences in dyadic interactions with caregivers, will also exhibit systematic structural variations. These variations, in turn, will be expressed as individual differences in infants' ways of coping with emotion and relating to caregivers.

Working models are relatively stable constructs. They guide the individual's behavior not only within the confines of the relational contexts in which they were formed but also in analogous interpersonal interactions at subsequent developmental stages. Relationships involving the giving and receiving of instrumental or emotional support arouse affective responses reminiscent of those experienced in early childhood and activate the social-cognitive interpretive structures associated with such affects. As a result of their repeated activation, primordial working models continue to structure the individual's social cognitions and interpretations of affective communication even into adulthood. Moreover, to the extent that working models of attachment become active at different times and in different situations, the individual's social interactions will exhibit some form of consistency or coherence across contexts. In short, people come to manifest characteristic interpersonal styles, whose origins can be located in their generalized representations of their relational histories.

What kinds of relational experiences contribute to the evolution of a working model that supports positive socioemotional functioning? In Bowlby's (1973) view, optimally adaptive working models are fastened through bonds with attachment figures who afford consistent nurturance, effective help in coping with negative affects, and freedom to contemplate a full spectrum of emotions in self and other. The means by which these ends are achieved vary depending on the individual's age or developmental stage. During infancy and early childhood, attachment figures provide for physical needs in a sensitive manner, soothe during times of distress, and demonstrate accurate attunement to emotions, primarily through nonverbal channels. As children mature, attachment figures reflect with them on their own and others' affective experience and may support their autonomous coping efforts through engaging them in problem-solving discussions (see especially Bowlby, 1973, pp. 322–323; Bretherton & Munholland, 1999, p. 93).

In Bowlby's view, those with such relational histories come to expect that in general, others will respond supportively when they express need, sadness, or anxiety. Over time, such individuals also build a sense of self-worth and a confidence in their capacity to assuage their own negative affects. Their beliefs in the helpfulness of others and in their own affect regulation skills engender a sense that emotional experiences need not be feared. This comfort with the world of emotions leads to a valuing of affects as sources of information that help maintain valued relationships and clarify personal goals.

According to Bowlby, these ways of regarding affect and affect regulation are the identifying features of secure attachment. They are advantageous to the secure person in that they foster a habit of reflecting with interest on the psychological states of self and others. Moreover, they help the secure person to apprehend and tolerate all manner of emotional experiences and communications met with later in life. In appraisals of self and other in relation, the secure person feels no impulse to censor or overemphasize any category of emotion for defensive purposes. As a result of this reflective attitude and lack of attentional bias, the individual will be able more readily to recognize moments when current socioemotional experience cannot be accurately depicted or understood through the application of existing so-cial-cognitive structures. Instead of becoming dysregulated by these mo-ments of recognition, the individual will be stimulated by them to reorganize current representations of relationships, creating *new* interpretive catego-ries that place past history and recent events in meaningful relation to one another (cf. Piaget, 1966, 1970, 1985, on perturbations as stimulating in-creases in the complexity of cognitive structures).

In short, the approach to emotion that a person learns though partici-pating in a relationship with a sensitive attachment figure helps to build a working model that remains an *open system*: The individual's ability to per-ceive, reflect on, and metabolize a variety of affective experiences allows him or her continually to integrate environmental feedback and thus to build increasingly complex social-cognitive structures. These more complex struc-tures, in turn, assist individuals in generating appropriate responses to an ever-widening array of environmental challenges. Thus, it can be seen that the defining characteristic of a secure working model is that it retains a *capacity for development*.

By contrast, children are at risk for forming internal working models with unfavorable implications for long-term adjustment if caregivers fail to respond in consistent, empathic, and supportive ways to manifestations of emotion, especially of distress. These caregiver tendencies are thought to contribute to insecure attachments. Insecurity consists in a sense that sig-nificant others cannot be relied upon for assistance in regulating negative affects and in a lack of self-soothing skills. This lack of trust in self and others fosters a propensity to regard feelings of need, sadness, and fear as dangerously disruptive. As a means of coping with this basic anxiety about emotions and relationships, insecure individuals are thought to develop some form of bias in their attention to emotional information; the precise nature of this bias depends on specific aspects of interaction patterns within the caregiver–child dyad.

If, for example, a parent systematically ignores, dismisses, or punishes a child when he or she expresses attachment-related affects, the child inter-nalizes the message that these emotions are objectionable or shameful and that he or she must suppress their display in order to forestall rejection. In effect, the child's experiences teach him or her that the only safe way to cope with his or her own need or unhappiness is through denial. In consequence, the child habitually excludes attachment-related affects from the internal working model of self and other in relation and develops a strong, fear-driven investment in maintaining such exclusion. If the caregiver's responses to the child's displays of attachment-related emotions are inconsistent or intermittently reinforcing rather than routinely dismissive, the child learns that, although he or she may at times be unable to elicit assistance whatever is tried, the best hope of doing so is to maximize the intensity and duration of the negative affective expressions. Thus, the caregiver's unreliability and the child's adaptation to it cause the child to become anxiously fixated on his or her own distress. The child's internal working model of self and others reflects this preoccupation, overemphasizing the experiences of sadness, helplessness, dependency, and abandonment at the expense of memories involving his or her own mastery or others' supportiveness.

Because insecure approaches to affect regulation involve creating and maintaining biases in the perception of emotional information, they limit the individual's ability to receive affect-laden communications inconsistent with his or her existing relationship schemas. Therefore, novel relationship experiences that might inspire secure people to reevaluate and reorganize their relationship representations will not prompt the same response in insecure individuals. Instead, insecure people, motivated by the need to make new affective experiences controllable through familiar means, will tend to distort information as they overassimilate it to the extant social-cognitive structures. Insecure working models of self and other in relation are, then, *closed systems,* and as such, they are characterized by limitations in their development over time.

Attachment theory's ideas on the origins, nature, and functioning of insecure versus secure working models may be summarized as follows: People's predominant affect regulation strategies, which they establish through interactions with their first caregiver, influence their modes of interpreting relationships. These modes of interpretation guide their conduct in subsequent interpersonal interactions and thus impart a cross-contextual continuity to their functioning. The nature of this continuity differs, however, depending on whether the individual is insecurely or securely attached: Insecure people form a fixed interpretive template, which they apply more or less indiscriminately to situations in their current life; the repeated imposition of this model may lead them into stereotyped social behaviors that are sometimes a poor fit to their changing relational world. In contrast, secure people are identified by their continual, active engagement in constructing and reconstructing their relationship representations. In their case, one would not expect to see rigidly repetitive behavior patterns. Instead, the common theme uniting their functioning in disparate situations is their increased likelihood of success—success in making emotional connections with others, in recovering from setbacks, and in meeting new challenges. The attachment perspective, then, sees secure working models as conferring adaptive advantage largely by virtue of their capacity for increasing in complexity, a capacity that depends on the individual's ability to engage freely in the contemplation of interpersonal affects.

Attachment Research Relevant to the Concept of Internal Working Models: A Brief Overview

Since attachment research was first launched in the late 1970s, workers in the field have generated myriad studies to test hypotheses embedded in or suggested by the internal working model construct outlined above. A comprehensive survey of this vast literature is beyond the scope of this chapter. The selective review that follows is intended simply to underscore key concepts in attachment theory regarding the development, implications, and properties of relationship representations.

Ainsworth's pioneering investigation (Ainsworth, Blehar, Waters, & Wall, 1978), well known to all students of attachment theory, was the first to document relationships between infants' reunion behavior and primary caregivers' parenting styles in the Strange Situation procedure desired to evoke attachment-related affects. Once Ainsworth et al. had illuminated the secure, avoidant, and anxious–ambivalent patterns of infant attachment, numerous studies traced connections between caregiver behaviors and infant attachment status, noting that maternal sensitivity (e.g., Cox, Owen, Henderson, & Margand, 1992), prompt responsiveness to distress (e.g., Crockenberg, 1981), interactional synchrony (Isabella & Belsky, 1991), and warmth (e.g., Bates, Maslin, & Frankel, 1985) were all correlated with security, whereas absence of these qualities was linked with insecurity (see Belsky, 1999a, for review). Furthermore, experimental studies showed that, in cases where clinical interventions enhanced caregiving sensitivity in participating mothers of babies, these increases in sensitivity led, in turn, to a heightened probability that the mothers' infants would develop secure attachments to them (van Ijzendoorn, Juffer, & Duyvesteyn, 1995). Thus, the overall pattern of results was consistent with attachment theory's assertion that caregiving styles played a causal role with respect to attachment status. A recent meta-analytic study revealed, however, that dimensions of maternal behavior accounted for only a modest to moderate portion of the variance in attachment status (DeWolff & van Ijzendoorn, 1997; see also review in Belsky, 1999a).

In addition to facilitating the exploration of links between parenting and attachment status, Ainsworth's development of the Strange Situation permitted the examination of a second premise of attachment theory, namely that attachment status should be related to children's levels of social competence in settings beyond the caregiver–child dyad and in later phases of development. Infant attachment status was shown to predict children's socioemotional functioning in at least three domains. Researchers demonstrated, first of all, that young children who were securely attached to their mothers in infancy interacted more harmoniously with their siblings than did children with insecure attachment histories (e.g., Teti & Ablard, 1989). Second, security of attachment at 12 to 18 months appeared to have favorable implications for children's relationships with friends. Compared to peers judged insecure in infancy, school-age children rated secure earlier in their lives established more extensive friendship networks and had greater success in sustaining positive relationships with their friends (Grossman & Grossman, 1991). Finally, children who were securely attached as infants seemed to be at an advantage in dealing with peers who were not close friends. For example, those with secure early attachments tended to be well liked by peers and to receive high ratings from adult observers on measures of social participation, social dominance, and conflict resolution (Grossman & Grossman, 1991; LaFreniere & Sroufe, 1985). They were also less likely either to victimize or to be bullied by peers than were children rated insecure as babies (Troy & Sroufe, 1987; see Belsky, 1990; Belsky, 1999b; Berlin & Cassidy, 1999; Sroufe, 1986; and Thompson, 1999, for reviews).

Attachment scholars typically accounted for results like those cited by inferring the operation of working models, as had Bowlby. Specifically, researchers posited that the observed correlations between early attachment status and later social behaviors were mediated by social-cognitive structures, which emerged from early caregiver–child relationships, maintained themselves over time, and organized children's social interpretations and interactions long after infancy. In particular, secure attachments were thought to foster interpersonal attitudes and coping skills supporting the development of flexible, optimally adaptive internal working models.

Several patterns in the literature on the Strange Situation and children's adjustment provided substantiation for this idea. School-age children with secure attachment histories proved more likely than those previously judged insecure to attribute positive characteristics to others and to regard them as potential sources of support in times of need (e.g., Cassidy, Kirsh, Scolton, & Parke, 1996; Grossman & Grossman, 1991). Children who were secure as infants had more favorable views of themselves as well: They evinced higher self-esteem, agency, and self-confidence, while manifesting a willingness to acknowledge their own vulnerabilities (e.g., Cassidy, 1988; Grossman & Grossman, 1991; see also Thompson, 1999, for review). Their approaches to managing negative affects, moreover, were found by some researchers to be more effective and adaptive (e.g., Cassidy, 1994; Isabella, 1993; Sroufe, 1979). Perhaps most interestingly, children judged secure in infancy displayed more comfort and less resistance than others when asked to contemplate their own attachment-related affects or to talk about topics likely to evoke such affects (e.g., Grossman & Grossman, 1991; Main, Kaplan, & Cassidy, 1985). For example, Main et al. found that six-year-olds rated secure at age one were able to discuss the theme of children's separation from parents in a relaxed, reflective fashion, whereas insecure children responded to the same theme with avoidance, displays of sadness, or disorganization. Taken together, these findings are consistent with Bowlby's notion that positive caregiver–infant relationships promote basic trust and positive affect regulation skills, which allow the individual to attend in an unbiased fashion to feelings summoned up in interpersonal contexts.

A more recently emerging line of work, focusing on adults' conceptions of their attachment bonds with their own first caregivers, has contributed in important ways to the extension and elaboration of the working model construct. With a view toward studying Bowlby's notion that adults' representations of early attachment experiences should predict aspects of their current functioning, Mary Main outlined a system for eliciting and classifying such representations. The Adult Attachment Interview (AAI) was designed to evoke as thorough an account as individuals could give concerning the quality of their relationships with principal caregivers during childhood. Respondents were asked to include consideration of remembered distress, loss, rejection, and separation experiences. Through examining the discourse strategies that they used to address these affect-laden topics, respondents could be assigned to one of three categories of adult attachment status, each reflecting a "state of mind with respect to attachment" (see description of the AAI and accompanying coding system in Main, Kaplan, & Cassidy, 1985).

Adults designated secure according to Main's system manifested some attitudes and skills reminiscent of those identified in children with secure attachment histories. For example, secure adults openly avowed their need for emotional support and placed a high value on attachment relationships. They tended to be balanced and compassionate in their evaluations of others and of themselves as children. Like secure children asked to discuss attachment-related themes, they readily recalled and reflected on a wide range of affects in themselves and others. If their affective memories were painful, they managed to contain them rather than becoming overwhelmed or avoiding discussion of them; thus, they showed affect tolerance and freedom from attentional bias, as had children rated secure in infancy. These two strengths helped secure adults to arrive at meaningful, plausible integrations of their remembered relational experience. Moreover, they evinced an awareness that they themselves had actively construed their accounts and that alternative constructions were possible. Main referred to these combined manifestations of integrative insight, self-awareness, and flexibility by the single term *coherence*. She identified coherence as the discourse property most indicative of security in adults. It follows, then, that respondents whose discourse led Main to develop her two insecure categories (dismissing and preoccupied) exhibited a limited ability to provide coherent accounts of their attachment experiences and appeared to lack a sense of their own agency as authors of the histories they presented in the AAI. Individuals who inspired Main's dismissing category described their early attachment relationships in idealized, abstract terms that were contradicted or unsupported by their specific memories; to the extent that experiences of negative affect were recollected, their impact on the self was dismissed as unimportant. Preoccupied individuals, in contrast, appeared unable either to contain or to avoid negative affects evoked during the AAI: They seemed flooded by predominantly unhappy memories, and as a result, their versions of their personal histories were both ruminative and confused.

Research using the AAI yielded impressive evidence for the predictive utility of adults' current state of mind with respect to attachment. Studies relating adult attachment status to parenting behaviors indicated that secure mothers were more likely than insecure ones to perceive and match their infants' affects accurately (Haft & Slade, 1989). Secure mothers were also found to be more supportive and effective in helping their children to complete laboratory tasks (Crowell & Feldman, 1988). Adult attachment status proved to be correlated not only with parenting styles but with socioemotional adjustment broadly construed (e.g., Hesse, 1999; Kobak & Sceery, 1988). For example, secure individuals were found to be less likely to manifest psychiatric disorders: Dismissing attachment status, conversely, was associated with affective disorders, and preoccupied status was linked with character pathology (see Hesse, 1999, for a review of the literature on adult attachment status as a predictor of socioemotional adjustment).

In sum, the empirical literature has converged to establish that attachment security—both as assessed in the Strange Situation and as measured in the Adult Attachment Interview—forecasts adaptive outcomes. Moreover, existing evidence is consistent with Bowlby's position that security of attachment predicts positive adjustment largely because it entails a capacity for flexibility in the representation of relationships. This ability may derive from other skills and characteristics found in conjunction with attachment security—namely, a propensity to value connections with others, a strong sense of self-efficacy, a high level of affect tolerance, and a habit of reflecting with minimal bias on affect-laden information from the past and present.

Available data also indicate that although caregiving quality makes a relatively modest contribution to the variance in attachment status, it cannot be regarded as its sole determinant. This overall finding may be one of the reasons why a growing number of attachment scholars now argue that it is time for the field to expand the scope of its attention beyond the caregiver–child dyad, devoting more energy to a systematic exploration of the ways in which other relational dynamics (e.g., Berlin & Cassidy, 1999; Hesse, 1999), particularly those within the family (e.g., Belsky, 1999a; Byng-Hall, 1990,

1995, 1999; Marvin, 1992; Marvin & Stewart, 1990), can shape attachment-related processes.

Family contextual factors have not been wholly neglected by attachment researchers over the years. Indeed, a substantial subgroup have included measures of marital quality in their studies. However, this work has typically construed dimensions of marriage as distal variables, expected to affect attachment status indirectly through their impact on parenting (e.g., Goldberg & Easterbrooks, 1984; Howes & Markman, 1989; Lewis, Owen, & Cox, 1988; see Belsky, 1999a, for review; see also Hazan & Shaver, 1987, for a notable exception). Research along these lines does not help uncover factors that would account for the variance in attachment status not explained by parenting, nor does it embody the approach advocated by commentators like John Byng-Hall. Byng-Hall (1990, 1995, 1999) stressed the potential value of considering aspects of family dynamics, like coparenting collaboration or whole-family emotional climate, as *direct* influences on children's working models of relationships.

These ideas regarding the importance of family process converge with a trend that has been gathering momentum in the wider discipline of developmental psychology over the past 2 decades: integrating family systems concepts into research on individual socioemotional adjustment in general. The following part of this chapter briefly describes the conceptual underpinnings of this movement, identifies some major lines of empirical investigation based on these ideas, and concludes by commenting on the possible relevance of this body of work to the understanding of working models and representational flexibility.

The Case for Greater Holism: Empirical Studies on Family Process and Child Development

In a ground-breaking 1981 article, developmentalist Jay Belsky called upon his colleagues to adopt a more holistic perspective on the family as a context for children's development. Belsky presented a conceptualization of the mother–father–infant triad as a system composed of qualitatively distinct units—individuals, marital processes, and parent-child dyadic relationships—which were all linked through patterns of reciprocal influence. In keeping with this view, Belsky argued that dynamics within any of the family system's constituent parts merited examination as possible determinants of children's functioning.

This hypothesis gave rise to several new research endeavors. In one of these, connections between marital dynamics and child outcomes were explored. Investigations along these lines suggested not only that marital variables were linked to children's adjustment but also that marital quality made contributions to child outcomes that were unmediated by the effects of parent-child interactions (see, e.g., E. M. Cummings, 1994, and Emery, Fincham, & Cummings, 1992, for reviews and commentary on theoretical implications).

A more recently emerging literature inspired by developmental psychologists' turn toward holism concerned *coparenting* processes and their impact on children. The concept of coparenting refers to the transactions occurring between two adults as they work together to raise a child or children for whom they share responsibility (see, e.g., Gable, Belsky, & Crnic, 1992; McHale, 1995; McHale, Kuersten, & Lauretti, 1996; Weissman & Cohen, 1985). Coparenting partnerships may be formed by children's two biological parents, whether married (e.g., Lewis, Beavers, Gossett, & Phillips, 1976; Katz & Gottman, 1996; McHale, 1995), divorced (e.g., Buchanan, Maccoby, & Dornbusch, 1991), or single; by grandmother–mother dyads (e.g., Chase-Lansdale, Brooks-Gunn, & Zamsky, 1994; Wakschlag, Chase-Lansdale, & Brooks-Gunn, 1996); by same-sex couples (e.g., Patterson & Chan, 1999); or by any other pair of adults who make a commitment to joint child-rearing. Thus far, however, research on this topic has concentrated primarily on the description and analysis of coparenting alliances formed by heterosexual spousal partners.

Although coparenting dynamics are structured largely by the two adult participants and could therefore be seen as dyadic, the coparenting construct is an implicitly triadic or polyadic one, in that all the interactions it comprises pertain to or express the partners' shared connection to one or more children. Thus, the concept of coparenting represents an attempt to move one step beyond Belsky's 1981 model of the family system as a group of interacting individuals and dyads and to consider triadic dynamics themselves as qualitatively distinct units of analysis, in the manner recommended by such family theorists as Patricia Minuchin (1985, 1988; see also Nichols & Schwartz, 1998).

In the available empirical findings on coparenting dynamics, three overall patterns may be discerned, all of which help to establish the construct validity of the coparenting concept. First, whether assessed via self-report (e.g., Abidin & Brunner, 1995; Block, Block, & Morrison, 1981; Brody & Flor, 1996; Floyd & Zmich, 1991; Jouriles et al., 1991; McHale & Rasmussen, 1998) or through observations of family interactions (e.g., Belsky, Putnam, & Crnic, 1996; Brody & Flor, 1996; Fivaz-Depeursinge et al., 1994; Fivaz-Depeursinge, Frascarolo, & Corboz-Warnery, 1996; Lindahl, 1998; McConnell & Kerig, 1999; McHale, Johnson, & Sinclair, 1999; McHale & Rasmussen, 1998), coparenting quality has clear implications for child outcomes: Cooperative, harmonious coparenting predicts children's positive socioemotional adjustment (e.g., Block et al., 1981; Jouriles et al., 1991; McHale, Lauretti, & Talbot, 1998), and conflicted or otherwise negative coparenting predicts a variety of internalizing and externalizing child behavior problems (e.g., McConnell, & Kerig, 1999; McHale & Rasmussen, 1998). A second group of findings suggests that, as family systems theories would assume, coparenting dynamics are empirically distinguishable from dimensions of dyadic parent–child relationship quality and cannot be adequately approximated by summing data that pertain to each partner's parenting in one-on-one interactions with children (Belsky, 1979; Buhrmester, Camparo, Christensen, Gonzalez, & Hinshaw, 1992; Clarke-Stewart, 1978; Eslinger, Magovcevic, & McHale, 1997; Gjerde, 1986; McHale, Kuersten-Hogan, Lauretti, & Rasmussen, 2000). Thirdly, coparenting and marital processes also seem to be distinct from one another in terms of their respective impacts on children's adjustment (Jouriles et al., 1991; McHale & Rasmussen, 1998; Snyder, Klein, Gdowski, Faulstich, & LaCombe, 1988).

In brief, contextually oriented developmentalists have made a compelling case for their position that marital and coparenting dynamics have an important bearing on child outcomes. But can the existing evidence shed light on more specific questions from the field of attachment concerning the impact of family contextual variables on the flexibility–rigidity dimension of children's relationship representations? The next two sections address this issue by using the empirical literature to reflect on two hypotheses regarding the manner in which family processes may act upon working models. The next part of this chapter reviews data pertaining to the proposition that marital and coparenting dynamics may affect the development of children's social-cognitive interpretive structures via their influence on the child adjustment variables identified by attachment theory as the foundations of representational flexibility.

Although attachment theory originally conceived of representational flexibility–rigidity as a property belonging to dyadic working models of attachment, it seems likely that individuals' characteristic approach to observing and processing affect-laden information would manifest itself in any type of relationship representation that they formed. Thus, structural flexibility–rigidity is conceptualized in the following discussion as an attribute that is relevant to the description of all working models, whether polyadic or dyadic.

It will also be argued that family dynamics beyond the caregiver–child dyad may have implications not only for individuals' general ability to revise their interpretive structures, but also for the particular ways in which the flexibility–rigidity dimension is reflected in their approach to construing *relations among contemporaneous relationships*. Malcolm Watson's (Watson & Amogott-Kwan, 1983, 1984; Watson & Fischer, 1993; Watson & Getz, 1990a, 1990b) work on children's understanding of family roles will serve as a framework within which findings from the empirical and clinical family literatures are organized and interpreted.

MARITAL AND COPARENTING DYNAMICS AS INFLUENCES ON THE FOUNDATIONS OF REPRESENTATIONAL FLEXIBILITY

As suggested earlier, attachment theory maintains that the secure individual's ongoing evaluation and reconstruction of working models is made possible by certain essential attitudes and capacities. Secure persons trust that others will generally be willing and able to respond to their needs in a positive, helpful way, and they also exhibit a consistent sense of self-efficacy, especially with regard to managing their own emotions. These assumptions about self and others may support the solid affect regulation skills that are often ascribed to the secure individual. They may likewise contribute to the sense of ease and comfort with which they typically contemplate their affective experiences and memories. These four capacities operating in concert foster secure persons' habit of reflection on interpersonal themes, and they obviate any need for them to engage in defensive distortions or exclusions of affect-laden information. The following discussion will consider what empirical family studies have to say about the role of marital and coparenting dynamics in contributing to or impeding development in the four bases of representational flexibility.

Children's Attitudes Toward Others

Data suggesting that marital quality shapes children's expectations regarding the availability and helpfulness of their parents came from the work of E. Mark Cummings and his colleagues (Davies & Cummings, 1998; Davies, Cummings, Meyers, & Heindel, 1999; El-Sheikh & Cummings, 1995). This group of researchers surmised that exposure to marital conflict might have adverse consequences for children's sense of emotional security within the family. To test this hypothesis, they designed experimental analogue studies in which they considered how different levels of interadult background anger affected children's attitudes and appraisals about the adults involved. In each investigation, children in a control group watched brief video clips of a couple engaged in amicable interactions, whereas children assigned to an experimental condition viewed a series of videotaped vignettes involving a couple in the throes of hostile, unresolved disputes. The children who were presented with scenes of discord proved more likely to predict an unhappy, conflict-ridden future for the couple they saw. This result was obtained in separate studies involving school-aged children (El-Sheikh & Cummings, 1995) and adolescents (Davies et al., 1999).

The investigators saw their findings as providing insight into the states of mind that marital conflict might engender in children. They reasoned that if children in the studies expected the worst for couples whose arguments they viewed, then children who frequently saw similar altercations between their parents might develop equally pessimistic expectations about their parents' marriages. These perceptions might lead children to fear that their parents were too preoccupied with their own relationship difficulties to serve as reliable sources of support. Davies and Cummings generated more direct evidence of this supposition in a 1998 study on 6-to-9-year-old children who had been exposed to varying degrees of marital conflict in their homes. Results indicated that children who had more extensive histories of exposure to marital discord were more likely than peers with different backgrounds to see interparental strife as threatening to their own well-being and as detrimental to family relationships in general.

Children's Confidence in Themselves and in Their Affect-Regulation Skills

We know of no studies that specifically focus on associations between marital or coparenting quality and children's sense of self-efficacy with respect to affect regulation. However, some investigators have considered related issues. For instance, El-Sheikh and Cummings (1995) found that school-aged children who had been exposed to episodes of unresolved interadult anger in a laboratory setting were more likely than children in a control group to tell interviewers that they felt sad and expected to feel sad in the future. This observation suggests the possibility that children who often witness their parents engaged in analogous conflicts may not only experience depressed mood as a result but may also tend to see themselves as relatively powerless to change their emotional states through efforts of their own. In addition, Eslinger et al. (1997) noted that young adults who recalled experiencing high degrees of coparenting conflict in their families of origin were more likely than peers raised by cooperative coparenting teams to report feelings of low self-efficacy and low self-esteem. Eslinger et al. observed, moreover, that participants' coparenting histories made contributions to the variance in self-concept measures even after the effects of early parent–child relationship quality were accounted for.

Emotional Reactivity and Self-Regulation

Among all the child outcome variables believed to influence representational flexibility, those having to do with emotional reactivity and self-regulation have received the greatest attention within the literatures on marital conflict and coparenting. Researchers on marital conflict have consistently demonstrated that children from infancy through adolescence experience distress and heightened arousal in response to background interadult anger (e.g., E. M. Cummings, Zahn-Waxler, & Radke-Yarrow, 1981; see also E. M. Cummings, 1994, for review). In addition, an abundance of evidence supports the conclusion that children who have a history of exposure to interparental conflict are more likely than peers without such histories to display negative emotional reactivity when they witness interadult anger outside the home. Affective displays assessed include crying, facial and verbal expressions of sadness or anxiety, muscular tension, and freezing (e.g., E. M. Cummings, Iannotti, & Zahn-Waxler, 1985; J. S. Cummings, Pellegrini, Notarius, & Cummings, 1989; E. M. Cummings, Vogel, Cummings, & El-Sheikh, 1989; Davies & Cummings, 1998). The intensity of children's reactivity in extrafamilial settings appears to depend on the frequency (E. M. Cummings et al., 1985; E. M. Cummings et al., 1981; Johnston, Gonzalez, & Campbell, 1987) and intensity (J. S. Cummings et al., 1989; E. M. Cummings et al., 1981; Johnston et al., 1987) of the interparental conflict in their home environments, as well as on the degree to which conflict resolution occurs (E. M. Cummings, 1987; J. S. Cummings et al., 1989; E. M. Cummings et al., 1985; E. M. Cummings et al., 1981). E. M. Cummings (1994) interpreted the connection between conflict properties and children's manifestations of reactivity as an indication that repeated episodes of destructive interparental strife lowered children's thresholds for dysregulation, increasing the likelihood that they might respond to relatively minor episodes of extrafamilial conflict with strong, potentially overwhelming negative responses.

A wealth of data also documents links between the quality of triadic coparenting interactions and children's ability to modulate affects and impulses. A high degree of coparenting harmony seems to promote the growth of adaptive self-regulation skills in children (Block et al., 1981; McHale, Krasnow, & Slavick, 1997). For example, in a study on coparenting in families with toddlers, McHale et al. (1997) found that couples whose coparenting was characterized by high levels of cooperation and low levels of verbal sparring were more likely than other couples to have children who showed optimal degrees of impulse control when performing challenging teaching tasks: Children of parents with more cooperative coparenting styles tended to approach task performance with persistence, high frustration tolerance, and positive affect.

Conversely, disturbances in coparenting predict deficiencies in children's capacity for self-regulation. One dynamic that appears detrimental in this regard is hostile-competitive coparenting, in which partners compete for control of the triadic family interaction, vying for their child's attention, undermining one another's parenting initiatives, and sometimes trading sarcastic or critical remarks (e.g., Haley, 1988; Katz & Gottman, 1996; Kerr & Bowen, 1988; McHale, 1995; S. Minuchin, 1974). Cross-sectional (Jouriles et al., 1991; McConnell & Kerig, 1999) and longitudinal studies (Belsky et al., 1996; Block et al., 1981; McHale & Rasmussen, 1998) have linked the hostile-competitive pattern to disinhibition or impulse control problems in children. Some research has uncovered associations between this coparenting style and children's difficulties in coping with anxiety as well (Block et al., 1981; Jouriles et al., 1991; McConnell & Kerig, 1999).

A second coparenting style that has negative implications for children's modulation of anxiety is the skewed pattern, in which one partner withdraws from the triadic interaction, while the other becomes involved with the child to the point of enmeshment (McConnell & Kerig, 1999; McHale & Rasmussen, 1998; for descriptions of skewed coparenting, see, e.g., Haley, 1988; Jackson, 1965; Katz & Gottman, 1996; Lewis, Tresch-Owen, & Cox, 1988; McHale, 1995; S. Minuchin, 1974). McHale and Rasmussen (1998) observed, for example, that coparenting partners who displayed highly discrepant levels of involvement in triadic interaction with their 1-year-old infants were more likely than other parents to have children who manifested problems in coping with anxiety 3 years later.

Freedom Versus Attentional Bias in Contemplating Affective Experiences

As yet, relatively few studies have attempted to discern relationships between marital or coparenting processes and children's capacity for calm, unbiased reflection on affective themes. However, results from these investigations are intriguing, suggesting that further inquiry into this topic is well warranted. To begin with, researchers have reported that in families whose coparenting interactions are characterized by high levels of cooperation and agreement between parents, children manifest a sense of comfort and an absence of distress when discussing negative emotions, whether experienced by themselves (Block et al., 1981) or by fictional characters in stories about families (McHale et al., 1999). Conversely, in instances when families ranked low on coparenting cooperation, children manifested uneasiness when talking about such affects as anger or sadness. McHale et al. (1999) found, in particular, that preschoolers who had experienced uncooperative coparenting dynamics in their homes responded with behavioral signs of resistance or avoidance when asked to complete story stems about family conflict. These avoidant behaviors included fidgeting, changing the topic of discussion, asking to discontinue the task, and chanting, "I don't know, I don't know" in response to interviewers' questions.

Although research indicates that a *lack* of coparenting cooperation predicts children's tendency to turn their attention away from negative emotions, investigators have also noted that the positive *presence* of disturbances in marriage and coparenting fosters children's anxious preoccupation with themes of anger and conflict. According to McHale et al. (1999), preschoolers from families exhibiting skewed coparenting patterns plus low levels of warmth were more likely than their peers to feature intrafamilial acts of aggression when telling stories about happy, sad, mad, and worried families in the context of a laboratory exercise. The effects of triadic process variables on children's portrayals of aggression were significant even after controlling for the influence of maternal and paternal parenting styles.

Children exposed to overt displays of hostility in marital and coparenting interactions seem to manifest a similar fixation of attention on angry emotionality: Cummings and colleagues have demonstrated that, in comparison to controls, children with histories of exposure to verbally (Davies & Cummings, 1998) or physically aggressive (J. S. Cummings et al., 1989) interparental conflict tend to show an exaggerated vigilance in response to viewing simulated hostile encounters between their mothers and researchers: Children were identified as manifesting vigilance if they turned from their ongoing play activity to a close observation of the enacted conflict (J. S. Cummings et al., 1989; Davies & Cummings, 1998), or if the quality of their affective displays shifted abruptly when the conflict scenario ensued (J. S. Cummings et al., 1989).

Related findings were obtained by Grugan and McHale in a 1997 study involving first-year college students. Participants viewed a series of 30-second video clips showing coparenting partners at play with their toddlers. Some of these family triads manifested warm, cooperative styles of interaction, whereas others showed subtle signs of competition or hostility, such as verbal sparring. Students with self-reported histories of high exposure to interparental conflict in their families of origin were more likely than those with histories of low exposure to attribute hostility to the coparenting interactions they observed. Thus, it appeared that angry emotionality had become especially salient to those individuals who regularly witnessed conflict between their parents during the course of their upbringing.

MARITAL AND COPARENTING DYNAMICS AS INFLUENCES ON MANIFESTATIONS OF FLEXIBILITY SPECIFIC TO POLYADIC RELATIONSHIP REPRESENTATIONS

Although family-level processes beyond the caregiver–child dyad may enhance or diminish a person's overall capacity for reconstructing working models of any description, they may also have a more specific relevance to his or her polyadic relationship representation. Individuals' participation in multiperson relational dynamics within their family of origin may directly affect their subsequent assumptions about how they can or should situate themselves with respect to two or more significant others who are also emotionally connected to one another. Some kinds of triadic or whole-family processes may be particularly beneficial in freeing a person to reexamine, reconfigure, and extend his or her working models of self in relation to several significant others, whereas other types of whole-family interaction patterns may engender qualitatively distinct types of distortion or rigidity in multiperson relationship representations. As yet, research permitting the assessment of this conjecture is quite limited. However, as the following discussion will attempt to show, Malcolm Watson's theoretical and empirical work (Watson & Amgott-Kwan, 1983; Watson & Fischer, 1993; Watson & Getz, 1990a, 1990b) on the development of family-role understanding in children offers a rich heuristic for reflection on this question.

Watson and his colleagues (Watson & Amgott-Kwan, 1983, 1984; Watson & Fischer, 1993; Watson & Getz, 1990a, 1990b) conducted a series of studies intended to define the stages through which children develop an increasingly complex conceptualization of family and social roles. According to their research, children between the ages of 5 and 6 have just begun to grasp the concept that one individual can simultaneously occupy different roles with respect to different people. For example, when considering the place that their mother occupies within the family, they can now see that the person who is a parent to them can also be a spouse to their father. Watson and colleagues refer to this insight as a recognition of *family role intersections* (Watson & Amgott-Kwan, 1983; Watson & Fischer, 1993). Attainment of this stage would appear necessary for a child to construct a truly triadic relationship representation, in which each member of the triad is described in terms of his or her connection to each other member.

Only by about age 12 do children reach the most advanced stage of role understanding, acquiring the ability consistently and correctly to *deconstruct* or qualify the ideas that they have formed about family-role intersections. This skill is based on the realization that although some clusters of family roles are typically filled simultaneously by one person, the roles are nonetheless separable. A child who has reached this stage can understand that although a father may be married to his child's mother, it is possible for him to withdraw from his role as spouse while remaining in his role as father (Watson & Amgott-Kwan, 1984). The child is also equipped to appreciate that the father can maintain his affectional bond with his child, even if no such connection exists between him and the child's mother. Thus, the child functioning at this level now has the cognitive capacity to rearrange his representations of connections among members of the family triad in ways that preserve the internal consistency of those representations. Watson commented that although children typically proceed to these stages at the ages indicated, there may be considerable variation in any given child's rate of progress. Moreover, the level of family-role understanding that children display when given contextual support typically exceeds their functional levels of understanding, which are subject to transient fluctuations.

Might the quality of marital or coparenting dynamics facilitate or impede development in children's family-role understanding, thereby affecting their ability to think flexibly about their triadic relationship representations? Watson and Fischer's (1993) study on divorce as a factor related to 5-year-olds' conceptualization of family roles provides a starting place from which to approach this issue. As noted above, Watson and his associates had shown in prior research that children of age 5, whatever their family circumstances, might be expected to have some trouble perceiving the separability of parental and spousal roles. Watson and Fischer's divorce study provided the additional insight that family structure, as well as age, was associated with children's comprehension of these issues. The researchers reported that as compared with age-mates from intact families, children whose parents had recently divorced functioned at a lower level when asked to explain distinctions and connections among family roles. In particular, these children had greater difficulty seeing how two parents could both continue to be parents if they were no longer married to one another; similarly, these children found it harder to comprehend that both their parents could still love them if they did not love each other.

In reflecting on the meaning of this outcome, Watson and Fischer surmised, first of all, that divorce was probably especially distressing to this young age because of their already limited capacity for deconstructing social-role intersections. Their position on the developmental trajectory of social-role understanding made them vulnerable to assuming that the dissolution of their parents' marital relationship must entail the dissolution of the other family relationships in which the parents were involved. Children's fears of losing one or the other parent could disrupt and distort their perceptions about events in their families, thus making it even more troublesome for them than it would otherwise have been to differentiate between marital and parental roles.

An additional finding of Watson and Fischer's study was that social-role understanding among the children of divorced parents varied considerably and was correlated with children's expressions of positive feelings about the current state of relationships within their families. In their interpretation of this observation, the authors speculated that perhaps those children who voiced positive feelings were experiencing less concern about their own security and therefore suffered from less anxiety-induced confusion about roles within their families. Watson and Fischer also advanced a corollary hypothesis relating to the specific effect of triadic family processes on children's representations of multiperson family relationships. They reasoned that children's levels of positive or negative feelings about the family may depend largely on the extent to which divorcing parents maintain boundaries between their own dyadic relationship on the one hand and their involvements with parenting and coparenting on the other. If each parent works to reassure the child of his or her ongoing availability, endorses the child's continued attachment to the other parent, and participates in cooperative coparenting, they may allay the child's fear of loss. In so doing, they may decrease the degree of rigidity and incoherence in the child's triadic relationship representations. Conversely, if parents fail to exercise such restraint, allowing marital discord to disrupt their parenting and coparenting, then they may exacerbate their child's sense of insecurity, which in turn may hinder development of flexibility in his or her triadic working models.

Watson and Fischer's argument suggests that it is coparenting quality, rather than family structure per se, that affects the ease and accuracy with which children make distinctions between spousal and parental roles. This conclusion seems especially plausible, because the most commonly observed coparenting disturbances (i.e., hostile-competitive and skewed coparenting) appear to provide living proof of the potentially distressing beliefs to which children are prone at lower levels of social-role understanding: When coparenting partners vie with one another for their child's allegiance, or when one partner forms a cross-generational coalition that excludes the other, the child may quite reasonably take this behavior as evidence that it is indeed impossible for him or her to maintain positive emotional connections with two parents who are at odds with one another. Such children may make slower progress than their peers in learning to differentiate between marital and parental roles in general. In addition, as regards the specific content of their triadic relationship representations, they may fall prey to the painful conviction that their only options within the family are to side with one parent, intervene to resolve their parents' conflict, or withdraw from the family triad altogether.

We are unaware of any empirical work that explores the effects of marital or coparenting quality, whether positive or negative, on children's progress through the stages of family-role understanding. However, data from the marital conflict literature do provide some indirect support for the idea that children who repeatedly witness interparental strife are slower than their peers to master the skill of deconstructing family-role intersections. It has been observed that children with histories of exposure to marital conflict are more likely than those who lack such histories to react in maladaptive ways to their parents' disputes (e.g., E. M. Cummings et al., 1981; Johnston et al., 1987; see E. M. Cummings, 1994, for review). Some children try to side with or protect one parent against the other (e.g., Carlson, Cicchetti, Barnett, & Braunwald, 1989; J. S. Cummings et al., 1989; O'Brien, Margolin, John, & Krueger, 1991), whereas others try to mediate between parents (e.g., Grych & Fincham, 1990). Still others distance themselves from both parents, seemingly in despair of retaining the attention and interest of either one. These patterns of coping seem to signal a belief that coparenting partners in conflict with one another cannot maintain their separate bonds with their children. In other words, they are behaviors that bespeak an inability to distinguish between spousal and parental roles. The fact that such behaviors occur with greater frequency in children with higher levels of past exposure to interparental discord may indicate that such discord is detrimental to the development of children's social-role understanding.

What might be the long-term effects of dysfunctional marital or coparenting processes on the flexibility of an individual's multiperson relationship representations? This topic, which has been virtually untouched within the domain of empirical family studies, figures prominently in the family therapy literature (e.g., Lerner, 1986; Nichols & Schwartz, 1998). Clinically oriented family theorists have advanced the view that even after individuals acquire the cognitive ability to appreciate that they can sustain attachments to two people who are not favorably disposed toward each other, they may still carry an emotional legacy from negative triadic interactions in their family of origin. This legacy may take the form of rigid beliefs and anxious feelings about what role they should adopt in the relationship systems to which they belongs as an adult. For example, a person who was embroiled in overtly competitive coparenting dynamics in childhood may exhibit a diminished tolerance for conflict among significant others in her or his present life. The person may harbor the expectation that conflicts between close loved ones or friends will spread to include him or her, as they did in the family of origin, and that this contagion will damage the relationships with those involved. This fear may impel the person to take an inordinate share of responsibility for keeping the peace among the people around him or her. As for individuals who were involved in a cross-generational coalition in childhood, their early experiences may have engendered the belief that whenever they form new emotional connections, friends and loved ones may feel betrayed and punish them with abandonment, as one or both parents may have threatened to do. Consequently, they may become hesitant and overcautious in seeking out social contacts, perhaps even remaining enmeshed with members of their family of origin well into adulthood. According to family theorists, a third possible long-term result of childhood exposure to dysfunctional coparenting is that the individual may simply avoid close relationship.

CONCLUSION: SUMMARY AND RECOMMENDATIONS FOR FUTURE RESEARCH

Attachment research of the past 15 to 20 years has provided compelling evidence that individuals' positive socioemotional adjustment is promoted by a propensity for reflecting on and revising the working models with which they interpret affect-laden interpersonal experiences and memories. Workers in the field of attachment have traditionally implied, through their choice of emphasis, that the quality of early maternal care is perhaps the most crucial influence on representational flexibility and on the subsidiary psychological attributes from which it emerges. This chapter has used theoretical commentary and data from the fields of family psychology and attachment to extend attachment theory's original model for the development of representational flexibility.

According to the expanded framework proposed here, the parent–child dyad is only one of several family subsystems that could affect the child's ability to reshape relationship representations in response to novel information from the interpersonal environment. Other family factors, especially marital and coparenting quality, could also make distinct contributions to the development of representational flexibility. The new model assumes, moreover, that the effects of marital, coparenting, or whole-family processes on the flexibility dimension are mediated through the same variables that attachment theory has viewed as mediators for the effects of parenting styles. These variables include the individual's attitudes regarding the availability of support from others, self-efficacy, self-regulation skills, and freedom from attentional bias in contemplating emotional experiences. A further key premise of the expanded model is that marital or coparenting dynamics will have a specific impact on manifestations of representational flexibility seen only in the individual's polyadic relationship representations.

The current state of research on family processes and relationship representations does not permit any firm and final judgment regarding the validity of this conceptual scheme. Few of the relationships it delineates have been conclusively proven to exist, except for the links between parenting styles and child outcomes. Evaluation of the model will require, first of all, that investigations be conducted to assess the effect of marital and coparenting quality on representational flexibility. Second, research must ascertain whether any effects observed are in fact mediated by the four attitudes and skills outlined above. Third, some studies should include measures of parenting quality as well as of coparenting and marital dynamics in order to determine whether these three factors each have independent effects on the mediating and dependent variables of interest. Studies of this kind would be particularly valuable, because they would offer means of examining interactions among measures of relationship quality in different family subsystems. They would thus make it possible to discern whether harmonious dynamics in one subsystem served to protect representational flexibility from negative processes occurring elsewhere in the family.

Perhaps the most speculative premise of the expanded model is the idea that marital or coparenting dynamics have especial relevance for the manner in which the individual represents relations among contemporaneous relationships. As a first step in investigating this general hypothesis, it would be important to trace connections between marital or coparenting quality and children's skills in thinking flexibly about the role of any one family member with respect to two others. Furthermore, it is as yet unclear precisely how this skill relates to the more general capacity for revising working models that is described by attachment theory. Therefore, it would be helpful to conduct research whose purpose was simply to explore connections between attachment-based measures of representational flexibility and measures like Malcolm Watson's, which may tap features specific to whole-family or polyadic relationship representations.

Attachment theory's idea of representational flexibility has captured the imagination of many scholars, who view the capacities it designates as important indices of individual psychological well-being. This rich and subtle construct may be rendered still more coherent, compelling, and useful if it can be situated within the broader, more ecologically valid context provided by family systems theory and research.

REFERENCES

Abidin, R. R., & Brunner, J. F. (1995). Development of a parenting alliance inventory. *Journal of Clinical Child Psychology, 24,* 31–40.

Ainsworth, M. D. S., Blehar, M. C., Waters, E., & Wall, S. (1978). *Patterns of attachment: A psychological study of the Strange Situation.* Hillsdale, NJ: Lawrence Erlbaum.

Bates, J. E., Maslin, C. A., & Frankel, K. A. (1985). Attachment security, mother–child interaction, and temperament as predictors of behavior-problem ratings at age three years. *Monographs of the Society for Research in Child Development, 50*(1–2, Serial No. 209), 167–193.

Belsky, J. (1979). The interrelation of parental and spousal behavior during infancy in traditional nuclear families: An exploratory analysis. *Journal of Marriage and the Family, 41,* 62–68.

Belsky, J. (1981). Early human experience: A family perspective. *Developmental Psychology, 17,* 3–23.

Belsky, J. (1990). Parental and nonparental child care and children's socioemotional development: A decade in review. *Journal of Marriage and the Family, 52,* 885–903.

Belsky, J. (1999a). Interactional and contextual determinants of attachment security. In J. Cassidy & P. R. Shaver (Eds.), *Handbook of Attachment* (pp. 249–264). New York: Guilford Press.

Belsky, J. (1999b). Modern evolutionary theory and patterns of attachment. In J. Cassidy & P. R. Shaver (Eds.), *Handbook of Attachment* (pp. 141–161). New York: Guilford Press.

Belsky, J., Putnam, S., & Crnic, K. (1996). Coparenting, parenting, and early emotional development. In J. P. McHale & P. Cowan (Eds.), *New directions in child development: Vol 74. Understanding how family-level dynamics affect children's development: Studies of two-parent families* (pp. 45–55). San Francisco: Jossey-Bass.

Berlin, L., & Cassidy, J. (1999). Relations among relationships: Contributions from attachment theory and research. In J. Cassidy & P. R. Shaver (Eds.), *Handbook of attachment* (pp. 688–712). New York: Guilford Press.

Block, J. H., & Block, J. (1980). The role of ego-control and ego-resiliency in the organization of behavior. In W. A. Collins (Ed.), *Minnesota symposia on child psychology: Vol. 13* (pp. 39–102). Hillsdale, NJ: Erlbaum.

Block, J. H., Block, J., & Morrison, A. (1981). Parental agreement–disagreement on childrearing orientations and gender-related personality correlates in children. *Child Development, 52,* 965–974.

Block, J. H., & Kremen, A. M. (1996). IQ and ego resiliency: Conceptual and empirical connections and separateness. *Journal of Personality and Social Psychology, 70,* 349–361.

Bowlby, J. (1958). The child's tie to his mother. *International Journal of Psychoanalysis, 29,* 1–23.

Bowlby, J. (1959). Separation anxiety. *International Journal of Psychoanalysis, 41,* 1–25.

Bowlby, J. (1960). Grief and mourning in infancy. *The Psychoanalytic Study of the Child, 15,* 3–39.

Bowlby, J. (1969). *Attachment and loss: Vol. 1. Attachment.* New York: Basic Books.

Bowlby, J. (1973). *Attachment and loss: Vol. 2. Separation.* New York: Basic Books.

Bowlby, J. (1980). *Attachment and loss: Vol. 3. Loss, sadness and depression.* New York: Basic Books.

Bowlby, J. (1988). *A secure base.* New York: Basic Books.

Bretherton, I., & Munholland, K. A. (1999). Internal working models in attachment relationships: A construct revisited. In J. Cassidy & P. R. Shaver (Eds.), *Handbook of attachment* (pp. 89–111). New York: Guilford Press.

Brody, G., & Flor, D. L. (1996). Coparenting, family interactions, and competence among African American youths. In J. P. McHale & P. Cowan (Eds.), *New directions in child development: Vol 74. Understanding how family-level dynamics affect children's development: Studies of two-parent families* (pp. 77–91). San Francisco: Jossey-Bass.

Buchanan, C. M., Maccoby, E. E., & Dornbusch, S. M. (1991). Caught between parents: Adolescents' experience in divorced homes. *Child Development, 62,* 1008–1029.

Buhrmester, D., Camparo, L., Christensen, A., Gonzalez, L. S., & Hinshaw, S. P. (1992). Mothers and fathers interacting in dyads and triads with normal and hyperactive sons. *Developmental Psychology, 28,* 500–509.

Byng-Hall, J. (1990). Attachment theory and family therapy: A clinical view. *Infant Mental Health Journal, 11,* 228–236.

Byng-Hall, J. (1995). Creating a secure family base: Some implications of attachment theory for family therapy. *Family Process, 34,* 45–58.

Byng-Hall, J. (1999). Family and couple therapy: Toward greater security. In J. Cassidy & P. R. Shaver (Eds.), *Handbook of Attachment* (pp. 625–645). New York: Guilford Press.

Carlson, V., Cicchetti, D., Barnett, D., & Braunwald, K. (1989). Finding order in disorganization: Lessons from research on maltreated infants' attachments to their caregivers. In D. Cicchetti & V. Carlson (Eds.), *Child maltreatment: Theory and research on the causes and consequences of child abuse and neglect* (pp. 494–528). New York: Cambridge University Press.

Cassidy, J. (1988). Child-mother attachment and the self in six-year-olds. *Child Development, 59,* 121–134.

Cassidy, J. (1994). Emotion regulation: Influences of attachment relationships. *Monographs of the Society for Research in Child Development, 59,* 228–249.

Cassidy, J., Kirsch, S. J., Scolton, K. L., & Parke, R. D. (1996). Attachment and representations of peer relationships. *Developmental Psychology, 32,* 892–904.

Chase-Lansdale, P. L., Brooks-Gunn, J., & Zamsky, E. S. (1994). Young African American multigenerational families in poverty: Quality of mothering and grandmothering. *Child Development, 65,* 373–393.

Clarke-Stewart, K. A. (1978). And daddy makes three: The father's impact on mother and young child. *Child Development, 49,* 466–478.

Cox, M., Owen, M. T., Henderson, V. K., & Margand, N. A. (1992). Prediction of infant-father and infant-mother attachment. *Developmental Psychology, 28,* 474–483.

Crockenberg, S. B. (1981). Infant irritability, mother responsiveness, and social support influences on the security of infant–mother attachment. *Child Development, 52,* 857–869.

Crowell, J. A., & Feldman, S. S. (1988). Mothers' internal models of relationships and children's behavioral and developmental status: A study of mother-child interaction. *Child Development, 59,* 1273–1285.

Cummings, E. M. (1994). Marital conflict and children's functioning. *Social Development, 3,* 16–36.

Cummings, E. M., Iannotti, R. J., & Zahn-Waxler, C. (1985). The influence of conflict between adults on the emotions and aggression of young children. *Developmental Psychology, 21,* 495–507.

Cummings, E. M., Vogel, D., Cummings, J. S., & El-Sheikh, M. (1989). Children's responses to different forms of expression of anger between adults. *Child Development, 60,* 1392–1404.

Cummings, E. M., Zahn-Waxler, C., & Radke-Yarrow, M. (1981). Young children's responses to expressions of anger and affection by others in the family. *Child Development, 52,* 1274–1282.

Cummings, J. S., Pellegrini, D. S., Notarius, C. I., & Cummings, E. M. (1989). Children's responses to angry adult behavior as a function of marital distress and history of interparent hostility. *Child Development, 60,* 1035–1043.

Davies, P. T., & Cummings, E. M. (1998). Exploring children's emotional security as a mediator of the link between marital relations and child adjustment. *Child Development, 69,* 124–139.

Davies, P. T., Cummings, E. M., Myers, R. L., & Heindel, S. (1999). Adult conflict history and children's subsequent responses to conflict: An experimental test. *Journal of Family Psychology, 13,* 610–628.

DeWolff, M., & van Ijzendoorn, M. (1997). Sensitivity and attachment: A meta-analysis on parental antecedents of infant attachment. *Child Development, 68,* 571–591.

El-Sheikh, M., & Cummings, E. M. (1995). Children's responses to angry adult behavior as a function of experimentally manipulated exposure to resolved and unresolved conflict. *Social Development, 4,* 75–91.

Emery, R. E., Fincham, F. D., & Cummings, E. M. (1992). Parenting in context: Systemic thinking about parental conflict and its influence on children. *Journal of Consulting and Clinical Psychology, 60,* 909–912.

Eslinger, O., Magovcevic, M., & McHale, J. P. (1997). *Coparenting conflict and sense of self during adolescence.* Paper presented at a meeting of the Eastern Psychological Association, Washington, DC.

Fairbairn, W. R. D. (1952). *Psychoanalytic studies of the personality.* London: Routledge & Kegan Paul.

Fivaz-Depeursinge, E., Burgin, D., Corboz-Warnery, A., Lebovici, S., Stern, D., Byng-Hall, J., & Lamour, M. (1994). The dynamics of interfaces: Seven authors in search of encounters across levels of description of an event involving a mother, father, and baby. *Infant Mental Health Journal, 15,* 69–89.

Fivaz-Depeursinge, E., Frascarolo, F., & Corboz-Warnery, A. (1996). Assessing the triadic alliance between mothers, fathers, and infants at play. In J. P. McHale & P. Cowan (Eds.), *New directions in child development: Vol. 74. Understanding how family-level dynamics affect children's development: Studies of two-parent families* (pp. 27–44). San Francisco: Jossey-Bass.

Floyd, F. J., & Zmich, D. E. (1991). Marriage and the parenting partnership: Perceptions and interactions of parents with mentally retarded and typically developing children. *Child Development, 62,* 1434–1448.

Gable, S., Belsky, J., & Crnic, K. (1992). Marriage, parenting, and child development: Progress and prospects. *Journal of Family Psychology, 5,* 276–294.

Gjerde, P. (1986). The interpersonal structure of family interactional settings: Parent–adolescent relations in dyads and triads. *Developmental Psychology, 22,* 297–
304.

Goldberg, W., & Easterbrooks, M. A. (1984). The role of marital quality in toddler
development. *Developmental Psychology, 20,* 504–514.

Grossman, K. E., & Grossman, K. (1991). Attachment quality as an organizer of
emotional and behavioral responses in a longitudinal perspective. In C. M.
Parkes, J. Stevenson-Hinde, & P. Marris (Eds.). *Attachment across the life cycle*
(pp. 93–114). London: Tavistock/Routledge.

Grugan, P., & McHale, J. P. (1997). *Links between recollections of family conflict and
current problem-solving behavior in college-aged students.* Paper presented at the
Biennial Conference of the Society for Research in Child Development, Washington, DC.

Grych, J. H., & Fincham, F. D. (1990). Marital conflict and children's adjustment: A
cognitive contextual framework. *Psychological Bulletin, 2,* 267–290.

Haft, W. L., & Slade, A. (1989). Affect attunement and maternal attachment: A pilot
study. *Infant Mental Health Journal, 10,* 157–172.

Haley, J. (1988). *Problem-solving therapy.* San Francisco: Jossey-Bass.

Hazan, C., & Shaver, P. (1987). Romantic love conceptualized as an attachment
process. *Journal of Personality and Social Psychology, 52,* 511–524.

Hesse, E. (1999). The Adult Attachment Interview: Historical and current perspectives. In J. Cassidy & P. R. Shaver (Eds.), *Handbook of attachment* (pp. 395–
433). New York: Guilford Press.

Howes, P., & Markman, H. J. (1989). Marital quality and child functioning: A longitudinal investigation. *Child Development, 60,* 1044–1051.

Isabella, R. A. (1993). Origins of attachment: Maternal interactive behavior across
the first year. *Child Development, 64,* 605–621.

Isabella, R. A., & Belsky, J. (1991). Interactional synchrony and the origins of infant-mother attachment: A replication study. *Child Development, 62,* 373–384.

Jackson, D. (1965). Family rules: Marital quid pro quo. *Archives of General Psychiatry, 12,* 589–594.

Johnston, J. R., Gonzalez, R., & Campbell, L. E. G. (1987). Ongoing postdivorce
conflict and child disturbance. *Journal of Abnormal Child Psychology, 15,* 493–
509.

Jouriles, E. N., Murphy, C. M., Farris, A. M., Smith, D. A., Richters, J. E., & Waters,
E. (1991). Marital adjustment, parental disagreements about child rearing, and
behavior problems in boys: Increasing the specificity of marital assessment.
Child Development, 62, 1424–1433.

Katz, L. F., & Gottman, J. M. (1996). Spillover effects of marital conflict: In search
of parenting and coparenting mechanisms. In J. P. McHale & P. Cowan (Eds.),
*New directions in child development: Vol. 74. Understanding how family-level dy-
namics affect children's development: Studies of two-parent families* (pp. 57–76).
San Francisco: Jossey-Bass.

Kerr, M. E., & Bowen, M. (1988). *Family evaluation.* New York: W. W. Norton.

Kobak, R. R., & Sceery, A. (1988). Attachment in late adolescence: Working models, affect regulation, and representations of self and others. *Child Development, 59,* 135–146.

LaFreniere, P. J., & Sroufe, L. A. (1985). Profiles of peer competence in the preschool: Interrelations between measures, influence of social ecology, and relation to attachment history. *Developmental Psychology, 21,* 56–69.

Lerner, H. G. (1986). *The dance of anger: A woman's guide to changing patterns of intimate relationships.* New York: Harper & Row.

Lewis, J. M., Beavers, W. R., Gossett, J. T., & Phillips, V. A. (1976). *No single thread: Psychological health in family systems.* New York: Brunner/Mazel.

Lewis, J. M., Owen, M., & Cox, M. (1988). The transition to parenthood: Vol 3. Incorporation of the child into the family. *Family Process, 27,* 411–421.

Lindahl, K. M. (1998). Family process variables and children's disruptive behavior problems. *Journal of Family Psychology, 12,* 420–436.

Lorenz, K. (1957). *Instinctive behavior.* New York: International Universities Press.

Main, M., Kaplan, N., & Cassidy, J. (1985). Security in infancy, childhood, and adulthood: A move to the level of representation. *Monographs of the Society for Research in Child Development, 50,* 66–104.

Marvin, R. S. (1992). Attachment- and family systems-based intervention in developmental psychopathology. *Development and Psychopathology, 4,* 697–711.

Marvin, R. S., & Stewart, R. B. (1990). A family systems framework for the study of attachment. In M. T. Greenberg, D. Cicchetti, & E. M. Cummings (Eds.), *Attachment in the preschool years: Theory, research, and intervention* (pp. 51–86). Chicago: University of Chicago Press.

McConnell, M., & Kerig, P. (1999, April). *Inside the family circle: The relationship between coparenting and child adjustment in two-parent families.* Paper presented at the Society for Research in Child Development, Albuquerque, NM.

McHale, J. P. (1995). Coparenting and triadic interactions during infancy: The roles of marital distress and child gender. *Developmental Psychology, 31,* 985–996.

McHale, J. P., Johnson, D., & Sinclair, R. (1999). Family dynamics, preschoolers' family representations, and preschoolers' peer relationships. *Early Education and Development, 10,* 373–401.

McHale, J. P., Krasnow, A., & Slavick, M. (1997). *Parenting style, marital quality, and family process as predictors of toddlers' personality styles.* Paper presented at the American Psychological Association, Chicago, IL.

McHale, J. P., Kuersten, R., & Lauretti, A. (1996). New directions in the study of family-level dynamics during infancy and early childhood. In J. P. McHale & P. Cowan (Eds.), *New directions in child development: Vol. 74. Understanding how family-level dynamics affect children's development: Studies of two-parent families* (pp. 5–26). San Francisco: Jossey-Bass.

McHale, J. P., Kuersten-Hogan, R., Lauretti, A., & Rasmussen, S. (2000). Parents' reports of coparenting and observed coparenting behavior during the toddler period. *Journal of Family Psychology, 14,* 220–236.

McHale, J. P., Lauretti, A., & Talbot, J. A. (1998, April). *Attachment quality, family-*

level dynamics, and toddler adaptation. Paper presented at the biennial meeting of the International Conference on Infant Studies, Atlanta, GA.

McHale, J. P., & Rasmussen, J. L. (1998). Coparental and family group-level dynamics during infancy: Early family precursors of child and family functioning during preschool. *Developmental Psychology, 10,* 39–59.

Minuchin, P. (1985). Families and individual development: Provocations from the field of family therapy. *Child Development, 56,* 289–302.

Minuchin, P. (1988). Relationships within the family: A systems perspective on development. In R. A. Hinde & J. Stevenson-Hinde (Eds.), *Relationships within families: Mutual influences* (pp. 7–25). Oxford: Clarendon Press.

Minuchin, S. (1974). *Families and family therapy.* Cambridge: Harvard University Press.

Nichols, M. P., & Schwartz, R. C. (1998). *Family therapy: Concepts and methods* (4th ed.). Boston: Allyn & Bacon.

O'Brien, M., Margolin, G., John, R. S., & Krueger, L. (1991). Mothers' and sons' cognitive and emotional reactions to simulated marital and family conflict. *Journal of Consulting and Clinical Psychology, 59,* 692–703.

Patterson, C. J., & Chan, R. W. (1999). Families headed by lesbian and gay parents. In M. E. Lamb (Ed.), *Parenting and child development in "nontraditional" families.* Mahwah, NJ: Lawrence Erlbaum.

Piaget. J. (1966). *The psychology of intelligence.* Totowa, NJ: Littlefield.

Piaget, J. (1970). *Structuralism.* New York: Basic Books.

Piaget, J. (1985). *The equilibration of cognitive structures.* Chicago: University of Chicago Press.

Sandler, J., & Rosenblatt, B. (1962). The concept of the representational world. *Psychoanalytic Study of the Child, 17,* 128–145.

Snyder, D. K., Klein, M. A., Gdowski, C. L., Faulstich, C., & LaCombe, J. (1998). Generalized dysfunction in clinic and nonclinic families: A comparative analysis. *Journal of Abnormal Child Psychology, 16,* 97–109.

Sroufe, L. A. (1979). The coherence of individual development: Early care, attachment, and subsequent developmental issues. *American Psychologist, 34,* 834–841.

Sroufe, L. A. (1986). Bowlby's contribution to psychoanalytic theory and developmental psychopathology. *Journal of Child Psychology and Psychiatry, 27,* 841–849.

Teti, D. M., & Ablard, K. E. (1989). Security of attachment and infant-sibling relationships: A laboratory study. *Child Development, 60,* 1519–1528.

Thompson, R. A. (1999). Early attachment and later development. In J. Cassidy & P. R. Shaver (Eds.), *Handbook of attachment* (pp. 265–286). New York: Guilford Press.

Troy, M., & Sroufe, L. A. (1987). Victimization among preschoolers: Role of attachment relationship history. *Journal of the Academy of Child and Adolescent Psychiatry, 26,* 166–172.

van Ijzendoorn, M., Juffer, F., & Duyvesteyn, M. (1995). Breaking the intergenerational cycle of insecure attachment: A review of the effects of attachment-based interventions on maternal sensitivity and infant security. *Journal of Child Psychology and Psychiatry, 36,* 225–248.

Wakschlag, L. S., Chase-Lansdale, P. L., & Brooks-Gunn, J. (1996). Not just "ghosts in the nursery:" Contemporaneous intergenerational relationships and parenting in young African-American families. *Child Development, 67,* 2131–2147.

Watson, M. W., & Amgott-Kwan, T. (1983). Transitions in children's understanding of parental roles. *Developmental Psychology, 19,* 659–666.

Watson, M. W., & Amgott-Kwan, T. (1984). Development of family-role concepts in school-age children. *Developmental Psychology, 20,* 953–959.

Watson, M. W., & Fischer, K. W. (1993). Structural changes in children's understanding of family roles and divorce. In R. R. Cocking & K. A. Renninger (Eds.), *The development and meaning of psychological distance* (pp. 123–140). Hillsdale, NJ: Erlbaum.

Watson, M. W., & Getz, K. (1990a). Developmental shifts in Oedipal behaviors related to family role understanding. *New Directions in Child Development, 48,* 29–45.

Watson, M. W., & Getz, K. (1990b). The relationship between Oedipal behaviors and children's family role concepts. *Merrill-Palmer Quarterly, 36,* 487–505.

Weissman, S., & Cohen, R. S. (1985). The parenting alliance and adolescence. *Adolescent Psychiatry, 12,* 24–45.

PART III

Life Cycle Transitions: Child and Adolescent Perspective

CHAPTER 3

Attachment Theory Applied to Adolescents

STACY CRETZMEYER

Over 40% of beginning college students drop out (Witherspoon, Long, & Chubick, 1999), and a growing body of recent research suggests that secure parental attachment and family emotional support yield advantages in the transition and adjustment from high school to college life. One particular dimension of parental–adolescent attachment that the literature shows as being of central significance is perceived family emotional support (Kenny, 1990; Kenny & Donaldson, 1992; McCarthy, Brack, Brack, Liu, & Carlson, 1998; Windle & Miller-Tutzauer, 1992). This chapter reviews the basic aspects of attachment theory (Bowlby, 1988) as applied to adolescents, specifically, late adolescents, and suggests implications for counselors, marriage and family therapists, and student affairs personnel in working with this particular population.

CRITICAL FACTORS IN ADOLESCENT ATTACHMENT

Traditional developmental theory proposes that adolescence is characterized by the developmental tasks of resolving identity and intimacy (Erikson, 1968). According to Erikson, there are eight psychosocial stages that manifest as "crises or critical issues to be resolved" (Slavin, 1988, p. 38). Adolescents face the challenge of resolving the crisis of identity versus role confusion, and late adolescents or young adults face the crisis of intimacy versus isolation (Erikson, 1968). Although female developmental theorists have challenged Erikson's stage theory as failing to fully address the developmental experience of women (Gilligan, 1982), the majority of traditional research literature "portrayed identity work as masculine, involving separa-

65

tion, and intimacy work as feminine, involving connection" (Horst, 1995, p. 275).

Current research literature suggests that connection and secure attachment bonds are important and necessary for both women and men in adolescence (Kenny, 1994; Lapsley, Rice, & FitzGerald, 1990; Lopez, 1995). Indeed, contrary to previous assumptions, secure parent–child attachment during adolescence has been highly correlated with social competence (Kenny, 1990).

Erikson's theory "conceives of identity as psycho-social. We deal with a process 'located' in the core of the individual and yet also in the core of his communal culture. The development of identity involves an individual's relationship with his cultural context" (Stevens, 1983, p. 61). Thus, the crisis is both personal and social and is precipitated by interactions with the individual's environment. Stevens suggested that Erikson's theory factored in the role that environment plays in both causing crises and in the resolution of crises.

The transition to college has been described as a catalyst in bringing about this personal and social crisis (Gerdes & Mallinckrodt, 1994). Students who have insufficient social and emotional support from their family of origin have been characterized as manifesting mild to severe adjustment problems in college (Gerdes & Mallinckrodt). Family functioning has been identified as a critical factor in college student adjustment (Buelow, 1995), and some of the more frequent crises in early college years that manifest themselves as loneliness are, in fact, struggles with social adjustment. In fact, depression has been identified as one of the primary psychiatric disorders observed among college-age students (Gerdes & Mallinckrodt).

Lopez (1995) mentioned a number of researchers who have attemped to link adults' current attachment styles to their perceptions of early relationship issues with their parents. Gerdes and Mallinckrodt (1994) noted the negative impact that marital conflict between adolescents' parents, as well as the adolescents' own conflicted or overinvolved attachment relations with their parents, can have on their own coping behaviors, including personal and social adjustment. Students' experiences of parental–adolescent attachment bonds and their experience of family emotional support have direct bearing on the resolution of this developmental "crisis," on the quality of peer relationships, and on the overall well-being associated with students' successful transition to college (Buelow, 1995).

According to Bowlby (1988), "no concept within the attachment framework is more central to developmental psychiatry than that of the secure base" (p. 3). Bowlby delineates three different patterns of attachment and their determinants. The first pattern is *secure attachment,* in which individuals express confidence that their caregivers (or parent figure) will be consistently available and responsive during adverse or stressful situations. This pattern promotes healthy development in children. Persons who grew up feeling unsure about their parents' responsiveness or availability and who experienced solicitude on some occasions but "threats of abandonment" on other occasions are said to have experienced *anxious–resistant* attachment. The third pattern, *anxious–avoidant* attachment, results from the caregiver's constant ignoring or rebuffing the child when he or she is in need of comfort or protection. This pattern of attachment is considered the most destructive to the individual over time. Bowlby states that when the pattern of attachment is stable over time, it tends to persist. He indicated that,

> As a child grows older, however, clinical evidence shows that both the pattern of attachment and the personality features that go with it become increasingly a property of the child himself or herself and also increasingly resistant to change. This means that the child tends to impose it, or some derivative of it, upon new relationships. (p. 5)

As the child progresses to adolescence and adulthood, seeking more autonomy, Ainsworth (1989) suggested that the attachment to parent figures still persists, and in secure attachment, young adults are likely to maintain an ongoing close association with their parents, even though their parents eventually become less involved directly in their lives. This is also true with parent surrogates to whom young persons may attach themselves. These parent surrogates, who may be a grandparent, a teacher, a coach, or even an older sibling, play a vital role in the lives of the young adults and often provide the security that their own parents failed to provide. When individuals are provided with that secure base from which they can explore the world, they have the greatest potential for social competence, cooperation, and stability in adult relationships (Bowlby, 1988).

Attachment theory, according to Lopez (1995), offers hueristic value in determining a framework for discussing the behavior of adolescents and adults in relationship. Later research studies of adult development have pointed to the continuity and persistence of attachment schemas developed in childhood, inasmuch as "attachment schemas and related behaviors tend to evoke environmental responses that reinforce and thus maintain the existing schema" (Lopez, p. 12). The implication is that adolescent behaviors in social situations in college are likely to reflect the individual's persistent approach toward others in the world. Lopez stressed that even though internal working models endure over time, they are still responsive to influences from environmental or developmental change. Therefore, unhealthy or insecure attachment schemas may actually be transformed as a result of effective intervention.

According to Kenny (1994), the literature is beginning to reflect a "reconceptualization of the separation-individuation process of adolescence" (p. 399), placing less emphasis on individuation and more emphasis on the relational perspective, which stresses that "a balance between individuation and parental connectedness is most facilitative of adaptive functioning. Individuation is believed to occur within a caring offspring relationship, which is transformed during adolescence from patterns of unilateral adult authority to patterns of mutuality" (Kenny, p. 399). Windle and Miller-Tutzauer (1992) underscore the notion that in healthy family functioning, parents can play a vital role in helping to facilitate the transition to adulthood:

> In contrast to historically earlier perspectives that portrayed adolescence as a highly turbulent developmental phase characterized by heightened conflict in parental-adolescent relations, more recent perspectives have suggested that parent-adolescent relationships remain highly supportive and emotionally significant as parents often facilitate adolescents in coping with often stressful transitional events. (p. 777)

Unfortunately, for students whose family-of-origin experiences have been minimally supportive, there is a far greater likelihood of poor academic performance and dropping out (Strathil, 1988). College counselors are increasingly becoming aware of the influence of students' pre-college experiences on their overall commitment to college, as well as on their level of social and academic integration.

McCarthy et al. (1998) have linked patterns of attachment bonds with internal working models, or schemas, in terms of how the effects of these interactions impact the level of functioning of college students. They suggest that students' perceptions of their experience of family support have direct bearing on levels of motivation and performance in college. According to McCarthy et al. higher levels of parental attachment and greater family support are related to successful adjustment of college students, including successful career development, academic achievement, and students' perceptions of having successful personal coping resources. Conversely, Windle and Miller-Tutzauer (1992) found that perceived lack of family emotional support has been associated with poor or disrupted family functioning. This dimension of family functioning—perceived family emotional support—is extremely relevant to the late adolescent, college-age population, for it has direct bearing on how a student assesses his or her ability to cope with the challenge of a major life transition. Windle and Miller-Tutzauer suggest that:

> An arguably understudied dimension that may be of particular relevance to adolescent parent, rather than adolescent–parent, relations is perceived family social support. That is, the physical, cognitive, and social capa-

bilities of middle and late adolescents far exceed those of children, and adolescents are confronted with a range of novel situations and interpersonal events that may be facilitated by actual . . . and perceived family social support. (p. 778)

It is critical to ascertain the student's perception of, rather than the acutal level of, support. According to Kenny (1994), students' descriptions of parental attachments indicate levels of perceived support. Kenny applies the principles of attachment theory to adolescents and posits that:

If attachment theory is useful in understanding family ties among late adolescents and young adults, students' overall descriptions of their parental attachments will resemble the secure attachment type. . . . That is, students will describe positive feelings in interaction with parents and will view their parents as simultaneously supporting their autonomy and being available as a source of support when needed. Characteristics of secure attachment will be associated with social competence. (p. 400)

Based on attachment theory, McCarthy et al. (1998) emphasized that these perceptions are founded upon a set of "internally organized expectations" called "working models [which] are, in effect, internal mental templates that help us predict and manage interactions with the outside world and are hypothesized to be the mechanism by which attachment experiences affect a person throughout life" (p. 137). These "working models," which are formed in early childhood, "continue into adulthood and affect how individuals view themselves and others in interpersonal relationships and perceptions of self" (McCarthy et al., 1998).

RESEARCH SUMMARY OF POSITIVE EFFECTS OF SECURE ATTACHMENT AND FAMILY EMOTIONAL SUPPORT

The literature points to the positive effects of secure attachment on adolescents, in particular, on students' transition from high school to college. Kenny's (1987) study of first-year college students identified family support as the source of security for adolescents as they eventually transition to college (Lapsley et al., 1990). Building on this premise, Lapsley et al. were the first to study attachment with regard to overall college adjustment. Using both a first-year student sample and an upper-level student sample, they found that parental and peer attachment were significant predictors of personal-emotional adjustment in both the first-year and upper-level samples. A noteworthy finding in the research has been the absence of gender differences in secure attachment to parents (Lapsley et al., 1990; Windle & Miller-

Tutzauer, 1992), with men and women reporting comparable levels of trust with their parents.

In a study of 159 college students in their senior year, Kenny (1990) found that students' views of the quality of parental interactions was positive and that they viewed their parents as encouraging autonomy and providing emotional support. However, they found women's ratings of parental support to be slightly higher than men's ratings. These results suggest that we need to reconsider the conceptualization of how young adults achieve independence from the family of origin during the college years. The findings of this study were limited because Kenny's sample of students was not socioeconomically or culturally diverse.

Kenny and Donaldson's (1991) study of first-year college students advanced the research involving adaptive and maladaptive dimensions of family functioning relative to adjustment of college freshmen students. According to their findings, parental closeness and support, indicative of secure attachment, were found to be "adaptive for women" (p. 484), and "positive attachment to parents in the absence of both family anxieties over separation and parental marital conflict [were] associated with social competence and low levels of psychological symptoms" (p. 484). The findings of this study were limited because there was a very small male sample.

Next, Kenny and Donaldson (1992) focused specifically on attachment and separation relative to the adjustment of first-year college women. Still focusing on the application of "attachment theory to college student development . . . [and] stimulated by dissatisfaction with traditional psychoanalytic models which focus only on separation-individuation" (Kenny & Donaldson, p. 431), the researchers found that most college women perceive themselves to be "positively and closely attached to their parents" (p. 435). Kenny and Donaldson's findings are consistent with contemporary perspectives on adolescent development and women's development, suggesting that healthy functioning involves interdependence rather than complete autonomy and separation, whereas sources of anxiety, guilt, or resentment can contribute to low levels of functional and emotional adaptation. Kenny and Donaldson suggest that perspectives from other family members, as well as behavioral observations of parent–college student interactions, might lead to greater understanding of healthy attachment. They also emphasize that there are some gender differences: In general, female college students are more closely attached to their parents than male college students and are also less independent of their parents.

Holmbeck and Wandrei (1993) proposed that there might be predictive value in identifying the indicators of individual and relational functioning for college students' level of adjustment (p. 74). The results of their study of family variables indicated that the level of family attachments definitely impacts the degree of adjustment to college (Holmbeck & Wandrei). Further, their findings in general proved true for both women and men, with gender differences found only in the less well-adjusted subjects. "The findings of this study suggest that less well-adjusted men may be more disconnected from significant others, whereas less well-adjusted women may exhibit higher levels of separation anxiety and enmeshment seeking" (p. 77).

Rice et al. (1995) conducted both a cross-sectional and longitudinal examination of attachment and separation-individuation relative to college student adjustment. The results of this study further substantiated the findings of Lapsley et al. (1990) that there are no significant differences between first-year students and upper-level students in quality of attachment to parents. Further, those students who had benefited from secure attachments to parents were at "considerable" advantage in adjusting to college. However, some significant inconsistencies surfaced when cross-sectional and longitudinal results were compared. For instance, "social-interpersonal adjustment and strong feelings of anger, resentment, and separation anxiety were more likely to be influenced by current perceptions of attachment to parents and less likely to be associated with previous perceptions of attachment. In contrast, aspects of academic and emotional adjustment were linked to current and prior attachment bonds" (Rice et al., p. 472). Acknowledging the absence of parents' reports of attachment relations in the research literature relative to attachment bonds and adjustment to college, Rice et al. encouraged future efforts toward including parent reports prior to, during, and after the transition to college.

Kenny's (1994) study focused specifically on young adults in trade and technical school programs, which constituted a departure from her previous research and an effort to study attachment in students of different socioeconomic backgrounds. The results of this investigation again supported the idea that there needs to be a balance between individuality and connectedness in healthy adaptive functioning. The study also revealed few gender differences in perceptions of parental attachment, "with the exception of the perception of parents as a source of emotional support. Perhaps women's need for parental connection is understood better in terms of a willingness to receive help and solve problems through interaction with parents, rather than in the expression of positive feelings toward parents" (Kenny, p. 401).

All of the studies mentioned above have incorporated self-report data from student subjects, and the results have emphasized the perceptions of students at the college level. Because functional and dysfunctional patterns in the family of origin play such a definitive role in the development or impairment of secure attachment and the consequent adjustment or maladjustment of the individual, it is necessary to focus on perceptions and patterns of perceptions.

McCarthy et al. (1998) have indicated that many students "seem entrenched in certain chronic appraisal patterns" (p. 149) concerning present life circumstances and the emotions that surface as a result. Referencing Bowlby, McCarthy et al. discussed how the internal working models, which are internal cognitive templates, persist into adulthood and assist individuals in managing interactions that occur within relationships.

Information on racial and ethnic differences in adolescent–parent attachment and perceived family emotional support was conspicuously absent in the literature. We urge more empirical research in this area. Moreover, although some recent studies have touched upon gender differences in secure attachment and college student adjustment (Kenny, 1994; Lapsley et al., 1990; Lopez, 1995), results were somewhat conflicting in terms of family emotional support, suggesting that further investigation is needed in the area of gender differences. One approach might involve the longitudinal study of male and female student subjects who participate in an initial study of their perceived level of attachment, an evaluation of their college adjustment and success over time, and an assessment of gender differences in critical variables relevant to that adjustment and success.

IMPLICATIONS FOR COUNSELORS, MARRIAGE AND FAMILY THERAPISTS, AND STUDENT AFFAIRS PERSONNEL

The transition from high school to college can be challenging for even the most highly motivated and emotionally secure adolescents. Recent research suggests that late adolescents entering college who have strong parental attachment bonds and have experienced consistent family emotional support are better equipped for successful adjustment to college and are more motivated to stay in college (Kenny & Donaldson, 1991; Kenny & Donaldson, 1992; McCarthy et al., 1998; Rice et al., 1995). Student readiness varies from student to student and is affected by a variety of factors, including their prior experiences with their families, which can even affect their attitudes about attending college at all (Coté & Levine, 1997). Secure parental attachment and strong parental support have been linked to "measures of social competence, psychological functioning, adjustment to college, and career development" (Kenny & Donaldson, 1992, p. 432) in college students, whereas "lower levels of perceived family social support by adolescents are associated with indicators of disrupted family functioning, higher levels of parental role stress" (Windle & Miller-Tutzauer, 1992, p. 786), and difficulties in adjustment to college.

McCarthy et al. (1998) noted the alarming rate at which students are seeking out college counseling centers for issues regarding abuse and other family-of-origin stresses. These historical factors can seriously harm the student's sense of competence, self-esteem, and perceived ability to succeed (McCarthy et al., 1998; Witherspoon et al., 1999). It becomes the challenge of university counseling and student affairs professionals to identify, within the limits of confidentiality, those students with insecure or problematic family bases and who are susceptible to adjustment difficulties in college (McCarthy et al.) inasmuch as early assessment would enable advisors and counselors to better respond to their needs (Witherspoon et al., 1999). One approach, in terms of instrumentation, in obtaining adolescent accounts of attachment styles might be the use of the Inventory of Parent and Peer Attachment, which has been used to measure attachment to mother, father, and peers (Armsden & Greenberg, 1987; McCarthy, Brack, & Brack, 1996). Involving parents in the assessment process would further assist counselors in university counseling centers to obtain a holistic understanding of the individual and his or her life experiences (Witherspoon et al.), and the incorporation of parents in transition-oriented programs and seminars would afford students the opportunity to work through unresolved issues related to adjustment while enhancing healthy connections (Kenny & Donaldson, 1992). Programs and interventions designed to help students capitalize on their strengths and come to terms with what was lacking in the development of healthy attachment in their family of origin could be implemented at the outset of the student's university career, thereby enhancing socio-affective integration (Holmbeck & Wandrei, 1993; Witherspoon et al.).

The notion that parental or parent-figure reports are a major contribution to the overall understanding of family issues affecting the adolescent transitioning to college (Rice et al., 1995) has important implications for marital and family therapists. It is often the case that parental perceptions of student readiness for college differ broadly from that of their college-bound son or daughter (Cretzmeyer, 1999). In fact, discrepancies between parental perceptions of family emotional support and their student's perception of level of family emotional support might be focused on early in family counseling sessions to assess level of attachment and to investigate to what degree the adolescent experienced a "secure base."

Although attachment theorists argue that "adult accounts of attachment styles should be consistent with attachment levels in childhood and early adolescence" (McCarthy et al., 1996, p. 318), Lopez's position, that powerful environmental or developmental changes or interventions can begin to reverse the damage of unhealthy attachment patterns in childhood, has positive implications for marital and family therapists. Robert Marvin, in a recent interview with Erdman and Caffery (2000), discussed the importance of clinicians being trained specifically in attachment theory and bemoaned the fact that there are not more attachment-based interventions being developed. However, Krause and Haverkamp (1996) point to Bowlby's emphasis on the importance of incorporating attachment theory in the counseling relationship in order to bring about therapeutic change. Bowlby (1988) identified five key tasks to be used in individual, family, and group psychotherapy, which are (a) establishing a safe base, (b) exploring past attachments and current relational difficulties, (c) exploring the client–counselor relationship, (d) linking the past with the present, and (e) revising internal working models (p. 87).

The work of the therapist should involve facilitating the process of "*updating* working models," realizing that the extent to which they can be revised varies on an individual basis (Krause & Haverkamp, 1996). The most accurate way for the clinician to adapt to individual client differences in attachment style is for the therapist to assess the therapeutic needs of the client and the "client's attachment history" early in the counseling relationship (Krause & Haverkamp).

The fifth task in the counseling process, *revising internal working models* (Bowlby, 1988), is arguably the most important task of the clinician working within the attachment theory framework. The therapist must help clients understand that their internal working models, which may have at one time served them well, were created from past parental experiences and may no longer be appropriate to their current situation (Krause & Haverkamp, 1996). New attachment information (i.e., the client's experience in the counseling relationship) can serve to update or revise the previously established working models from which the client has been approaching life thus far (Krause & Haverkamp). From this therapeutic experience, the goal is that the client will be able to generalize to other emotionally important relationships.

Krause and Haverkamp (1996) have focused specifically on adult child–elderly parent issues, applying attachment theory to this dyad. In particular, attachment theory may be applied in counseling to help the adult child resolve issues that have thus far gone unresolved in the parent–adult child relationships. This is a potential area for further research in the field of attachment theory, particularly with the gradual aging of the general population and the increasing number of adult caregivers of aging parents. This research paradigm might be extended to investigate how individual differences extend into adulthood (Erdman & Caffery, 2000) and may be transformed through counseling on attachment issues, combined with grief therapy.

Marvin cautions that attachment research and attachment-based clinical work are very specialized (Erdman & Caffery, 2000) and that even training in the Adult Attachment Interview necessitates in-depth clinical training. Given the factors that impact adolescents, especially in relation to their transition to college life and beyond, such training may prove to be invaluable for university-based counselors and therapists.

Transition-oriented programs and seminars, incorporating anecdotal information from both parents and their incoming students, may identify some of the strongest indicators of future stress for college students. For example, students who report that their parents divorced when they were very young or that a parent died may be targeted for participation in a "University 101" class, a "Student Success Seminar," or other group-oriented experiences, in which the student has an opportunity early on for forging strong friendships and supportive relationships with faculty and staff as well as peer educators. Such seminars are designed to establish group cohesiveness, to build trust, and to enhance self-esteem. At new student orientation seminars or retreats, parents of incoming students might be encouraged to provide written, self-report data pertaining to periods of family stress during their son or daughter's childhood or early adolescence that may have affected the child's ability to form strong attachments. If a death, divorce, or other trauma occurred during the child's early years, this information may be useful for counselors to whom these students may later be referred. The incoming student also may provide such anecdotal information in self-exploration exercises with a counselor or other student affairs personnel. Students who report that they experienced early ruptured parental relationships and have conflicted perceptions of family emotional support as they enter college may be targeted by advisors or peer educators for front-end services, such as a series of "introductory developmental" sessions in the college counseling center or participation in a student success seminar.

Being able to predict or hypothesize about current and future client behaviors (Erdman & Caffery, 2000), based upon information about the early attachment history of adolescents, is perhaps one of the most exciting trends in attachment-focused research. University counseling centers could provide the perfect setting for conducting such research, and those with approved on-site training programs could offer specialized postdoctoral work in attachment theory research and clinical specialization.

REFERENCES

Ainsworth, M. D. (1989). Attachments beyond intimacy. *American Psychologist, 44*, 709–716.

Armsden, G., & Greenberg, M. (1987). The inventory of parent and peer attachment: Individual differences and their relationship to psychological well-being in adolescence. *Journal of Youth and Adolescence, 16*, 427–454.

Bowlby, J. (1988). Developmental psychiatry comes of age. *American Journal of Psychiatry, 145*, 1–10.

Buelow, G. (1995). Comparing students from substance abusing and dysfunctional families: Implications for counseling. *Journal of Counseling & Development, 73,* 327–330.

Coté, J. E., & Levine, C. (1997). Student motivations, learning environments, and human capital acquisition: Toward an integrated paradigm of student development. *Journal of College Student Development, 38,* 229–243.

Cretzmeyer, S. (1999). *A comparative study of early recollections and the college student inventory in assessing parents' vs. child perceptions of family emotional support in the first year of college.* Unpublished doctoral dissertation, University of South Carolina, Columbia.

Erdman, P., & Caffery, T. (2000). An interview with Robert Marvin: Linking systems and attachment theory. *The Family Journal: Counseling and Therapy for Couples and Families, 8,* 309–316.

Erikson, E. (1968). *Identity: Youth and crisis.* New York: Norton.

Gerdes, H., & Mallinckrodt, B. (1994). Emotional, social, and academic adjustment of college students: A longitudinal study of retention. *Journal of Counseling and Development, 72,* 281–288.

Gilligan, C. (1982). *In a different voice: Psychological theory and women's development.* Cambridge, MA: Harvard University Press.

Holmbeck, G. N., & Wandrei, M. L. (1993). Individual and relational predictors of adjustment in first-year college students. *Journal of Counseling Psychology, 40,* 73–78.

Horst, E. A. (1995). Reexamining gender issues in Erikson's stages of identity and intimacy. *Journal of Counseling and Development, 73,* 271–278.

Kenny, M. E. (1987). The extent and function of parental attachment among first-year college students. *Journal of Youth and Adolescence, 16,* 17–27.

Kenny, M. E. (1990). College seniors' perceptions of parental attachments: The value and stability of family ties. *Journal of College Student Development, 31,* 39–46.

Kenny, M. E. (1994). Quality and correlates of parental attachment among late adolescents. *Journal of Counseling and Development, 72,* 399–403.

Kenny, M. E., & Donaldson, G. A. (1991). Contributions of parental attachment and family structure to the social and psychological functioning of first-year college students. *Journal of Counseling Psychology, 38,* 479–486.

Kenny, M. E., & Donaldson, G. A. (1992). The relationship of parental attachment and psychological separation to the adjustment of first-year college women. *Journal of College Student Development, 33,* 431–438.

Krause, A. M., & Haverkamp, B. E. (1996). Attachment in adult child–older parent relationships: Research, theory, and practice. *Journal of Counseling and Development, 75,* 83–92.

Lapsley, D. K., Rice, K. G., & FitzGerald, D. P. (1990). Adolescent attachment, identity, and adjustment to college: Implications for the continuity of adaptation hypothesis. *Journal of Counseling and Development, 68,* 561–565.

Lopez, F. G. (1995). Attachment theory as an integrative framework for family counseling. *The Family Journal: Counseling and Therapy for Couples and Families, 3,* 11–17.

McCarthy, C. J., Brack, G., & Brack, C. J. (1996). Relationship of cognitive appraisals and attachment to emotional events within the family of origin. *The Family Journal: Counseling and Therapy for Couples and Families, 4,* 316–326.

McCarthy, C. J., Brack, G., Brack, C. J., Liu, H. T., & Carlson, M. H. (1998). Relationship of college students' current attachment to appraisals of parental conflict. *Journal of College Counseling, 1,* 135–153.

Rice, K. G., FitzGerald, D. P., Whaley, T. J., & Gibbs, C. L. (1995). Cross-sectional and longitudinal examination of attachment, separation-individuation, and college student adjustment. *Journal of Counseling & Development, 73,* 463–474.

Slavin, R. (1988). *Educational psychology: Theory into practice.* Englewood Cliffs, NJ: Prentice-Hall.

Stevens, R. (1983). *Erik Erikson: An introduction.* New York: St. Martin's Press.

Strathil, M. L. (1988). *The college student inventory.* Iowa City, IA: USA Group Noel-Levitz, Inc.

Windle, M., & Miller-Tutzauer, C. (1992). Confirmatory factor analysis and concurrent validity of the perceived social support-family measure among adolescents. *Journal of Marriage and the Family, 54,* 777–787.

Witherspoon, A. D., Long, C. K., Chubick, J. D. (1999). Prediction of college student dropouts using EDS scores. *Journal of College Student Development, 40,* 82–86.

CHAPTER 4

Adolescence and Attachment

From Theory to Treatment Implications

SUSAN K. MACKEY

For many years I have been interested in incorporating relationship issues into a systemic orientation of therapy with families of adolescents. I had focused my treatment approaches on developing a connection between the parents and adolescent through a focus on parental nurturance (Mackey, 1996). The basis for that approach is my belief, supported by research findings (Allen & Land, 1999), that a secure attachment between parents and adolescent is the basis for successful adolescent differentiation. The most difficult cases that a therapist faces with adolescent families are those in which the problems did not begin with the transition to adolescence but much earlier. When problems begin early on, they often reflect long-term difficulties in the parent–child attachments. A closer look at attachment theory can guide our treatment in some of these most difficult cases.

ATTACHMENT THEORY

John Bowlby (1969) developed the theory of attachment, which is the exploration of affectional bonds between parent and child. He believed that the nature of the attachment between the primary caretaker and child formed the basis of how the child formed relationships in the future as well as the nature of the child's internal representation of self. A secure attachment formed the basis of good relationships and self-esteem, whereas an insecure attachment led to problems in both self-esteem and relationships.

Ainsworth, Behar, Waters, and Wall (1978) explored the nature of attachments experimentally by developing an observational procedure called the Strange Situation. The experimenters would have the child and mother come to a naturalistic lab setting and then have the mother leave for a brief period and observe how the child dealt with both the separation and the reunion. From these observations the experimenters named three categories of attachment: secure attachment, ambivalent attachment, and avoidant attachment. With a secure attachment the child is comfortable exploring the new situation using the mother as a secure base. The child is upset briefly when the mother leaves but seeks connection upon her return and is easily comforted. The child who is ambivalently attached cries the most, is clingy and demanding, and explores little. This child is very upset with the mother's separation and is difficult to sooth after separation, acting both clingy and angry simultaneously. Finally, the avoidantly attached child is least responsive to the mother's presence or absence, ignoring her upon her return and periodically being irritable and angry.

Researchers have subsequently linked attachment styles to later developmental behavior, including behavior in preschool (Sroufe, 1983), the nature of adult romantic relationships (Hazen & Shaver, 1987), and parenting styles (Main & Goldwyn, in press). The categories named by Ainsworth and her colleagues have been confirmed by other researchers who have expanded on the original three with their own variations. Sroufe (1983), in his studies of preschool children, found three types of avoidant children: (a) the lying bully who blames others; (b) the shy, spacey loner who appears emotionally flat; and (c) the obviously disturbed child with little interest in his or her environment. Sroufe also found two ambivalent types: (a) the fidgety, impulsive child with poor concentration who is tense and easily upset by failures; and (b) the fearful, hypersensitive, clingy child who lacks initiative and gives up easily. Bowlby (1988) identified four patterns of insecure attachment in adults: (a) anxious–overly dependent; (b) insistent self-reliance; (c) insistent caregiving at the expense of not receiving; and (d) detachment from feelings and memories.

Main and Goldwyn (in press) analyzed data that was collected using the Berkeley Adult Attachment Interview and again found the two types of insecure attachments. The first, which was the avoidant type, was named "dismissing of attachment." Similar to Bowlby's categorization, these adults were insistently self-reliant and could name few feelings or memories from childhood. The second category, which corresponded to ambivalent attachment, were adults who were preoccupied with their unresolved childhood hurts and angers. These adults were not able to talk with much insight and instead became lost in their feelings about their childhood experiences. Main (1997) also found a high degree of concordance between the infant Strange Situation categorizations and Adult Attachment Interview classifications of persons at age 19, suggesting a continuity of attachment patterns within a family from infancy to adolescence.

Finally, Roger Kobak (1999) used the Adult Attachment Interview with teenagers. He found that secure teens could handle conflicts with their parents. They were more assertive and empathic, could understand their parents' points of view, and made an easier transition to college than insecurely attached adolescents. He found that "dismissing" adolescents were seen by peers as more hostile, condescending, and distant, and the "preoccupied" adolescents were seen as more anxious, introspective, and ruminative.

In a book comprehensively reviewing attachment literature and citing an interview with Kobak, Robert Karen (1994) concluded that "this study suggests that young adults continue to be aided by the secure base they have had at home. It gives them the strength to do the adult equivalent of exploration—take risks, face challenges, be open to the new" (p. 384). Karen, a clinical psychologist, goes on to say that he believes that the lack of a secure base leaves one "struggling with a profound and painful loneliness." The following section will explore the development of attachment patterns in adolescence.

Attachment in Adolescence

Researchers and clinicians agree that adolescent differentiation and autonomy is developed most successfully in the context of a secure relationship. In the course of the progress of attachment from infancy to adolescence, an overarching organizational pattern for attachment behavior develops that predicts future behavior in new attachment relationships (Allen & Land, 1999; Main & Goldwyn, in press). Another characteristic of adolescent development is the differentiation of self (Allen & Land; Bowlby, 1973). This, along with the development of formal operational thinking, allows the adolescent's view of relationships to become more internally based. Adolescents become skilled in considering the nature of their own and others' attachment patterns, can differentiate between those styles, and can adapt their behavior in response to those differences (Allen & Land).

Family therapists who work within a family therapy framework also recognize the complementary behaviors in parents and in family interactions that reflect the nature of the attachments within the family. The development of cognitive abilities in the form of formal operational thinking lays the foundation for an adolescent to develop a "goal-corrected partnership" with both parents (Bowlby, 1973; Kobak & Duemmler, 1994); however, just the opposite may occur in families with insecure attachments.

In a goal-corrected partnership, each individual is weighing his or her individual needs against the goals of the relationship. This is possible when each member of a partnership has empathy, the ability to think in terms of the other person's perspective and to imagine how others feel in a particular situation. Ideally, the parents and adolescent are able to balance their needs for connection with the normative developmental task of adolescence, which involves a decreasing reliance on the attachment to parents in service of individuation and differentiation as a preparation for living autonomously. With a difference of opinion, secure teens and their parents evidence the ability to engage in productive, problem-solving discussions balancing the need for autonomy with that for connection. Allen, Kupermine, and Moore (1997) suggested that this ability to successfully balance autonomy and connectedness in the face of disagreements may be considered a stage-specific manifestation of attachment security in adolescence.

In insecurely attached families, the differentiation process results in emotional cut-off or escalating power struggles with little evidence of accurate empathy or of a goal-correcting partnership. Research findings indicate that insecure teen–parent dyads are more likely to be characterized by avoiding problem solving, maintaining higher levels of disengagement and dysfunctional anger, using pressuring tactics that undermine autonomy, and adolescents having lower levels of confidence in interactions (Becker-Stoll & Fremmer-Bombik, 1997; Kobak, Cole, Ferenz-Gillies, Flemming, & Gamble, 1993). Such behavior patterns can easily frustrate and anger the therapist or anyone who works with these adolescents and families. Understanding these behaviors as attachment styles in both the parents and adolescents can provide understanding to guide treatment approaches and insure the therapist's empathy. We will explore how insecure attachment manifests itself in adolescence by looking at the two major categories of insecure attachment—ambivalently attached adolescents and avoidantly attached adolescents.

Ambivalently Attached Adolescents

The ambivalently attached adolescent fits the previous descriptions: anxious, ruminative, and needy. With parents they often alternate between being needy and being demanding in an angry way. Like the infants in Ainsworth's Strange Situation, they can be angry and difficult to sooth but can insist on attention at the same time. Like Sroufe's (1983) ambivalent preschoolers, these adolescents are immature, impulsive, and sensitive to failure and can give up easily. They can be overly dependent and clingy with friends and, in their insecurity, become easy targets of victimization and exploitation. They are focused on their own hurt and anger and, therefore, can either be overly self-critical or, alternatively, defensive and blaming of others. Allen and Hauser (1996) found that these adolescents demonstrate passive thought processes. Rosenstein and Horowitz (1996) further noted that the preoccupied focus on parents of the ambivalently attached adolescent may lead to failure to learn to regulate negative self-affect. The preoccupied attachment style in adolescence has also been linked to internalizing problems, particularly depression (Allen, Moore, Kupermine, & Bell, 1998; Kobak, Sudler, & Gamble, 1991), as well as to externalizing symptoms (Allen & Kupermine, 1995). Allen and Land (1999) pointed out that the ambivalently attached adolescent may well use hostile, self-destructive, and infuriating behavior as a way to both engage parental attention and to express anger and resistance.

Similarly, the parents of these adolescents are characteristically both emotional and inconsistent. They "care" but report that they have "had it" and alternate between giving attention and being intensely hurt and angry. The parents' own insecurities hinder them from tuning in accurately to the adolescent's perspectives or feelings, so the attention that they do give can be intrusive or inaccurate and reflect more on the parents' needs than the adolescent's. An example would be taking a vegetarian daughter to a restaurant that specializes in barbecue as a special treat. In my clinical experience, these parents vary in their degree of self-understanding. They often fit the descriptions of Main and Goldwyn's (in press) "preoccupied" adult in that they may alternate between not being able to own their part at all and being immobilized by self-imposed guilt over being a "bad" parent. Allen and Land (1999) concluded that for ambivalently attached families, the normal pressures of adolescent development "create a chronic state of activation of the attachment system, thus increasing the impact of an insecure parental relationship on the adolescent" (p. 324) at a time when the adolescent is trying to reduce the centrality of the parental relationship in his or her life.

Avoidantly Attached Adolescents

Avoidantly attached adolescents can be the most difficult with whom to work. They have "written off" their needs for connection with their parents and present themselves as invulnerable. They are characterized by a tendency to avoid discussion or even consideration of any strong emotion, particularly fear, anger, disappointment, hurt, and loneliness, and to minimize their problems. Like Sroufe's (1983) preschoolers they can be either depressed loners or bullies who are hostile to authority in general, and they impulsively "act out" their needs for gratification in the moment with little self-insight or thought to the consequences of their actions. Research findings indicate that they are more likely to be substance abusing and conduct disordered (Rosenstein & Horowitz, 1996). They are often angry, aggressive, withdrawn, and less capable of problem solving. They have few close friends, and the friendships they do have are either shallow or marked by exclusivity and jealousy. Becker-Stoll and Fremmer-Bombik (1997) found that dismissing adolescents demonstrate the least autonomy and relatedness in interactions with parents, leaving little room for any change in the relationship.

Similarly, the parents are often unavailable both physically and emotionally. If the child is involved in acting-out behavior, they minimize the seriousness as a normal part of adolescence and something he or she will "grow out of," or they may have "written off" the adolescent and see the child as a "bad seed." They are defensive or simply unwilling to see how they contribute to the problem and become distant and uninvolved in the child's life. They can either minimize the child's problems or be defensive regarding their contribution to the problems. They see problems as someone else's responsibility, most typically the child or school personnel. If they are financially secure, they may be willing to finance tutors, therapy, or other interventions, assuming these activities do not interfere with their own personal agendas.

Exploring the Genesis of the Insecure Attachment

Exploring how and why the attachment became insecure often gives the therapist important data about how to proceed with treatment. It also helps the therapist to develop an empathic approach with both the adolescent and the parents, which is a necessary condition for effective treatment. Theorists propose several causes for insecure attachment. These will be explored in the following categories: early parent–child separation; lack of fit between parent and child personality or temperament styles; a child with a difficult temperament who is hard to nurture; difficulties in the parents' own attachment histories; narcissistically damaged or abusive parents; and the impact of loss and deprivation on the formation of the attachment.

Early Parent–Child Separation

John Bowlby's earliest observations involved children who were separated from their parents. Bowlby wrote that many of the most intense emotions arise during the formation, the maintenance, the disruption, and the renewal of affectional bonds. He went on to write that the threat of a loss of these bonds arouses anxiety, actual loss causes sorrow, and both situations are likely to arouse anger (Bowlby, 1977).

Because of the awareness and influence that attachment theory has had on hospital practices, it is less common today for parents and infants to be separated with a severe illness than in earlier years. Separation issues can play a part in adoptions, for example, determining whether a child was consistently nurtured prior to the adoption. Perhaps more common than adoption is the emotional separation caused by serious parental mental illness, particularly depression. Postpartum depression might influence the attachment with the mother if she withdraws from contact with the child. If the mother is unable to care for a child due to depression, the attachment process is dependent upon the availability of an alternative, consistent caretaker. In many cases, the father may also be unavailable due to the financial pressures of supporting the family.

Lack of Fit

Another common factor cited in the attachment literature that affects bonding is the quality of fit between the parents and the child. Children need parents to be responsive to their needs and to recognize their individuality. If the parents are very different in temperament from the infant this responsiveness will be more difficult to develop than in cases where the parents and infant are more similar. Brazelton and Cramer (1990) referred to this as synchrony. If the parent and child are of different temperaments, the parent needs to learn to respond to the infant's cues to correctly identify his or her capacities for attention, behavioral styles, and preferences for intake of external information, as well as the infant's typical responses. Brazelton and Cramer used the word "symmetry" to refer to children's ability to influence the parent's response to them.

The Difficult Child

Related to the idea of fit is research on the inborn individual differences of infants and innate temperament. Put simply, some children are born with capabilities that make them more or less vulnerable or invulnerable to the environment and, in some sense, easier or more difficult to love. Chess and Thomas (1987) thought that the origins of many behaviorally disordered children begins with temperament. They labeled about 10% of the infants they studied as "difficult." These children were characterized by generally negative moods, irregular body rhythms, and difficulties in adapting to change. In addition, they demonstrated both high withdrawal from, and intensity of response to, environmental stimulation. These are babies who are hard to care for and soothe, and they give less positive and more negative reinforcement to the parent. In other words, these children will push whatever buttons a parent might have.

Attachment in the Parents' Family of Origin

Clinical observations suggest that the attachment style in one's family of origin affects one's parenting style such that a person will tend to replicate the same parenting style. Brazelton and Cramer (1990) maintained that insecure attachment styles can be recreated through both reenacting one's past and by "evocation of the past through its opposite." An example of the latter is a parent who was strictly disciplined as a child and then who parents with lack of discipline and exaggerated gratification, which is as equally unresponsive to the real needs of the child as being overdisciplined.

In one study, Sroufe (1989) interviewed mothers about their attachment histories and found that if the interviewee portrayed her own mother as confident and competent, then she reported a secure attachment with her child. In another study (Ricks, 1985), mothers were asked how accepted or rejected they felt by their own parents, and these results correlated almost perfectly with whether their children were rated as securely or anxiously attached.

The Berkeley Adult Attachment Interview referred to earlier was devised by Carol George, Nancy Kaplan, and Mary Main. When Main and Goldwyn (in press) analyzed data from this interview, they found that if adults with unhappy attachment histories were able to talk articulately about them and demonstrate insight and understanding of their parents' behavior, then they were likely to be rated as "secure" as adults, and their children demonstrated secure attachments. However, the adults who were "dismissing of attachment" had three quarters of their children rated as avoidantly attached. The third category of adults in the study, classified by Main as "pre-occupied with early attachments" were more likely to have children who were ambivalently attached. The conclusion to be drawn from this study is that parents can escape their own attachment histories, but only through efforts to understand and work through their experiences.

Abusive and Narcissistically Disordered Parents

Alice Miller (1981, 1990), among others, has written about the effects of being raised with one or both parents who are narcissistic or abusive. The way in which Miller describes the internalization of abuse as "for your own good" resembles the denial of the dismissive adults described above. When parents have internalized these ideas they are likely to recreate the abuse with their own children.

Similarly, parents who suffer from narcissistic personality disorder are likely to treat their children as projections of themselves and attempt to get them to conform to the parents' projections in order to be loved. When the child is successful, the child grows up with narcissistic tendencies, having internalized the "false self," and sees self as worthy only in terms of how successfully he or she can project that image. The child is never confident that the "true self" might be enough (Masterson, 1990). If the child should fail to live up to the parental projections, then the child is treated as bad or inadequate, which can have devastating effects on the child's self-esteem and life history.

Loss and Deprivation

Other factors that can interact with attachment histories of parents include important losses, such as those of a parent, sibling, or child, or deprivation from the effects of poverty. One of the dangers with loss is that the child becomes the ghost, reincarnation, or replacement of the lost "other" (Brazelton & Cramer, 1990). The parents' projections onto the child can influence the development of a false self, which can be particularly damaging when the influence of the lost "other" is kept secret (e.g., in the case of suicide) or otherwise not acknowledged.

The deprivation of poverty can be a harsh reality that focuses parents' energies on basic needs for security, making them less available to focus on the emotional needs of their children. Robert Karen (1994), in his book summarizing attachment literature, reported on an interview with Sroufe about mothers in poverty whom he had studied. Sroufe said, "I personally haven't seen a mother that I would want to blame for the outcome. The poor single mothers in our study all want the best for their kid. They maybe can't do it. They may be so beaten down by their histories and their circumstances that they're doing a terrible job, but I've never seen one that didn't want to do it right" (p. 378).

The harsh effects of poverty are evident in the present but can also act as a ghost for parents who have grown up poor themselves. Parents can react sometimes through excessive gratification, trying to create the perfect childhood for their own children, overextending themselves until they feel exploited (Brazelton & Cramer, 1990), and raising children who expect immediate gratification.

ESTABLISHING A TREATMENT FRAME

To establish a treatment frame that incorporates attachment issues, the therapist needs to collect data about the history of the problems and interventions with the adolescent, the developmental history of the adolescent with a focus on attachment, and the parents' attachment histories. The therapist

should explore in depth any evidence of factors that contribute to an insecure attachment that were listed in the previous section.

Detailed History of the Problem and Interventions

The therapist can start with taking a detailed history of the problem, including all medical, psychological, and educational assessments and the nature
and degree of success of previous interventions, including those within the
school settings. The therapist needs to acquire permission to speak to anyone involved with the adolescent, especially school personnel who have had
significant contact. Both the parents' and adolescents' views on the successes
and failure of all types of interventions are important. Generally there are
mixtures of both—some tutors, counselors, or teachers who have been more
successful than others. Those with successful experiences will be able to
offer important suggestions. The therapist should determine whether the
approaches have been strictly behavioral or if there has been an attempt to
focus on relationship issues as well, and if so, what the results were.

Detailed Developmental History of the Child

Along with collecting a history of the problem and treatment, the therapist
should also collect a developmental history of the child, with a focus on
attachment issues. Special interest should be paid to the parents' and others'
assessment of the child's innate temperament. Questions to consider might
include the following: How did the parents respond to the child's temperament? How similar does each parent view the child's temperament to his or
her own? Did each parent feel synchrony or symmetry in his or her relationships with the child? What was the early history of child care? Was the child
viewed as difficult, and if so, how? Was there any early or chronic illnesses
on the part of the child or parent, including postpartum depression? How
did the child make each parent feel? How early were the parents aware of
any problems with emotional relatedness? Were there any significant losses
in the history of the child, for example, grandparents, siblings, friends, or
even pets? What is the history of the child's peer relationships? The answers
to these questions should be considered both from the parents' and the
adolescent's perspectives.

Parental Attachment Histories

The therapist should also collect histories from each parent on his or her
own development and families of origin. I find it most helpful to do this
with both parents together, because they each tend to chime in with their

own perspectives on the spouse's history and family relationships. Questions to ask might include the following: Where were they raised, how well off were they, and what were any cultural or religious influences? How do they describe their present and past connections to their family of origin? How would they describe their own parents' styles of parenting? What were the roles of each parent? Were there other caretakers, and if so, what were their caretaking styles like? Who was the parent close to; who not? What was each parent's history of both problems and successes, including school and peer histories?

In collecting these histories, the therapist listens with an ear toward how to classify both the parents' and the adolescent's attachment styles in light of the previously mentioned work by Main and Goldwyn (in press). In the "secure" category, parents are able to talk articulately about their history with insight and understanding. If they were wounded by their parents, they are able to describe how they have worked through it and are neither cut off nor embroiled in their feelings about it. "Avoidantly" attached adults will not want to talk about their histories and will be dismissive of possible connections. They will have trouble remembering early experiences with their parents and will answer in guarded ways without much elaboration. They may even seem somewhat hostile to the questions and may present their parents in either vague terms or even as idealized. When pressed for details about nurturance and attention, they may reveal problems or hurts that they will play down or view as things that "made me strong." "Ambivalently" attached adults, conversely, will be very emotional and likely to discuss hurts in great detail, not infrequently becoming overwhelmed by their emotions. It will be as if they have not moved on at all, and they may have either completely cut off from, or have current problematic relationships with, their families.

Establishing Mutual Goals, Form, and Framework of Treatment

Although the therapist can benefit from the use of an attachment framework to guide therapeutic interventions, the adolescent and parents may be less comfortable with such a framework. Parents will usually be oriented toward concrete goals and will want their children to be more successful in school, both socially and behaviorially. They usually want them to know how to accept limits, cooperate, and behave respectfully. The extent to which the therapist can introduce attachment issues depends on how dismissive the parent and adolescent are: Both secure and ambivalently attached parents will probably be open to this frame, and goals and tasks can be directly related to issues of the child–parent bond. However, both the parents and adolescents in avoidantly attached families are likely to be unresponsive and even hostile to attachment frames, and introducing these themes or tasks needs to be done slowly in the context of a supportive therapeutic environment or to be reframed in other behavioral terms (e.g., less conflict and more respect reframed as benefitting both the parents and adolescent).

There are two main objectives in setting the goals of treatment with families with longstanding problems. One is to set small, realistic goals, and the second is to establish that the accomplishment of those goals relies on the participants' following through with the counseling strategies. If the therapist does not emphasize that success in treatment lies less in the hands of the therapist than in the hands of the clients, the therapist will end up in a defensive posture with the parents. The initial starting point has to be one that combines hope with realistic expectations about what can be accomplished.

Finally, in terms of the format for treatment, I recommend that most of the treatment involve work with the subsystems individually. When joint sessions are planned, they need to be carefully choreographed ahead of time. The frequency of the sessions depends on the family's resources, of both time and funds (e.g., HMO limitations) for treatment. The family needs to be told overtly whether or not the amount they are willing to invest, especially in terms of time, is sufficient to accomplish the established goals. In other words, the therapist needs to make clear what goals are reasonable given the resources the family is willing to commit. Committing the adolescent and parents to a bottom line is important, because inconsistent treatment is ineffective.

The following sections will look at treatment issues separately for the parental, adolescent, and family subsystems. The therapist, while working with the separate subsystems, is also working to coordinate the treatment so the therapy is consistent across the subsystems.

WORKING WITH THE PARENTAL SUBSYSTEM

For the purposes of this chapter, I am going to separate working on behavioral goals from working on relationship issues in therapy. In practice, this distinction is somewhat arbitrary, and the therapist is commonly working on both at any given time. The attachment categories previously introduced will also be used to guide the following treatment strategies.

Working Behaviorally

Most families who have had problems for some time have been previously exposed to behavioral interventions. The history of interventions already explored will guide how the therapist incorporates behavioral interventions. Families with avoidant attachments are generally undercontrolling and unwilling to participate in behavioral work. If they are unwilling, the goal is to establish some limits and consequences, with a focus on rewards for the adolescent.

In contrast, ambivalent families are anxious to focus on behavior. These families are characterized by a long history of chronic, angry power struggles, and they frequently approach therapy with the secret hope that the therapist will effect a "scared straight" cure. The parents typically are overcontrolling and inconsistent setting limits. Struggling for control, they demand structure, but then they give up or fail to follow through, usually with a great deal of yelling and drama on all sides.

The first issue I address with ambivalent parents is that of "control." I want to have an honest discussion with the parents about what they are able to and not able to control with respect to their adolescent. I ally with the parents about how much more difficult it is to raise an adolescent in this day and age. I stress the cultural factors that put parents less in control of what their children are exposed to; how popular culture contributes to what I term the "death of hierarchy," leaving many children with little respect for adult authority; and how few supports there really are for parents whose adolescents are out of control. I stress that only the adolescent directly controls his or her behavior, and that typically many of the stances parents have taken, although with the best intentions of helping, may have inadvertently contributed to the problem behavior.

For example, often parents who have attempted to be most controlling have also participated in sheltering their child by intervening with school and legal systems in protective ways. The concept of "enabling" can be helpful. The frame is established that in trying to control their children's behavior and then rescuing them from consequences, they have given their child the message that it is the parents' rather than the adolescents themselves who take responsibility for the behavior. This message gives the children a false sense that the parents will always be able to protect them from the consequences of their behavior and that therefore they do not need to learn from their mistakes. The adolescent has not learned to accept the failures as his or her own but continues to blame the parents. The only way for adolescents to learn to accept failures as their own is for the parents to acknowledge what they cannot control and to concentrate instead on things they can control.

A major goal for the therapy is to have the parents reframe their displays of anger in a new view in which they equate a nonangry stance with being "in control" of themselves. These strategies are particularly necessary with ambivalently attached parents, whose emotions are likely to run high, and parents who use anger with adolescents "for their own good." Parents need to understand that it is impossible to control the adolescent's behavior directly. They can demonstrate a good example themselves by being in control of their own emotions and behavior, especially around the adolescent. I help parents look at how they may be spending their energies in "no-win" battles and exhausting themselves. I also help them look at how to focus their energies on the few resources they do control. For example, they may still control the use of a car, a telephone, and access to money or other resources. I ask the parents to consider what the key issues are and how they want to focus those resources as rewards or consequences.

School performance is one of the areas that is frequently a focus of over- or inconsistent control. I stress that frequently the parents accept too much responsibility for the adolescent's schoolwork and put themselves in a position of constantly nagging and reminding. Evenings become a battleground, with the parent determined to have the adolescent do his or her schoolwork and the adolescent focused on how to avoid the work and the parents' wrath. I urge parents to have the courage to let their adolescents fail on their own and accept the consequences. The parents should concentrate their efforts on cooperating with school consequences (e.g., not calling in as sick for the adolescent when he or she just wants to stay home because of incomplete work that is due). I urge parents to back out of any attempts to help the adolescent with homework by reading it, offering suggestions, or monitoring its completion. Parents should, instead, focus their efforts on limiting external interferences, such as telephone usage, television time, and going out, to provide conditions under which the homework could be completed if the adolescent expends the effort. Often the therapist needs to explain the approach to the adolescent's school counselor so they are all on the same page and not giving the parents contradictory messages. The parents and adolescent have to be fully prepared for the adolescent's failure. It is only by failing on his or her own that the adolescent will understand the consequences of his or her own behavior and not be able to blame it on parental interference. In my experience, the adolescent usually does at least as well as he or she has done in the past.

Another important concept for parents is that consequences teach the idea of cause and effect but do not necessarily control any particular instance of behavior. With parents, I frequently use the example of speed laws: Just because people are aware that there is a consequence for speeding does not mean they obey the speed limit. However, most people accept a speeding ticket as a consequence of "getting caught" and as a result may even reduce their speeding behavior, at least temporarily. I point out that adolescents are frequently willing to take their chances on "getting away with" any particular instance of behavior; however, that does not mean that conse-

quences have no effect. Taking my analogy further, I point out that the attitude of the highway patrol officer who gives you the speeding ticket may
contribute to your feelings about the situation. A calm, polite officer leaves
the responsibility with speeders, whereas an angry, nasty officer is likely to
leave speeders focused on the officer's behavior instead of their own.

Ambivalently attached parents often have the most difficulty "backing
off" and need the most work with the therapist in a supportive, nonblaming
therapeutic alliance. Referring to their own families of origin helps them see
themselves as agents of change for the family pattern with their own children rather than the source of blame. Conversely, avoidantly attached parents may accept little responsibility for their adolescent's behavior and be
difficult to engage in treatment. Their emotional tone may be generally calmer,
but they may need to be more involved in setting limits if they have been
uninvolved.

Working with Relationship Issues

As before, the goals will be different with the two different types of insecurely attached parents. With avoidantly attached parents and adolescents
the goal is to build connection between the adolescent and each parent.
Because these parents avoid discussing the effects of attachment in their
lives, the therapist should help them gain an understanding of these effects.
In a previous article (Mackey, 1996), I detailed a list of guidelines for structuring small, nurturant tasks for parents. Each parent and the adolescent is
asked to spend from 5 to 15 minutes of conflict-free time together daily
involved in a mutually agreed upon activity as a way to foster connection.
The difficulty with avoidant families is keeping them on task, so making the
task small and manageable is important. They may avoid a direct connection frame initially, so the tasks can be presented in the beginning as a way
to reduce conflict and increase respect within the family relations.

These focused connection times are also important with ambivalently
attached families but for different reasons. For ambivalently attached families, the goal is to teach appropriate boundaries, emphasizing the difference
between connection and support and intrusiveness. Along with the behavioral work already detailed, the structured nurturant tasks help parents pay
attention to what the adolescent actually wants instead of their own needs
or projections. In addition, it provides the security of knowing there is a
time to connect so the therapist can help them in "backing off" where they
are overinvolved. Whereas avoidantly attached parents are likely to already
be involved in their own lives, ambivalently attached parents may need help
in focusing on their own lives. A developmental life stage frame can help them
look ahead to when their adolescents will be leaving home and help them

focus on helping their adolescents learn to be independent. This "get a life" directive helps them refocus their energies on their own lives. They cannot just stop being so involved in their child's life—they need to redirect their energies. They may focus on such things as: the interests they have given up because of their children; changes they want to consider but have been putting off (e.g., changes in their jobs or going back to school); things they've always wanted to do and never had the time for; and ways they have stopped caring for themselves (e.g., how they are taking care of their own health, their diet, their exercise needs).

Another possible focus for the parents is the quality of their own relationship. The therapist can urge the couple to work on strengthening their marriage. They can be asked to consider to what degree they have focused on parenting rather than nurturing their marital relationship, and the therapy can be used as an opportunity to tend to their relationship.

When the parents are open to individual and couples work, they can often make progress in sorting through their own family-of-origin issues, which helps them become more appropriately involved with their own children. It can also help them accept and forgive themselves for their own mistakes in parenting. Some of the most healing moments in therapy can happen when the parent is able to acknowledge those mistakes in a family session with the adolescent (Mackey, 1996).

WORKING WITH THE ADOLESCENT

General Goals of Treatment

Sable (1992) suggested that therapy using attachment theory typically involves five tasks:

1. to provide clients with a secure base from which to explore various areas of their lives,
2. to encourage clients to examine the nature of current relationships with significant others,
3. to encourage clients to examine the client–therapist relationship,
4. to encourage clients to consider how current perceptions and expectations are a product of childhood and adolescent events and interactions with attachment figures, and
5. to enable clients to recognize that their models of self and others are not appropriate to the present and can be changed.

The approach suggested in the current chapter mirrors those tasks: The relationship with the therapist provides the secure basis from which adolescents can begin to take an honest look at themselves and their relationships (1, 2); the therapist–client relationship provides data for exploring relationship styles (3); the therapist encourages adolescents to examine how their perceptions and expectations are a product of interactions with their parents and other attachment figures (4); and finally, the therapist helps adolescents change the constraining aspects of both their models of themselves and their relationship patterns (5). In addition, family therapists working with adolescents have the advantage of direct, current access to the attachment figures.

The therapist should also help insecurely attached adolescents acknowledge and validate their loss and experience of emotional deprivation. The adolescents need to be able to face this pain and mourn it directly instead of acting it out. The failure of the parents can be talked about directly because of the attempts the therapist makes to help the adolescents get what they need emotionally from the parents in the family sessions. The anger that the adolescents are accustomed to expressing gives way gradually to sadness. The adolescents thus begin to make a difference for themselves as they are empowered to take charge of their emotional needs. The stated goal for the adolescents is to begin to control their lives and learn to "care" for self. A developmental life stage framework can be used to emphasize that the transition to adulthood involves a natural transference of reliance on parents for emotional needs to a reliance on self and peers.

With adolescents, behavioral change is addressed together with relationship issues, because adolescents' behaviors are tied to the relationship stance they take. Again, the two types of insecure attachment provide a framework for understanding both the adolescent's model of him or herself and also his or her behavior in relationships. The therapist helps the adolescent look at his or her common patterns of behavior that serve to divert the underlying pain and "keep him or her stuck."

Behavior/Relationship Patterns of Insecurely Attached Adolescents

Avoidantly Attached Adolescents

A pattern I call the "counterdependent" stance is typical of avoidantly attached adolescents in relationships. The goal inherent in this relationship style is to avoid letting anyone close to them emotionally. There are two subtypes, the bully and the codependent. Although both subtypes can be present in both genders, the prevalence of each type in either males or females is related to common gender role socialization. Typical socialization for males in our culture places a premium on competition and independence, whereas females are socialized to be more cooperative, caretaking, and "nice." Therefore, the first subtype, the bully, is more common in males.

The overt stance of the bully is "I don't care about anything or anyone but myself." The bully comes across as angry, defensive, and cynical. The therapist needs to be patient, avoid being drawn into power struggles, and look beneath the defensive structure for the underlying vulnerability. The therapist needs to take a stance of understanding the adolescent's need for protection, relate it to the family, and gently help the adolescent look at the consequences of his or her stand. The positive and affirming role that the therapist takes with the adolescent will serve as a secure base to explore the underlying loneliness. The adolescent will test this relationship in various acting-out ways, and the therapist must be honest and set with clear limits but always express belief in the adolescent's underlying strengths and potential to make other choices.

The second subtype, the codependent, is similar to a type described by Bowlby (1988). In this type, the counterdependency and avoidance of intimacy is much less obvious on the surface because it is manifested through overt caretaking of others. This adolescent directs her energy toward others at the cost of her own well-being. Apparently well liked by many peers, this adolescent attracts other needy adolescents and plays mother hen, frequently involving herself in situations that she is not equipped to handle. The caretaking allows her to dismiss her own feelings and attachment issues in a gender role–appropriate manner. Her caretaking behavior "looks" like connection, but it maintains both a "one-up" status along with an avoidance of her own feelings. She is much less likely to be engaged in defiant or acting-out behavior directed in opposition to authority figures. However, poor school performance is often common, and she can find herself at odds with authority figures over her loyalty to her "friends" if authority figures catch on to the consistent sacrifice of her own needs and well-being (e.g., homework assignments not completed because a friend "needed" her). This adolescent needs to be gently guided to help her see how her caretaking stance is a "one-up" position that keeps her protected from true intimacy and how serious the consequences are for her. She is often easier to connect with initially than the acting-out adolescent but has an equally hard time facing emotions or looking objectively at her own behavior.

Ambivalently Attached Adolescents

With adolescents who are ambivalently attached, the emotional deprivation is obvious to others. These adolescents are overt in their need for attention and will do whatever it takes to be the center of attention: Their motto is that any attention, no matter how negative, is better than none. They are needy, dependent, jealous, and demanding in relationships and can be narcissistic in the sense of having little sense for anyone else's feelings, needs, or boundaries. They frequently lie, and peers in relationships with them eventually confront their behaviors and lies. Once confronted, the neediness becomes even more exaggerated and less tolerated over time, developing a positive feedback loop. As discussed earlier, these adolescents are often sensitive to failure and give up easily. Ironically, the peer most likely to stay in a long-term friendship with an ambivalently attached adolescent is the codependent adolescent.

In therapy, these adolescents are likely to form "instant" and dependent relationships and test limits and boundaries with needy behavior. Their emotions are frequently volatile, and they are not likely to be either honest or have much insight into their own behavior. The therapist will need to be patient, calm, and caring in setting limits and, again, gently help the adolescent see the consequences of his or her stance in relation to self and others.

The Process of Treatment with the Adolescent

With all of the attachment styles described above, the relationship with the therapist serves as a secure base for the adolescents to develop insight into their relationships with both parents and peers and with their internal model of themselves. This self-knowledge or insight develops the basis of understanding how they can gain control of their lives through changing how they see themselves and others, how they care for themselves and others, and how they develop and realize personal goals, including relationship skills. These goals are consistent with the developmental tasks of adolescence: the development of identity, individuation, and autonomy.

With this general approach in mind, the process of therapy will be explored. The overarching framework for the therapeutic process is that of *self-focus*. From that framework we will look at how to help the adolescent develop *self-awareness*, then *self-in-relation awareness*. Awareness and self-knowledge provide the basis for *setting personal goals* for change. We will look at how to implement these goals and changes by helping adolescents take responsibility for self-care. This starts with the concrete notion of *care of the body* and proceeds to the development of *self-soothing and nurturance*. Finally, the last aspect of self-care is the ability to look for what one needs in the environment; therefore, exploring external *resources* is an important aspect to the treatment process.

Self-Focus

All of these adolescents need to be guided to a position of focusing on themselves and assuming the care for their selves, including their relationships, which is one of the benefits of a secure attachment history. Conversely, adolescents with insecure bases evidence insecurities in their sense of self and self-in-relationship as described above.

The focus on assuming responsibility fits within the developmental framework of the adolescent's discovery of identity and progression toward the independence of adulthood. The therapist can help the adolescent see the process of independence as one of making good choices for oneself. To make good choices,one needs to have a strong sense of identity or self and understand the costs of current choices of behavior, as well as what alternatives are. The therapist can communicate to adolescents that they hold within themselves the ability to truly control (within limits) their own lives and destinies and that the therapist believes in those abilities and will support them in achieving their goals. The notion of control is highly attractive to most adolescents, who can recognize that they are often just "re-acting" instead of acting in their lives.

I stress the idea that self-control comes out of self-knowledge and that they cannot control the behavior of others, only of themselves. In understanding what they can do differently, they can change their patterns.

Self-Awareness

An initial step in working alone with adolescents is to help them begin to become aware of their unique attributes and experiences. Preoccupied adolescents will need to learn to regulate their negative emotions, and avoidant adolescents to identify their own emotions. The avoidant adolescent needs to be approached slowly. One way to connect to avoidant adolescents is to begin by talking about their interests rather than their relationships. The therapist can assist the process of self-awareness through feedback to the client via observations about the adolescent. The therapist can make simple statements about the kind of clothes the adolescent wears and how she or he acts or expresses her or himself. The therapist can ask a lot of uncritical questions about how the adolescent spends his or her time and about preferences in music, television, movies, computer games, foods, and so on. Offering observations about how the adolescent is alike or different from his or her parents, friends, the therapist, and other adolescents provides "self-defining" feedback to the adolescent.

Avoidantly attached adolescents, however, may have more difficulty talking about themselves in general, so another avenue in therapy is to have art materials available. I have found nonverbal adolescents can be more willing to draw or color with crayons or markers, especially when these options are presented casually.

I call one helpful exercise the "Me" Collage. I have used this exercise with adolescents from 12 to18 years of age successfully. The therapist needs to provide a large variety of magazines, a glue stick, scissors, and a piece of posterboard. Give the adolescent time to go through the magazines and cut or tear out pictures that he or she thinks captures something about him or herself or that he or she just likes. The adolescent can arrange as many pictures as can fit onto the posterboard. The resulting collage can be discussed and modified over time. Collages can be done at various points in the treatment and compared over time.

Preoccupied adolescents can use the positive self-feedback to help build a more competent sense of self. The strong emotions they feel are readily apparent and often painful. The pain of those emotions is used as the reason to motivate the adolescent to set a goal of learning to manage them.

Self-in-Relation Awareness

As noted earlier, increased cognitive abilities place adolescents in the position of being able to consider and compare their various attachments to others. Therefore, at least in terms of cognitive abilities, they can begin to assess which relationships in their lives are "good" for their personal development and which are "unhealthy" in specific ways. Of course the nature of their attachment style determines how open, objective, and flexible the adolescent can be in considering relationships. Openness, objectivity, and flexibility can be stated as objectives in the discussions, and it will be the therapist's job to provide the adolescent with clear and concrete feedback regarding how he or she is doing with regard to the objectives. The nature of different relationships with each parent, sibling, teacher, and friend can be evaluated. Although one parent or adult may be deficient in some aspect, they may be helpful in others (mom is calmer about certain issues and dad about others). Friendships can be looked at as either healthy or unhealthy. Those that are deemed unhealthy can be analyzed to determine if there are aspects of the relationship that are appropriate and can be maintained in a safe way. For example, an adolescent can share his or her interests in music at school with a friend but not socialize with that same friend outside of school because of the pressure to smoke pot. Ideally, I help adolescents develop a set of informal criteria for themselves to evaluate their relationships.

Setting Personal Goals

Another step is to begin to help adolescents visualize some personal goals. To further appropriate differentiation, the therapist encourages the adolescent to "own" his or her therapy. Remember that both anxious and ambivalently attached adolescents have difficulty sticking with things and delaying gratification, and their goals may be highly unrealistic at the beginning. The therapist should accept whatever goals the adolescent offers, perhaps commenting on the ambitious nature of them and gently helping the adolescent judge if they are realistic or need to be scaled down. The adolescent needs to be advised that failures will be used as feedback to guide the process rather than as reasons to "give up." The therapist's job is to help the adolescent begin to take small, active steps toward those goals, thus making them real. To do that, the goals have to be broken down into steps that are small enough to be "do-able," and they must start where the adolescent currently "is" in a realistic way. The adolescent may need to start very small, especially when it comes to relationship issues and changing those behaviors.

School is often a loaded subject with adolescents. They often want to do better but do not want to engage in a power struggle or "fail." Talking with them concretely about what gets in the way of concentrating or completing work can make the struggle their own and not their parents' or the therapist's. As the therapist, you must communicate that you are willing to help them improve in whatever area they would like and help them think about those things in problem-solving ways. The therapist should avoid being invested in a particular strategy or communicating personal investment in the results.

When adolescents get to the point where the therapist really thinks that they are ready to begin doing something different, they are often still constrained by multiple fears. It is helpful for the therapist to remember how potent those fears can be and to work to get the adolescent to both articulate and face them. Adolescents can feel extremely vulnerable and may be hesitant to voice their fears because they are afraid of ridicule. It is the therapist's job to help them feel safe enough to voice their fears and eventually begin to challenge them. Whereas the preoccupied adolescent is well aware of his or her fears, the dismissing adolescent may need considerable time to develop an awareness and then be able to voice them aloud.

A helpful concept to remember is David Elkind's (1997) *imaginary audience*. At the development of formal operations, individuals can take multiple perspectives and therefore can imagine themselves from other perspectives. One result is that adolescents can become extremely "self-conscious" and think that any action they take is being judged by an imaginary audience. With the majority of adolescents in treatment, this audience is a harsh one filled with critics. The preoccupied adolescent is likely to be particularly focused on parents as critics, whereas the avoidant adolescent will focus on authority figures and peers as "jerks" and overtly dismiss the impact of any perceived criticisms. The therapist needs to help the adolescent realize that the worst critics are frequently internal. Cognitive behavioral techniques in which the therapist helps the adolescent give the critics voices and then confront them are often helpful.

Care of the Body

The most concrete way to help adolescents care for themselves is to teach them to take good care of their bodies. Sports or any form of physical exercise is good for stress and depression. Adolescents need to be encouraged to enjoy activities for the sake of the activity itself, rather than for the end product. They do not need to be "good" to enjoy the feeling of running or even walking. I encourage them to start very small and gradually work up to more if they do not regularly do anything physically beyond gym class.

Food can be an important metaphor, especially for girls. Social pressure on girls to be thin has been widely documented; however, I also see an increasing number of teenage boys feeling pressured about their appearance. If the adolescent focuses on appearance, I try to help him or her focus on "eating healthy" and engaging in exercise instead of dieting. I refer to the data regarding the negative effects of dieting and help the adolescent talk about the choices he or she wants to make. I help them confront the negative and unrealistic images in the media by bringing information about the average body and talking about how unrealistic those media images are. I encourage females to begin to identify "anorectic" models in ads and encourage males to identify the kind of effort required to attain the body of most male models or actors, who have access to personal coaches. I then encourage the adolescent to practice talking back to the ads and to confront internalized messages that are unrealistic.

Another important need for adolescents is for nonsexual physical contact. Not infrequently, parents withdraw from physical contact as their adolescent develops secondary sexual characteristics. I believe that this inadvertently sends the message that all physical contact is sexual. I encourage adolescents to seek nonsexual physical contact (e.g., hugging). Finally, in terms of having adolescents get in touch with their own bodies, I may also encourage them to consider meditation, yoga, or any kind of self-defense classes to help them feel empowered.

None of the suggestions offered here should be "assigned" as homework. Avoidantly attached adolescents, with their fierce independence, will resist direct suggestions, and ambivalently attached adolescents need to make their own choices to develop appropriate boundaries. Suggestions should be offered as resources for the adolescent's consideration and with numerous examples to consider. The therapist must be cognizant of the overall goal, which is for the adolescent to make choices for him or herself. In the best-case scenarios, adolescents will find their own ways to fulfill their goals with new ideas or resources. When it is a resource the therapist has suggested, the adolescent needs to personalize it in some way to make it his or her own in order for it to work most effectively.

Self-Soothing and Nurturance

Self-soothing refers to how one calms oneself during the experience of unpleasant emotions. Many insecurely attached adolescents have never learned those skills and need concrete help in developing the ability to manage emotions without acting them out. First, I help adolescents identify the negative feelings and thoughts they are having and try to accept bad feelings as important information. Typically, I help adolescents learn to take time to calm themselves down before reacting (e.g., by counting to 10, leaving the situation if possible, deep breathing, etc.). Then I ask what he or she would like at those times. I encourage them to "be nice to themselves." Frequently adolescents, girls especially, retain childhood stuffed animals they can hug, but they are also often fond of candles, incense, and music. Small items that can be kept in their pockets can be used outside of home. I have had adolescents choose a wide variety of items to carry, ranging from pieces of an old baby blanket to balls that can be squeezed or key ring emblems that represent something special to them. I encourage them to make lists of things they can do for themselves when they are feeling bad and then do them as needed. Exercise or other physical activity can be an important self-soothing tool because it is a natural stress reliever and antidepressant.

Frankl (1998) noted that people survive in tough circumstances when they are able to establish meaning for themselves. I talk about Frankl's book, *Man's Search for Meaning,* and encourage my adolescent clients to find meaning for themselves. It can be music, books, film, art, writing, sports, or any kind of interest or activity. I also use Frankl's concept of being able to project themselves into the future and in envisioning who they will be in that future to bring meaning to a current time of difficulty (e.g., an adolescent who wants to be a musician may want to focus on improving his or her music now).

Work is an additional way that adolescents can develop self-esteem and self-reliance. Not infrequently, adolescents who have trouble with adults at home and at school can develop positive relationships in a work setting and derive a sense of accomplishment in their place of work. At this point, the parents' reactions are crucial. Too much overt interest on the parents' part can cause an adolescent to give the interest up because of the fear of the parent becoming either involved in the interest and co-opting it or else becoming critical of it. I caution the parents not to offer advice or comment on the interest unless the adolescent offers information or indicates a willing-ness for the parent to comment. Then all comments should be neutral or positive, never critical or even what is perceived by the parent as being "helpful."

Journal writing can be particularly helpful if the adolescent is moti-vated to keep one. Many homes have computers that can make the writing more pleasurable for the adolescent and that allows privacy to be guarded with a password. If the journal is handwritten, parents need to be told to keep "hands off" even if it is left out in plain view, and adolescents need to guard its privacy, even from close friends who might exploit information. In the journal they can also project themselves into their imagined future and develop and explore their hopes and dreams.

Resources

I work to help adolescents realize that they need to search for sources of support in their lives, which is especially true for the avoidant adolescent whose parents have been uninvolved. However, ambivalently attached ado-lescents can also benefit from appropriate and supportive connections. Friends of similar age as the adolescent are one source, but they need to look for positive adults in their lives as well.

In the work on self-in-relation the goal was to look at "healthy" versus "unhealthy" friendships. In developing resources for support, the adoles-cent must determine whether this person only wants to complain and shift blame to others for the problems in his or her life or is able to look at how he or she might contribute to problems. I often encourage adolesecnts to invite their friends to therapy sessions. Friends can be invaluable assets to the therapist because they often confirm many of the therapist's ideas. They can also offer new data.

Siblings are another possible resource for the adolescent. A common problem in families with insecure attachments is conflict between siblings who are competing for meager parental resources. If siblings can be encour-aged to see each other as supports for each other and see that each are sub-ject to similar deprivation, the siblings can be encouraged to nurture each other. Instead of competing for resources, they can work together to maxi-mize them. Work in session can be devoted to conflict resolution, sharing their experience of deprivation, and talking about similarities and differ-ences. They can be encouraged to develop common time together and to share support and resources.

Developing a support system within the sibling subsystem is more dif-ficult when there is a "favored" sibling. To make progress within the sibling subsystem, the "favored" sibling needs to understand the cost he or she pays for the "privileged" position in the family. These costs can include "foreclosure" of their identity to their parents, loss of relationship with siblings, and limited relationships with peers.

Extended family members can also be candidates for support for the adolescent. Frequently there are grandparents or aunts or uncles who have less conflictual relationships with the adolescent. These family members can be invited to sessions and coached on how to develop a more supportive relationship with the adolescent without further threatening the adolescent's relationship to the parents. Of course, when other resources are invited into therapy sessions, the parents need to see this as supportive of them rather than as threatening. Therefore, the therapist needs to seek the parents' support prior to contact with other family members.

Other possible resources include parents of the adolescent's friends, teachers, other school personnel, coaches, ministers, and personnel in local adolescent drop-in centers. A thorough understanding of the adolescent's typical day may reveal other hidden resources. The therapist may ask the adolescent to describe each day of the week hour by hour, including the weekends. This will help to identify people he or she may connect to during a typical week. One client I worked with had a supportive relationship with a school monitor who was a parent volunteer in the school and who, when I talked to her, had very helpful information about the adolescent's relationships at school and was willing to be of continued support to this young man.

I routinely arrange a staffing with as many school personnel as I can meet with, including the adolescent's teachers, counselor, and social worker. I often like to do this without the parents present in order to discuss the situation more openly and to elicit support for the adolescent. It is important to make sure that when discussing the parents' relationship to the adolescent at school to avoid putting the parents in such a light that school personnel are supported in a position of blaming the parents. If, after the school staffing, parents experience a more adversarial or unsupportive stance on the part of school personnel, then the treatment will be negatively affected. The parents' difficulties, therefore, need to be presented in a sympathetic manner without revealing too many personal details to school personnel.

Another very positive adjunct to adolescent therapy are adolescent groups that may be sometimes offered within the school and community agencies. Many self-help groups are often available to adolescents with specific symptomatology or problems, such as eating disorders, drug use, and divorced families. As a therapist, I keep a list of adolescent groups available in the communities where I practice. Many are even offered free or at very low cost.

FAMILY THERAPY

The work described thus far has been individual work with the parental and adolescent subsystems. In families with insecure attachments, the goals of any family therapy sessions need to be clearly understood and agreed upon by all participants. In the individual sessions the therapist coaches each of the participants so that their behavior in the joint sessions will provide changes in their typical ways of interacting. Whether the goals of the family session involve behavioral contracting or relationship issues, everyone should be clear ahead of time how they want to act in order to change their own behavior.

Goals

The goals of any session need to be well articulated and may include the following:

1. Behavioral contracting: Negotiating, clarifying, or changing some aspect of limits, consequences, or rewards.
2. Communication: Working on bringing down the emotional tone, especially anger, in discussions and working on respectful communication and empathic listening. "I" messages and active listening exercises are good tools for this goal.
3. Connection: Developing short, nonconflictual time for the adolescent to spend with each parent in an agreed-upon activity. Encouraging either the parent or the adolescent to apologize or to discuss with insight their contribution to problems within the relationship.
4. Interactional Sequences: Identifying the specific interactional sequences that are problematic and specifying the behavior change each participant will make to change the outcome of the sequence (e.g., changing a pattern of escalating fights).

Therapist's Role Within the System

Alliance Issues

One of the most difficult challenges to face the therapist in working with insecurely attached adolescent families is that of maintaining alliances with both the parents and the adolescent. Both the parents and the adolescent need to feel that the therapist can understand their experience of the difficult relationship. This can be difficult to do because both sides can be unreasonable and extreme in their beliefs much of the time. For many therapists, it is particularly difficult to witness how rejecting parents can be toward their own children. The therapist must work hard to understand the pain that was involved in creating the rejection without minimizing the impact of the rejection on the adolescent. The hypothesis of the "difficult child" can be helpful in this regard for both the therapist and the parents. Additionally, adolescents typically evidence black-and-white thinking and may demonstrate "stubbornness." Having been wounded, they are slow to acknowledge any change on the parents' part or show them any respect or affection. The responses from both the adolescent and the parents need to be framed as defensive and as a result of pain—the more extreme the reaction, the stronger the underlying pain. Helping the individual participants "control" and choose their behavior in family therapy sessions may be facilitated by additional individual sessions where they can be coached and may feel less vulnerable. Typical problems, reactions, and resistances can all be predicted and discussed in advance.

Both the adolescent and parent need to be coached to understand that the other's response is the individual's emotional experience of any particular situation. This goal—accurate empathy—is one of general communication. Active listening exercises are helpful. I work hard to coach each side not to participate in the predictable arguments about "what really happened." Instead I try to help each side understand that it is not what really happened that influences people, but each person's experience of what happened that determines an individual's response. This validates each person's experience of emotional events.

As the therapist, remember you are in a triangulated position. This position is often advantageous because the therapist can mediate disputes and "explain" the responses of the individuals to each other. But it is, of course, a difficult position if the therapist is not really clear with everyone about what will and will not be communicated to the other individuals. I always tell parents in the beginning that I will inform the adolescent of any communication from the parent and what stance I took on any part of the issue. Whenever I take a position with one individual that will be potentially difficult for anyone else, I try to talk to the person for whom it will be difficult first, or as soon thereafter as possible. I also remind everyone that things can be taken out of context and misunderstood, so each should always call and talk to me if they hear anything from someone else in the family about what I said that angers or upsets them in any way.

It is especially important to inform the adolescent that the therapist must have regular contact with the parents in order to be most helpful. Discuss thoroughly with the adolescent what is permissible for you to share with the parents. I actually review with the adolescent what I plan to say to the parent.

The therapist needs to remind the adolescent that he or she will have to share with the parent any behavior deemed dangerous. The most common issue in this regard is drug and alcohol use. I inform parents and adolescents that although occasional or experimental use is normal, I will inform the parents if I believe the adolescent is in trouble and certainly if I have evidence that they are driving under the influence of alcohol or drugs. The therapist should never be in the position of having protected the adolescent's confidence when the behavior could result in tragedy.

Role Model

Working with these families can be extremely difficult and frequently unrewarding. The therapist should retain an attitude of hope and not be discouraged by the predictable ups and downs of such cases. If the therapist begins to feel hopeless, this attitude will undoubtedly be communicated to the family, who will consequently view therapy as useless. This outcome is especially unfortunate for the adolescent.

To maintain hope, the therapist needs to make sure that he or she models the skills advocated for clients, including self-soothing, self-nurturance, and a balanced life outside of work. Some of the therapist's own experiences and struggles can serve as examples of how these things can be done or not done. If the therapist does not have clear, concrete examples about how to do what clients are asked to do, it is unlikely the client will be able to learn to do them.

Some of the therapist's most helpful feedback can come from his or her own experience with struggles as parents, especially if the therapist either currently has, or has raised, adolescents. The therapist can frequently empathize with many of the frustrations, concerns, and even anger that parents feel, even if it is at a lesser degree.

It is also important for the therapist to serve as a role model with regard to setting reasonable limits with the family. For example, the therapist should not allow abusive behavior from either the adolescent or the parents and should not allow him or herself to overreact and respond in kind. Modeling calm boundary setting with a certain amount of flexibility teaches the importance of not being rigid with adolescents. The flexibility must be genuine and not forced. Each therapist must define his or her own limits and be comfortable with them.

Advocate

The therapist needs to take an active position of advocacy for both the parents and the adolescent. When there has been an insecure or hostile attachment, there often has been a long history of problems in school and in the community. Both the parents and adolescent may have experienced judgmental and shaming attitudes from multiple sources and responded with defensive attitudes. The therapist can act as an advocate with these outside systems, which is often easier than it appears on the surface: Obvious solutions have frequently not been employed because of the attitudes of the warring sides. For example, each side may have developed uncooperative and rigid stances so that agreements cannot be reached. With a neutral third party, these agreements can be reached in a mutually beneficial way. In these situations the therapist serves as a mediator and "translator" to the different sides of any particular situation.

The therapist should also act as an advocate by informing the family about community resources for both the parents and the adolescent. Sometimes effort needs to be made to establish relationships with key resources. These families usually need more than just the support the therapist can provide, which the therapist should acknowledge to the family as well as to her or himself.

CASE ILLUSTRATION

Marion, the mother of two adolescents, Joe (14) and Abby (16), asked for a family session to deal with anger-control issues in the family, particularly relating to Joe's recent slipping performance in school and increasingly disrespectful behavior both at home and school. Marion said her husband, William, had finally agreed to family therapy after she threatened to leave him if he did not participate. The subsequent treatment took place over the course of about a year and a half with frequent breaks and very flexible scheduling.

I heard this family coming down the hall even before they reached my office, because William and Abby were involved in a heated exchange about the scheduling of the session, parking, and when they were going to leave. The parents' goals were to have both children do better in school and to be more respectful, and the children's goals were for the parents to "get off our backs" and "stop going postal." All participants agreed that they were all volatile in their own ways and had a long history of difficulties among them. Strengths apparent in this family were their obvious intelligence, displays of humor (especially from the son), and a positive connection between the siblings. The hurt, anger, and conflict between the parents were readily apparent, and they agreed to come in together without the children. I would schedule a separate session for the children together in light of their positive connection.

Alone, the parents were very open about both their disagreements about parenting and the longstanding conflicts in their marital relationship. Both parents described family histories reflecting an ambivalent attachment. William admitted that his parents were cold and his own father was abusive. Although he was reluctant to share insights about his family, Marion filled in with great detail. William mostly agreed, at times defending his parents as doing the best they could given the financial pressures with which his family had grown up. Marion had some insight into her own family but at times was overcome with emotion. Her father was nice but mostly absent, taking a back seat to his wife with regard to parenting. Marion experienced her mother as controlling, overprotective, and critical. Marion said she grew up being a "pleaser" and had taken that role with William, whom she felt had been emotionally abusive over the course of their marriage. William acknowledged his problems with anger but also felt his anger was at times justified in light of how unsupportive Marion was and how he felt marginalized and not respected by anyone in his family.

In exploring the history of problems in the family, they revealed that William had suffered severe depression that began shortly after Abby was born and was only recently being effectively controlled through medication. Due to concerns about needing to support the family on her own, Marion went back to school and earned her MBA at nights while William cared for the children.

In their session, the children echoed the history and expanded on their own roles in the family. Abby, like her parents, displayed a typical ambivalent attachment style. She was a fighter, and any request by her parents was deemed as "stupid" and automatically met with resistance. Yet her parents described the typical neediness and demandingness characteristic of an ambivalent attachment style. She admitted she had recently experimented with drugs and alcohol, and because she attended a small, private school her teachers were noticing a change in her performance and were concerned. Joe, conversely, demonstrated a detached attachment style. He avoided conflict, was generally less verbal, and downplayed any discomfort he felt in the family. The difference in attachment styles allowed the siblings to be close. Joe acknowledged that Abby's expression of anger in the family allowed him to maintain his more detached style, and Abby did not feel any competition from Joe for the emotional resources in the family. Everyone acknowledged that Joe used humor defensively to lighten tension in the family as a whole and avoid emotional interactions for himself.

In subsequent sessions, I worked to have the parents learn to listen more empathically to each other and set jointly agreed upon expectations and consequences for both children. Individually, William worked on anger management with the goal of being a different parent than his own father, and Marion worked at resolving some of her own hurt, both in regard to her own family and in terms of the years spent during William's depression. She also acknowledged she was inconsistent in limit setting both because she did not want to duplicate her own mother's "overcontrol" and because she wanted to make up to the children for her husband's verbal abuse when he was angry.

Concurrently, I worked with Abby and Joe to make different choices by setting goals for themselves. Abby was able to acknowledge her own neediness and began to change her interactions with peers, setting appropriate limits and being less demanding. She set a personal goal for herself to become involved in the theater department at school and subsequently earned a lead role in the spring play. This proved to be an invaluable source of support for her in terms of self-esteem, as well as in acquiring new friends who were supportive and positive and in relating to adults who were nurturant yet clear in their limits and expectations. Joe eventually was able to acknowledge his own anger and hurt. He talked about how he had "turned off" his emotions because he had been so frightened as a child when his father became angry. He was able to remember some specific incidents he had repressed that were very traumatic for him. He also was able to acknowledge that he felt angry at what he felt was his mother's abandonment when she went back to school, effectively "throwing me to the lions." The family came to understand how they had reinforced Joe's detached style by never acknowledging that Joe might have feelings of hurt, preferring to believe he had been unaffected by the family's turmoil.

The final step was coaching the parents to be able to listen and validate Joe's experience of his preschool years. Through this experience, Joe became much more able to acknowledge his own feelings and dependency needs and began to have real friends rather than just be the class clown as he had previously been. One of Joe's personal goals was to become involved in a sport, and he ended up choosing basketball and making the varsity team. His coach and teammates turned out to be important resources for him, and the camaraderie of the team gave him a place to begin to connect emotionally.

Abby is now a theater major in college, and Joe is in his junior year in high school, beginning to think of college choices for himself. William's depression continues to be stabilized through medication, and he feels he controls his anger but has joined a men's group for support and to further his work. Marion has just received a promotion at work and indicates the marriage is much closer; however, she wants to keep the door open to future therapy on an "as-needed" basis.

SUMMARY

A secure attachment between parents and child is the basis for the developmental task of differentiation in adolescence. Attachment theory has been used as a framework to understand why some families with adolescents can be particularly difficult if relationship issues are not taken into account in the therapeutic approach. In this chapter, we have looked at how the two forms of insecure attachment, ambivalent and avoidant attachments, manifest themselves in adolescents and in their parents. I have suggested that in adolescent cases in which there is a longstanding history of problems, the therapist collect a history of the treatment and problems with a focus on attachment issues.

The model focuses on working individually with the parental and adolescent subsystems to help them separate from unhealthy power struggles and to establish a more secure attachment. Work with the parent is directed at letting go and "getting a life" and setting appropriate boundaries with ambivalently attached parents, and strengthening a nurturant connection with avoidantly attached parents. Work with the adolescent is advised by their attachment style and focuses on developmental goals of identity and independence through self-knowledge, self-care, and self-control through making good choices for oneself. Effective work with families with insecure attachments relies on the therapist maintaining a secure alliance with both the adolescent and the parents.

REFERENCES

Ainsworth, M. S., Behar, M. C., Waters, E., & Wall, S. (1978). *Patterns of attachment*. Hillsdale, NJ: Erlbaum.

Allen, J., & Hauser, S. (1996). Autonomy and relatedness in adolescent–family interactions as predictors of young adults' states of mind regarding attachment. *Development and Psychopathology, 8,* 793–809.

Allen, J., & Kupermine, G. (1995, April). *Adolescent attachment, social competence, and problematic behavior.* Paper presented at the biennial meeting of the Society for Research in Child Development, Indianapolis, IN.

Allen, J., Kupermine, G., & Moore, C. (1997). Developmental Approaches to understanding adolescent deviance. In S. Luthar, J. Burack, D. Cicchetti, & J. Weisz (Eds.), *Developmental psychopathology: Perspectives on risk and disorder* (pp. 548–567). Cambridge, England: Cambridge University Press.

Allen, J., & Land, D. (1999). Attachment in adolescence. In J. Cassidy & P. Shaver (Eds.), *Handbook of attachment: Theory, research, and clinical applications.* New York: Guilford Press.

Allen, J., Moore, C., Kupermine, G., & Bell, K. (1998). Attachment and adolescent psychosocial functioning. *Child Development, 69,* 1406–1419.

Becker-Stoll, F., & Fremmer-Bombik, E. (1997, April). *Adolescent–mother interaction and attachment: A longitudinal study.* Paper presented at the biennial meeting of the Society for Research in Child Development, Washington, DC.

Bowlby, J. (1969). *Attachment and loss: Vol. 1. Attachment.* New York: Basic Books.

Bowlby, J. (1973). *Attachment and loss: Vol. 2. Separation: Anxiety and anger.* New York: Basic Books.

Bowlby, J. (1977). The making and breaking of affectional bonds. *British Journal of Psychiatry, 130,* 201–210.

Bowlby, J. (1988). *A secure base.* New York: Basic Books.

Brazelton, T. B., & Cramer, B. G. (1990). *The earliest relationship: Parents, infants, and the drama of early attachment.* New York: Addison & Wesley.

Chess, S., & Thomas, A. (1987). *Origins and evolution of behavior disorders.* Cambridge, MA: Harvard University Press.

Elkind, D. (1997). *All grown up and no place to go.* New York: Perseus Press.

Frankl, V. (1998). *Man's search for meaning: An introduction to logotherapy* (Rev. ed.). New York: Washington Square Press.

Hazen, C., & Shaver, P. (1987). Romantic love conceptualized as an attachment process. *Journal of Personality and Social Psychology, 59,* 511–524.

Karen, R. (1994). *Becoming attached: Unfolding the mystery of the infant–mother bond and its impact on later life.* New York: Warner.

Kobak, R. (1999). The emotional dynamics of disruption in attachment relationships: Implications for theory, research, and clinical intervention. In J. Cassidy & P. Shaver (Eds.), *Handbook of attachment: Theory, research, and clinical applications.* New York: Guilford Press.

Kobak, R., Cole, H., Ferenz-Gillies, R., Fleming, W., & Gamble, W. (1993). Attachment and emotional regulation during mother–teen problem-solving: A control theory analysis. *Child Development, 64,* 231–245.

Kobak, R., & Duemmler, S. (1994). Attachment and converstation: Toward a discourse analysis of adolescent and adult security. In K. Bartholomew & D. Perlman (Eds.), *Advances in Personal Relationships: Vol. 5. Attachment Processes in Adulthood* (pp. 121–149). London: Kingsley.

Kobak, R., Sudler, N., & Gamble, W. (1991). Attachment and depressive symptoms during adolescence: A developmental pathways analysis. *Development and Psychopathology, 3,* 461–474.

Mackey, S. K. (1996). Nurturance: A neglected dimension in family therapy with adolescents. *Journal of Marital and Family Therapy, 22,* 489–508.

Main, M. (1997, December). *Attachment: Theory, research, application.* Paper presented at the meeting of the American Psychoanalytic Society, New York.

Main, M., & Goldwyn, R. (in press). Adult attachment rating and classification system. In M. Main (Ed.), *A typology of human attachment organization assessed in discourse, drawings, and interviews.* New York: Cambridge University Press.

Masterson, J. (1990). *The search for the real self: Unmasking the personality disorders of our age.* New York: Free Press.

Miller, A. (1981). *The drama of the gifted child.* New York: Basic Books.

Miller, A. (1990). *For your own good: Hidden cruelty in childrearing and the roots of violence* (H. Hannum, & H. Hannum, Trans.). New York: Noonday Press.

Ricks, M. (1985). The social transmission of parental behavior. Attachment across generations. In I. Bretherton & E. Waters (Eds.), *Growing points in attachment theory and research. Monographs of the Society for Research in Child Development, 50*(Serial No. 209), 211–227.

Rosenstein, D., & Horowitz, H. (1996). Adolescent attachment and psychopathology. *Journal of Consulting and Clinical Psychology, 64,* 244–253.

Sable, P. (1992). Attachment theory: Application to clinical practice with adults. *Clinical Social Work Journal, 20,* 271–283.

Sroufe, L. A. (1983). Infant–caregiver attachment and patterns of adaptation in preschool: The roots of maladaption and competence. In M. Perlmitter (Ed.), *Minnesota Symposium in Child Psychology: Vol. 1.* (pp. 41–81). Hillsdale, NJ: Erlbaum.

Sroufe, L. A. (1989, February 10). Talk at City University of New York, Graduate Center.

PART IV

Life Cycle Transitions: Adult Perspective

CHAPTER 5

Linking Work, Love, Individual, and Family Issues in Counseling

An Attachment Theory Perspective

M. CAROLE PISTOLE

As a faculty member with experience teaching counselors and providing therapy in college counseling centers, I had an experience recently that stimulated my thinking about how work and love are linked and how addressing relationship agendas can produce gains across work, relationship, family, and individual functioning. In my Introduction to Mental Health Counseling class, a masters student asked, for the entire class, "Why are career classes included in mental health counseling curriculums?" After brief thought I heard myself telling the class that (a) I have rarely seen a client where work or career issues were not, at some point in the therapy, an important focus of therapeutic change, and (b) while in professional training learners develop their core knowledge from separate courses (e.g., career, human development, theories of counseling), but in working with clients, those artificially discrete knowledge bases become integrated. Professionals can and do make distinctions between career and personal counseling, and people do sometimes talk about their work and their personal life as if they were separated from one another. There is, however, an "interdependent relationship . . . between career and personal counseling" (Dorn, 1993, p. 419), because people are comprised of a personality organization within which love and work reflect related aspects of the person.

The contention in this chapter is that attachment theory, which focuses on emotionally important relationships, provides a powerful framework for conceptualizing and intervening with adults' struggles. Theory and research indicate that a relationship focus in counseling is beneficial for clients (Framo,

117

1996; Orlinsky, Grawe, & Parks, 1994; Strupp & Binder, 1984). In addition, both relationship and work difficulties are influenced by family emotional patterns (e.g., Bowen, 1985; Friedman, 1985). The chapter will begin first with a rationale for considering work as a central therapeutic issue and second with a synopsis of attachment, followed by a brief discussion of counseling with college students. In discussing the application of attachment theory, I will focus on college students because I have the most experience with this group and because the connections may be seen with particular clarity in college students due to their normative developmental issues. After case material illustrating the points, I will consider caveats as part of the conclusion of this chapter.

LINKING WORK AND PERSONAL ISSUES

Work is much more than a means to earn money and to support the financial independence of the self or the family (Bielski, 1996). Work can be viewed as a life anchor (Maida, Gordon, & Faberow, 1989), and work or career is an important element in personal development and contentment with life. Like family and love relationships, work is an important source of meaning for adults because it tends to "fulfill . . . fundamental emotional needs for identity, power, security, a sense of self-worth and purpose" (Bielski, p. 25). Unresolved career issues and difficulties in the workplace can be disruptive in people's lives and have a negative impact on both emotional and physical well-being and health (Dorn, 1993). In today's world characterized by technological innovations, sometimes with corresponding changes in work, career-related struggles are an important therapeutic concern (Bielski, 1996). For instance, an employer's plan to downsize in the workplace creates a stressful environment for all workers, and the loss of a job creates as much or more stress as a 65-hour workweek. Such work-related concerns may reverberate throughout the multigenerational family system, producing a variety of broad effects (Bowen, 1985). If a parent's job is downsized at work, the traditional-aged college student may find that counted-on funds for tuition are not available, or symptomatic behavior related to the parent's work-place stress may surface in the college student. Students of a nontraditional age may be in programs to facilitate a career transition because they were downsized or feared downsizing in a previous job. In addition, with the two-earner family becoming more prevalent, individuals' work-related distress can complicate relationship and family functioning (Bielski, 1996).

Another reason that work is a legitimate concern in counseling is that it is linked to family functioning. The family influences career beliefs, career choices, and the ways people organize their career experience (Dorn, 1993). For instance, some students choose their major and their career based on the parent's advice and guidance, or pressure, and the family's contextual matrix can also be salient in career decisions. Families who immigrate to this country and lack particular skills (e.g., language) required for access to organizations may establish their work through a family business that can then be bequeathed to children (Kaslow, 1993). In addition, family themes seem to pervade, anchor, and serve as a useful framework for understanding work (Chusid & Cochran, 1989). That is, people's family experiences operate as a "potent source for imparting meaning and structuring [work] situations" (MacGregor & Cochran, 1988, p. 146). Research indicates that (a) an individual's family drama can extend to and pervade work (Chusid & Cochran) and (b) positive and negative family members are aligned in people's perception with positive and negative coworkers, respectively, indicating that family roles are transferred to work (Zimmerman & Cochran, 1993). Relatedly, "emotional issues in . . . organizations have the same basic patterns as emotional issues in the family" (Bowen, 1985, p. 464). To reiterate, family experience is relevant to work in at least three ways: (a) people organize and structure the work setting and understand their experience by imparting meaning through their internal, family-based meaning systems; (b) people interact in the work setting using the same patterns that they exhibit in their family relationships (Weinberg & Mauksch, 1991); and (c) work systems operate similarly to family systems (Boverie, 1991; Friedman, 1985). In addition, some work organizations speak of themselves as a "family." It seems clear, then, that people's work is infused with elements that have emotional meaning, some of which is based in family and, therefore, parent–child relationships.

ADULT ATTACHMENT THEORY

Attachment theory (Bowlby, 1979, 1988) addresses central emotional relationships and the bonding and exploratory behavior that results in competence or mastery of the physical and social environment. As a developmental framework, it emphasizes beliefs about both the self and others and affect management associated with bonding, caregiving, and disruptions in connectedness. Attachment theory is, therefore, consistent with family systems theories (e.g., Bowen, 1985) that concern the experiencing of the self as both separate from and connected with important persons as a central organizing emotional theme. In addition, theorists have examined attachment as an aspect of the family as a systemic whole (Byng-Hall, 1995; Donley, 1993). From a counseling perspective, one of the strengths of attachment theory is its relevance for examining "the developmental antecedents and interpersonal features of client problems" (Lopez & Brennan, 2000, p. 294). In addition, it addresses the strong emotional reactions that occur in a variety of central relationships, such as between children and parents (Hazan & Shaver, 1994a, 1994b), adult love partners (Pistole, 1994, 1995), students and faculty (Lopez, 1997), and clients and counselors (Pistole & Watkins, 1995).

Bowlby (1988) proposed attachment as a lifelong developmental theory that influences personality organization. Attachment and caregiving are interrelated, complementary systems, with the attachment system serving the evolutionary function of physical and psychological protection. Attachment reflects bonding and a motivation to maintain proximity to a specific, preferred figure, usually a parent in childhood and often a romantic partner in adulthood. This person provides a sense of felt security through the safe haven (i.e., comforting and soothing) and secure base (i.e., anchorage and guidance as needed) aspects of caregiving. Although some separation from the attachment figure is tolerable, when the acceptable range is exceeded, the attached person experiences separation anxiety, which is characterized by anger, anxiety, and searching for the other person. If physical or psychological proximity is not reestablished, then grieving begins.

Attachment theory posits a link between the felt security derived through the attachment–caregiving relationship and exploratory behavior with its resulting sense of felt competence. According to Bowlby (1969), "exploration and investigation constitute a class of behaviour that is as distinct and important as are such recognized classes as feeding and mating" (p. 237). In describing exploratory behavior and its association with attachment, Bowlby observed that, because the elements that stimulate interest also trigger alarm, young children's approach to novel objects involves a shifting between approach and withdrawal. As the object is perceived as safe, the balance swings toward interest, and the object is explored. "In most creatures such a process is greatly speeded up in the presence of a friend; and in a young creature especially it is notably accelerated by the presence of mother" (Bowlby, 1969, p. 239). Bowlby noted that play is an extension of the exploration of objects.

Given that attachment remains important throughout the lifespan, work would be an adult version of exploratory behavior (Hazan & Shaver, 1990). Productive work and concomitant feelings of competence would be facilitated, particularly in new situations or with novel objects, by the physical or psychological presence of a protector (i.e., an attachment figure). The function of this person is especially important. The attachment system is activated when the person is (a) distressed, fatigued, or ill; (b) anxious about the availability of the attachment figure; or (c) coping with a new or stressful situation. A new job or work-related distress can then provoke the need for an attachment figure to anchor the exploratory process. When an attachment figure is unavailable, the person will engage in behavior that is de-signed to gain proximity so that the secure base or safe haven functions will be fulfilled. When seeking the attachment figure and the attachment func-tions, the person's exploratory system is inhibited along with concomitant work effectiveness and feelings of competence: "Attachment needs are pri-mary; they must be met before exploration can proceed normally" (Hazan & Shaver, 1990, p. 271). There are, however, individual differences in how people respond to attachment-related cues and situations.

Individual Differences in Attachment Organization

People differ in the quality of their attachment organization because of their internalized working model of the attachment–caregiving relationship (Bowlby, 1988). Theoretically, the organization of attachment-related infor-mation is developed from real-life interactions, rather than based on fanta-sies or drives (cf. Diamond & Blatt, 1994), and is a reasonably accurate reflection of childhood experience, at least as perceived from the child's per-spective (Bowlby, 1988). Because the model is based on interactions between the person and the caregiver, both the attachment and the caregiving sys-tems are represented in the working model. The working model can be suf-ficiently flexible to be updated to match current experiences. However, it may persist into adulthood as a prototype that is relatively resistant to change, in which case the early attachment organization may act as a template that interferes in updating the working model. For instance, processing of at-tachment-related information may be biased by selective attention to cues, or the person may behave in ways that elicit expectation-consistent responses from others. In this way, current attachment-related information may be distorted, resulting in stability in the working model; thus, nonsecure at-tachment experience may continue to compromise development (Klohnen & Bera, 1998).

Several elements of this cognitive–affective schema together compose the working model and provide leverage for change through counseling in-tervention. First, a person has a generally positive or negative belief about being worthy of care, as well as a positive or negative belief about the caregiver being the kind of person who will provide care when needed. In addition, the person develops characteristic strategies for regulating sensitivity to at-tachment-related cues and for managing emotion associated with attach-ment (Bretherton, 1985; Fuendeling, 1998; Main, Kaplan, & Cassidy, 1985).

Attachment Prototypes

Four prototypical styles of adults' attachment organization have been described in the theoretical and research literature. People with *secure* attachments believe that the self is lovable and the other will be accessible for care when needed (Bartholomew & Horowitz, 1991). Affect management is associated with problem-solving coping strategies (Mikulincer, Florian, & Tolmacz, 1990; Mikulincer, Florian, & Weller, 1993) and mutuality (Fuendeling, 1998), with caregiving being associated with openness to attachment-related cues and providing sensitivity and proximity (Kunce & Shaver, 1994). When *preoccupied* with attachment, individuals have a negative view of the self's lovability in conjunction with a positive, usually idealized (Feeney & Noller, 1990) belief in the other person. Affect management is characterized by hypervigilance and hypersensitivity to attachment-related information, emotionally focused coping strategies (Mikulincer et al., 1990, 1993), close monitoring of the partner (Bretherton, 1985), sensitivity to threat of separation, and criticism of the self (Fuendeling). Caregiving is characterized by low levels of sensitivity, high proximity (Kunce & Shaver), and inconsistent responsiveness to attachment-related cues (Ainsworth, Blehar, Waters, & Wall, 1978). With *dismissing–avoidant* attachment, the individual has a defensively positive belief about the self coupled with a negative view of the other. Affect is managed through distance, low intensity (Feeney & Noller), dismissing the importance of attachment, valuing independence, and emotional detachment. With *fearful–avoidant* attachment, the person has a negative belief about both the self and the other person. Distance is used to protect the self from fears of intimacy and rejection. The self is experienced as alone and unwanted, and others are expected to be rejecting and untrustworthy (Lopez, 1995). Affect is managed through withdrawal and underassertiveness, which seemingly is associated with fear of rejection accruing from provoking the other (Horowitz, Rosenberg, & Bartholomew, 1993). In general, both forms of avoidant attachment are associated with managing affect through distancing coping strategies and low levels of relying on others. These individuals may have little understanding of others' motivations because withdrawal interferes with emotional exchange and communication (Fuendeling). Also, with attention to attachment-related information being inhibited, those who avoid closeness may not recognize bids for proximity, or these cues may be rejected.

Competency

The safe haven and secure base functions provide the attached person with a sense of felt security, but the adequacy of that security differs systematically among the attachment organizations and, thereby, influences exploratory behavior and competency. When caregiving is inconsistent or rejecting, the security and the exploratory behavior that accrue from the secure base function are inhibited. With preoccupied attachment, monitoring of the inconsistently responsive partner interferes with attention to exploratory behavior and results in diminished mastery behavior and skills (Fuendeling, 1998). Similarly, avoiding attachment-related information carries a cost in physiological arousal that competes with exploratory behavior (Dozier & Kobak, 1992).

The connection between attachment and exploratory behavior as reflected in adults' work life has been examined. By construing a new job as falling "into the category of potentially dangerous, threatening, and/or stressful situations" (Nelson, Quick, & Joplin, 1991, p. 59) and assuming that people would try to form attachments within the organization with other newcomers and more senior colleagues, Nelson and Quick (1991) found that relationship supports were associated with positive adjustment for newcomers. Hazan and Shaver (1990) examined individual differences in attachment and work, finding that (a) preoccupied persons have more concern about work performance, feel underappreciated, fear they will be rejected for poor performance, use work to gain respect from others, and prefer to work with others; (b) avoidant persons prefer to work alone and may use work to avoid social life, and (c) secure persons are relatively satisfied with work, value it, but do not allow work to inhibit other personal relationships. In a study that used a clinical sample, Hardy and Barkham (1994) found similar results: People preoccupied with attachment were anxious about their performance and concerned over work relationships, whereas those with avoidant attachment seemed less satisfied with work and reported difficulties with social relationships. In this study, therapy resulted in improvements in both relationship problems and job satisfaction. Other theory (Quick, Joplin, Nelson, & Quick, 1992) and research (Raskin, Kummel, & Bannister, 1998) has explored individual differences in affect management in the work environment. Two points are worth noting: Those with secure attachment seem to function in a more self-reliant manner. They appear "autonomous because they display decisive, active behavior; yet they possess well-developed support networks that they draw on to achieve their effectiveness" (Quick et al., p. 51). In addition, Bowlby's (1988) theory seems to allow for the possibility that the work or the workplace itself is the attachment figure.

In sum, research has consistently shown systematic differences related to exploratory skills and behavior, such as curiosity and information processing (Mikulincer, 1997; Miller & Noirot, 1999), constructive thinking (Lopez, 1996), career maturity (Blustein, Prezioso, & Schultheiss, 1995), and adolescent development and adjustment to college (Kenny & Rice, 1995). Research also consistently finds more effective relationship functioning and positive relationship characteristics, such as trust and intimacy (Hazan &

Shaver, 1987; Levy & Davis, 1988), associated with secure attachment. Overall, secure attachment appears to promote more optimal development (Lopez & Brennan, 2000), including effective problem-solving and relationship behavior (Hazan & Shaver, 1994a, 1994b).

Attachment as a Therapeutic Framework

Attachment theory can also be used as a framework for providing therapy (Bowlby, 1988; Pistole, 1999; Pistole & Watkins, 1995). Attachment theory is useful in conceptualizing the therapeutic relationship as a caregiving–attachment relationship, with the counselor in the caregiving position and the client's bond being attachment. Similar to the parent–child relationship, the counselor is powerful vis-à-vis the client's vulnerability, and care from the counselor is triggered by the client's signals of distress. So, the counselor functions to provide both a secure base, offering guidance as needed, and a safe haven, offering comfort and soothing. Both counseling and attachment relationships are coconstructed (Bowlby, 1988), and the counselor's thoughtful response to the client's attachment organization may facilitate a more effective therapeutic relationship (Dolan, Arnkoff, & Glass, 1993; Dozier, 1990; Dozier, Cue, & Barnett, 1994). By attuning to the client's attachment-related signals and providing responses that can be perceived as availability, the counselor may enhance the opportunity for engaging the client and maintaining the relationship in a way that facilitates service delivery.

From an attachment perspective, counseling goals would include updating the attachment organization to greater security by targeting the elements of the working model: (a) the client's view of self as worthy of care, (b) the client's perception of the emotionally important person as able and willing to provide care when needed, and (c) the client's characteristic affect management strategies. For instance, with persons who are preoccupied with attachment, the counselor would address the negative sense of the self, the idealized view of the other person, and the strategies of overfocusing on attachment-related cues, seeking approval, hypermonitoring of the other person, and coping in an emotionally focused rather than a problem-focused way. With a person who demonstrates dismissing avoidance in interactions, interventions would target the defensively positive view of the self, the negative view of the other's accessibility, and the strategies that block recognition of attachment-related cues, such as dismissing the importance of or need for attachment relationships. When focusing on expectations of the other, the therapist should help clients learn to distinguish when others are willing to be available and also learn to interact in ways that receive the care. These goals may be accomplished more effectively if the counselor can see and connect similar responses across a variety of relationship contexts, including the client's relationship with his or her counselor, romantic partner, parents, the family as a unit, colleagues at work, and the work setting itself. Persons' caregiving responses to their own children can also be explored as a means for clarifying attachment-related patterns. If the client should demonstrate different organizations in some contexts, then exploring and contrasting these distinctions can be useful. Interventions that identify people who consistently try to be available and distinguish them from those who seem either rejecting or inconsistently available can be powerful, especially when linked to material that indicates the caregiver's response is about the self rather than a statement about the client's lovability. If the client can move to a more secure organization of attachment, exploratory behavior will be compromised less, with increasing effectiveness and corresponding increases in feelings of competence accruing.

THE APPLICATION OF ATTACHMENT THEORY TO COLLEGE STUDENT COUNSELING

As illustrated by the following case material, attachment theory can provide a systematic focus for the counselor in sorting through the seemingly varied concerns associated with individual, family, work, and love relationships. Because the client was a college student, however, discussion will focus briefly on college student counseling and the normative struggles that accompany the transition reflected in the educational environment.

College presents students with both personal and work-related (e.g., academic demands, career choice) development; simultaneously, families cope with the transition represented by college, facing career preparation, development of the college student, and changes or stresses for the family. Consistent with this transitional process, in the college counseling center, both traditional- and nontraditional-aged undergraduate and graduate college students typically present with developmental struggles related to relationship or family issues, often concomitantly with competency and identity concerns (Murray, 1996). Traditional-aged students' development includes resolving separation and connection issues with the family (Carter & McGoldrick, 1989), forming a central relationship to anchor life, and choosing and initiating a work life (Chickering, 1969; Erikson, 1968). Although there are cultural differences in the norms and meaning of family connectedness (McGoldrick, 1989), the goal is for the student to be launched into adult status and responsibilities, such as work. Family and relationship struggles are also typical of nontraditional-aged students because emotionally important relationships embody the meaning of people's lives (Marris, 1982); there is a change of status in becoming a student, with an increase in dependency (Barger & Mayo-Chamberlain, 1983); the student status can resonate with previous family developmental issues (cf. Johnson & Schwartz, 1989); and we live in a world with high rates of relationship dissolution. Similarly to younger peers, the older student may be involved in emotionally separating from family or from a marriage that is no longer satisfying (P. A. Grayson, 1989). Students' development may include resolving the dilemma of trying to maintain supportive connection with family, while not exposing themselves to pressure or too much separation from the family (P. Grayson, 1998). These issues may be exacerbated or ameliorated by the student's fit with and sense of belonging within the university environment, especially for people who have moved from their family or friends for educational purposes. For instance, shy students may be overwhelmed and lost within a large university, or, conversely, graduate programs may foster connection between students and reliance on one another for both academic and emotional–social support.

Work-related themes are also salient for both the traditional and nontraditional student. For college students, work consists of both jobs that earn financial support and also the academic or nonspecific elements included in the degree or professional preparation program that provide access to career paths. Therefore, college students' relationships with faculty or each other (e.g., on group projects or in cohort groups) can also be considered work-related issues, and these relationships in the academic environment may reflect parallel themes from family life (P. A. Grayson, 1989). For instance, students may have authority issues with faculty or siblinglike conflict with peers. In addition, both returning students and those traditional-aged students who are self-supporting have stresses related to part-time employment and full- or part-time study, especially if the university seems not to modify its expectations because of the competing demands that working students experience. Students with full-time jobs may find a full course load onerous, and they may be unable to gain admittance to or be as effective as they could be in either undergraduate or graduate programs that require full-time study. They may also be caught in a prioritizing dilemma. The student who relies on a job for financial support, including meeting tuition requirements, may feel a priority to his or her employment, whereas program faculty may see the student's primary responsibility as the program and professional or career development. Other struggles are encountered by nontraditional-aged students, especially undergraduate or graduate students who return to school to accomplish a career transition. Coming from a work environment back into school, these students frequently experience (a) threats to esteem from academic demands and fears of failure; (b) stress from juggling the multiple demands of being a student, part-time employee, spouse, parent, and so on; (c) discomfort from trying on professional roles and forming an expanded view of competence and professional identity; and (d) isolation from not fitting in with younger student colleagues (Barger & Mayo-Chamberlain, 1983).

In general, both older, returning students and younger students have similar individual, relationship, family, and work-related issues in the transition associated with college. Thus, in working with college clients, the counselor is faced with integrating several elements into a productive treatment plan. A multiprong focus can be useful; that is, the counseling may be helped by considering "each individual as a separate self, the complex family relationship system . . . , and the larger society" (Kaslow, 1993, p. 9), which means work as well as cultural or contextual elements. In addition, the therapeutic relationship merits thoughtful consideration.

CASE STUDY

Elaine was a 30-year-old, married, white, female masters student who self-referred to a college counseling center because she was having difficulty in a work relationship with her male faculty advisor. After working hard on a prethesis project, she had received unexpected criticism on her paper and felt rejected. She was too upset to be assertive, could not confront the professor, and was convinced that she could experience negative career consequences if she could not work cooperatively with him. Initial exploration of the problem revealed that the advisor was emotionally important to her, though her views of both herself and him were negative. Elaine wanted his approval and reacted to his comments as if he were telling her that she was not worthy and not competent, even though she could tell the counselor that there were positive comments on the paper and that he had previously provided her with positive feedback on her competence. Indeed, an example of his criticism was that he had written on her paper that she needed to rewrite it using the appropriate professional style (which seemed to the counselor to be appropriate academic feedback and mentoring). Elaine's comments about her family paralleled her view of the situation with the faculty member. The family had all rejected her, they were not supportive, and they criticized her even when she made efforts to fit in with the family's values (e.g., achieve a master's degree). In addition, she felt out of place with, unable to obtain support from, and rejected by her student cohort group, who was much younger.

The presenting material can be understood as Elaine seeming to (a) distort some of the professor's comments (i.e., see them as criticism and rejection of her rather than view them as supervisory feedback), (b) direct her attention to the negative aspects of the situation while minimizing the positive, (c) use her distortions to reinforce her own negative beliefs about herself and him, and (d) distance herself as a means to cope with her hurt feelings. Rather than viewing the advisor's behavior as work-related guidance, she reacted as if he were uncaring, unsupportive, and rejecting, though later she was aware that she cared for him and noted that he had at times been supportive. This pattern seemed to be consistent across her other work and family relationships. Elaine had distanced from her family, her academic peers, and the advisor because of perceived rejection. Moreover, she was underassertive in dealing with problems for fear of provoking further rejection. From an attachment perspective, goals for counseling included (a) establishing the therapeutic relationship by taking into account Elaine's fearful-avoidant attachment organization (Dolan et al., 1993; Dozier & Tyrrell, 1998; Pistole, 1999); (b) focusing on her experience with the therapeutic relationship, her family, her husband, her advisor, and other work relationships; (c) addressing her exploratory behavior and feelings of competence; and (d) attending to her affect management strategies across these aspects of her functioning.

Therapeutic Relationship

Elaine had indicated that, similar to her experience with the professor, she tended to feel criticized by women from whom she needed approval, and she linked this fear of rejection to her mother, previous female work supervisors, and a previous female therapist. Because Elaine reported being able to work through the fear of rejection and criticism with the previous therapist, the counselor asked her if she both could and would bring up, in the sessions, any feelings of criticism or rejection. This intervention provided the safe haven function of comforting and structuring consistent and appropriate emotional availability by letting her know that her attachment-related emotional concerns were heard and responded to. The intervention also used the secure base function: It guided, as needed, her assertiveness and her competence to say what she experienced, as well as help her notice that her competent behavior was not a threat to the attachment relationship. When Elaine did report feeling criticized, the counselor expressed appreciation for her bringing the issue up, discussed the purpose of the misunderstood interventions, explored the internal process that was associated with feeling rejected, and noted regret over Elaine's having the uncomfortable feelings. In these interventions, the counselor was available to Elaine, which contradicted the expectation that others cannot be counted on to be available when needed; provided feedback countering Elaine's belief that she was not worthy of care; and addressed the affect management strategies that maintained her fearful–avoidant attachment organization. After these interventions, Elaine reported that she did have good relationships with some women who, unlike her mother, were able to be supportive. This comment provided an opportunity to suggest that she was able to identify people who try to and can be available when needed.

Family of Origin

During the counseling, Elaine had discovered that her sister was having marital difficulties. Consistent with being underassertive with interpersonal difficulties, she worried whether it was okay to contact her and offer support, and Elaine also fretted that she would be inviting rejection by trying to be supportive. After considerable thought, she sent the sister a note with a brief comment that expressed her concern and a desire to be supportive. The counselor, targeting the affect management strategies, observed how worried Elaine was that she had not said the right thing and so would be rejected, and provided feedback that her solution seemed competent, that is, both appropriate and caring. Further, the counselor suggested that the competency of her behavior should be evaluated separately from whatever response the sister might choose. Elaine's reaction of voicing relief can be construed as the intervention having effectively fulfilled both safe haven and secure base functions. Nonetheless, Elaine also responded by explaining how the competent behavior was really her husband's because he had helped her with the wording. Using the secure base guidance function, the counselor directed her attention to how she was the one who wanted to make contact and be supportive and who did the final phrasing. This situation was framed as relying on her husband for support and guidance and then making her own decision, with a part of her own competent behavior being that she modified the husband's ideas to better fit who she is and what she can do. When Elaine later reported having heard from the sister, the counselor noted that her behavior had not provoked rejection as she feared and emphasized that her assertiveness had been useful, thereby pointing out that the fears of rejection were not fulfilled.

In a related incident, Elaine discovered that the family was supporting the sister's husband, even though it was upsetting to the sister. After both worrying and thinking, she contacted her mother and suggested that because the sister was going through a very difficult time, she needed the family to provide emotional support rather than be caring toward the husband. Mom responded with a superficial discussion of her daily activities. Elaine's behavior was framed as trying to elicit closeness for both herself and her sister, as well as emotional availability for her sister. Although Mom did respond to Elaine, she did not address the emotional issues or provide emotional support, which Elaine perceived as rejection of both herself and her sister, who Elaine perceived as valued by the family (unlike herself). The counselor suggested that, because both were rejected, perhaps Mom was not very good at caring; that is, perhaps Mom was uncomfortable with emotional material or lacked insight and psychological-mindedness. She could not be very available for care because she did not recognize such needs. Thus, the rejection resulted from Mom's inability to process and deal with emotional material rather than from Elaine's unworthiness. In addition, the counselor focused on Elaine's valuing and appreciating emotional life, a competence that her family seemed not to share. This self-respected quality was linked to her being worthy of care, even if it was difficult for her to believe. Also, the counselor suggested that withdrawing from the family was not a perfect, self-protective solution because Elaine was "carrying her mother around in her own head." Elaine responded to this idea by noting, in later sessions when she was criticizing herself, that it was as if she were responding to herself like her mother would. In these interventions, the counselor was indicating that Elaine's feeling of unworthiness was not justified; that is, Mom did seem to care, and her unavailability was about her own development rather than a comment about Elaine.

Mastery Behavior

Issues of competence were often connected to discussion of Elaine's husband, Elbert. She viewed her husband as stronger and wiser and supportive. She relied on him for safe haven, comfort functions, and secure base, anchor, and guidance functions. For example, the revised paper submitted to the professor was graded as excellent and ready for submission to a professional journal. Elaine noticed that there was no criticism in the feedback; however, Elbert noted that the feedback was an important statement about her competence. The counselor agreed that the advisor's feedback was evidence of competence and was glad that Elbert had pointed it out. Then the counselor observed that Elaine seemed to minimize the feedback about her competence and to rely on someone else to note it. The point of the intervention was to (a) address the affective strategy of discounting feedback about her competence in lieu of focusing mainly on fears of criticism or rejection and (b) emphasize how she relied on Elbert's guidance in order to be aware of her competence. The counselor questioned whether the feedback about competence had been integrated, indicated that relying on the husband and therapist for guidance and support was useful, and wondered whether there was a difference in relying on versus depending on Elbert, with "depending" meaning that she did not internalize a sense that she was competent and worthwhile, even when the evidence was unequivocal. The goal was to stimulate an affective strategy of noticing competence rather than being vigilant to criticism and rejection. Because the point was to increase her feelings of competence and positive sense of self, the counselor emphasized that what was important was the way Elaine saw it and that she was capable of determining what was a reasonably accurate view. Theoretically, fearful–avoidant attachment is consistent with a history of the attachment figure being unavailable and with the caregiving failures forcing the child to rely on his or her own resources, which are unequal to tasks and so reasonably result in feelings of incompetence, including being unable to elicit responsiveness from the caregiver (West & Sheldon-Keller, 1994). If guidance could help Elaine recognize that her husband was reasonably available to her, that she could elicit care, and that she made good judgments, then she could revise the attachment organization and feel more competent.

In addition, this material was tied to previous work-related experiences in which Elaine had reported (a) knowing that she had done a good job, usually in situations that had little or no new learning involved; (b) having performed competently, but needing support from her supervisor to feel she had done a good job; and (c) feeling, on one occasion, overwhelmed by the work expectations and being relieved when the project had been canceled. The counselor introduced the notion of "relative competence," that is, wondered if Elaine was competent enough and had growing edges, as would be appropriate to her student and changing career status. Because she sometimes knew when she had performed well, discussion centered on how the fear of being criticized might arise when she felt challenged. When Elaine was not sure of herself or when the task was difficult, she experienced more need for closeness, which often was sought from work supervisors, who would be the logical people to provide guidance. She also seemed to forget any previous instances of competence, as if competence meant perfection, which was an unachievable goal. The difficult work situations were framed as learning situations, which indeed would normatively be facilitated by attachment security. The counselor also used the secure base guidance function to note that (a) learning continues after graduation and in any new job situation, (b) recognizing her strengths and limitations is competent behavior, and (c) failing does not cancel previous achievements or skills. Elaine responded in future sessions by examining what she was learning in difficult work assignments and focusing on situations in which she had increased her skills. She was able to understand more clearly when she solicited feedback from supervisors because of being challenged to develop greater mastery. Within the attachment framework, this ongoing learning behavior is natural and not a reason to denigrate the self's worthiness.

Summary

Concerning the presenting issues, Elaine was able to assertively reconnect with the professor and revised her paper in a way that elicited strong feedback about her competence. In general, she moved from fearing rejection to noting that she did have skills and could remember that she could do things, even in new learning situations. She also began to recognize that some of her work-related fears seemed to be professional development (e.g., student status, change in career) that were confabulated with her family of origin attachment-related issues. In general, by termination of therapy, Elaine was more able to acknowledge herself as worthy of care, distinguish people who were able to be consistently available, work with available caregivers to attain support, notice her own competence, and "battle" her tendency to fear rejection and focus on negative aspects of personal- and work-related experiences. For example, she more clearly realized that, with her student cohort and others, she often withdrew because of fearing rejection before giving the others a chance to be supportive. In addition, she was able to distinguish when she was rejected from when she only perceived, rather than received, rejection, which increased her assertiveness in work and personal interactions.

CONCLUSION

As this case illustrates, the application of attachment theory can address college students' developmental issues by framing a theme that emerges across love, work, family, and personal domains. The clinical understanding of attachment presented herein has been synthesized across theory and different research methodology; therefore, counselors should attend to the nuances that may differ among clients rather than force clients into theoretical generalizations. In addition, attachment theory, as applied to client issues, is more complex than has been presented thus far. Clients can operate from more than one attachment organization because, theoretically, in infancy a different organization may develop with mother and with father, based on each parent's reactions to the child (Bowlby, 1988). In the case just presented, Elaine seemed to operate from a different attachment organization with her husband than with others in her life. She, in fact, stated that Elbert was different than other men she had dated, and she was able to note his supportiveness and her reliance on him. She attributed her picking a different kind of man to learning that had accrued from the previous therapy, which occurred following the break-up of a serious relationship. It is possible, therefore, that the previous counseling had influenced change in the attachment organization in reference to her love relationships, whereas these sessions focused more broadly due to the development associated with school and work-related issues. Regardless, counselors need to be attuned to the possibility that clients may manifest one organization in their central love relationships and another with the counselor or with work supervisors or mentors and use these differences to effect change to increasingly secure attachment.

Much of the counseling with Elaine concerned work-related settings—her on-campus academic work, off-campus jobs that provided income, required practical experiences, and previous work experience. These issues seemed to be intertwined with family-of-origin issues, as is consistent with family being a theme from which to impose meaning on work situations. On a few occasions, the work-related content was also tied to previous love relationships. Consistent with a systems point of view, changes in understandings and interactions in the work setting seemed to help her gain greater clarity with both her family and romantic relationships. As importantly, changes in Elaine's attachment-related behavior seemed to stimulate changes in the marital relationship.

This case does not address diversity issues, which may be more salient with some clients. Attachment is conceived as a universal human tendency (Bowlby, 1988), with secondary, insecure organization (avoidant, preoccupied) forming because the primary secure organization does not correspond well to cultural or other environmental realities (Main, 1990). There are two points here: First, the organization accruing from childhood experience was likely to have been useful in the past, but may be inappropriate or ineffective now, as was true with Elaine. There was evidence that she was actually rejected in childhood; certainly her mother's responses did not comprise warm, available caregiving while Elaine was in counseling, though her mother did seem to care. Second, an issue that emerged during therapy was Elaine's valuing of family and her husband's lack of valuing family. She was able to retain her value, despite his "guidance," by framing the value as a gender difference: Perhaps family is more important for women due to their relationship-oriented socialization (Gilligan, 1982). Other diversity issues might be more relevant to the person's ethnic or cultural background. Counselors need to remember that the attachment organization that was effective in the childhood cultural milieu may be somewhat ineffective in a different culture that is dominant in, for instance, the workplace or college campus.

Finally, this chapter has specially considered college student clients. Although college presents a transition and a developmental agenda for late adolescents, young adults, and older adults, there is reason to believe that the conceptualization discussed would be appropriate with the general adult population and apply, for instance, to individuals experiencing divorce, parenting problems, or personnel-related stresses in the workplace. The use of attachment theory allows therapists to consider and connect the effects of family functioning and the individual's functioning based on the meanings perceived in the relationship context, and, thereby, its use complements family systems theory.

REFERENCES

Ainsworth, M. D., Blehar, M. C., Waters, E., & Wall, S. (1978). *Patterns of attachment: A psychological study of the Strange Situation.* Hillsdale, NJ: Erlbaum.

Barger, R. R., & Mayo-Chamberlain, J. (1983). Advisor and advisee issues in doctoral education. *Journal of Higher Education, 54,* 407–432.

Bartholomew, K., & Horowitz, L. M. (1991). Attachment styles among young adults: A test of a four-category model. *Journal of Personality and Social Psychology, 61,* 226–244.

Bielski, V. (1996). Our magnificent obsession. *Family Therapy Networker, 20,* 22–35.

Blustein, D. L., Prezioso, M. S., & Schultheiss, D. P. (1995). Attachment theory and career development: Current status and future directions. *The Counseling Psychologist, 23,* 416–432.

Boverie, P. E. (1991). Human systems consultant: Using family therapy in organization. *Family Therapy, 18,* 61–71.

Bowen, M. (1985). *Family therapy in clinical practice.* Northvale, NJ: Aronson.

Bowlby, J. (1969). *Attachment.* New York: Basic Books.

Bowlby, J. (1979). *The making and breaking of affectional bonds.* London: Routledge.

Bowlby, J. (1988). *A secure base.* New York: Basic Books.

Bretherton, I. (1985). Attachment theory: Retrospect and prospect. *Monographs of the Society for Research in Child Development, 50*(1–2), 3–35.

Byng-Hall, J. (1995). Creating a secure family base: Some implications of attachment theory for family therapy. *Family Process, 34,* 45–58.

Carter, B., & McGoldrick, M. (1989). Overview the changing family life cycle: A framework for family therapy. In B. Carter & M. McGoldrick (Eds.), *The changing family life cycle* (pp. 3–28). Boston: Allyn and Bacon.

Chickering, A. W. (1969). *Education and identity.* San Francisco: Jossey-Bass.

Chusid, H., & Cochran, L. (1989). Meaning of career change from the perspective of family roles and drama. *Journal of Counseling Psychology, 36,* 34–41.

Diamond, D., & Blatt, S. J. (1994). Internal working models and the representational world in attachment and psychoanalytic theories. In M. B. Sperling & W. H. Berman (Eds.), *Attachment in adults* (pp. 72–97). New York: Guilford Press.

Dolan, R. T., Arnkoff, D. B., & Glass, C. R. (1993). Client attachment style and the psychotherapist's interpersonal stance. *Psychotherapy, 30,* 408–412.

Donley, M. G. (1993). Attachment and the emotional unit. *Family Process, 32,* 3–20.

Dorn, F. (1993). Career assessment: A social psychological perspective. *Journal of Career Assessment, 1*, 410–426.

Dozier, M. (1990). Attachment organization and treatment use for adults with serious psychopathological disorders. *Development and Psychopathology, 2*, 47–60.

Dozier, M., Cue, K. L., & Barnett, L. (1994). Clinicians as caregivers: Role of attachment organization in treatment. *Journal of Consulting and Clinical Psychology, 62*, 793–800.

Dozier, M., & Kobak, R. R. (1992). Psychophysiology in attachment interviews: Converging evidence for deactivating strategies. *Child Development, 63*, 1473–1480.

Dozier, M., & Tyrrell, C. (1998). The role of attachment in therapeutic relationships. In J. A. Simpson & W. S. Rholes (Eds.), *Attachment theory and close relationships* (pp. 221–248). New York: Guilford Press.

Erikson, E. H. (1968). *Identity: Youth and crisis.* New York: Norton.

Feeney, J. A., & Noller, P. (1990). Attachment style as a predictor of adult romantic relationships. *Journal of Personality and Social Psychology, 58*, 281–291.

Framo, J. L. (1996). A personal retrospective of the family therapy field: Then and now. *Journal of Marital and Family Therapy, 22*, 289–316.

Friedman, E. (1985). *Generation to generation: Family process in church and synagogue.* New York: Guilford Press.

Fuendeling, J. M. (1998). Affect regulation as a stylistic process within adult attachment. *Journal of Social and Personal Relationships, 15*, 291–322.

Gilligan, C. (1982). *In a different voice.* Cambridge, MA: Harvard University Press.

Grayson, P. (1998). A fast and bumpy ride: Students and therapy in an ever changing environment. *Journal of College Student Psychotherapy, 13*, 3–13.

Grayson, P. A. (1989). The college psychotherapy client: An overview. In P. A. Grayson & K. Cauley (Eds.), *College psychotherapy* (pp. 8–28). New York: Guilford Press.

Hardy, G. E., & Barkham, M. (1994). The relationship between interpersonal attachment styles and work difficulties. *Human Relations, 47*, 263–281.

Hazan, C., & Shaver, P. (1987). Romantic love conceptualized as an attachment process. *Journal of Personality and Social Psychology, 52*, 511–524.

Hazan, C., & Shaver, P. R. (1990). Love and work: An attachment-theoretical perspective. *Journal of Personality and Social Psychology, 52*, 270–280.

Hazan, C., & Shaver, P. R. (1994a). Attachment as an organizational framework for research on close relationships. *Psychological Inquiry, 5*, 1–22.

Hazan, C., & Shaver, P. R. (1994b). Deeper into attachment theory. *Psychological Inquiry, 5*, 68–79.

Horowitz, L. M., Rosenberg, S. E., & Bartholomew, K. (1993). Interpersonal problems, attachment styles, and outcome in brief dynamic therapy. *Journal of Consulting and Clinical Psychology, 61*, 549–560.

Johnson, E. A., & Schwartz, A. J. (1989). Returning students. In P. A. Grayson & K. Cauley (Eds.), *College psychotherapy* (pp. 316–333). New York: Guilford Press.

Kaslow, F. (1993). The lore and lure of family business. *The American Journal of Family Therapy, 21*, 3–16.

Kenny, M. E., & Rice, K. G. (1995). Attachment to parents and adjustment in late adolescent college students: Current status, applications, and future considerations. *The Counseling Psychologist, 23*, 433–456.

Klohnen, E. C., & Bera, S. (1998). Behavioral and experiential patterns of avoidantly and securely attached women across adulthood: A 31-year longitudinal perspective. *Journal of Personality and Social Psychology, 74,* 211–223.

Kunce, L. J., & Shaver, P. R. (1994). An attachment-theoretical approach to caregiving in romantic relationships. In K. Bartholomew & D. Permian (Eds.), *Advances in personal relationships: Vol. 5. Attachment processes in adulthood* (pp. 205–237). London: Jessica Kingsley.

Levy, M. C., & Davis, K. E. (1988). Lovestyles and attachment styles compared: Their relations to each other and to various relationship characteristics. *Journal of Social and Personal Relationships, 5,* 439–471.

Lopez, F. G. (1995). Attachment theory as an integrative framework for family counseling. *The Family Journal, 3,* 11–17.

Lopez, F. G. (1996). Attachment-related predictors of constructive thinking among college students. *Journal of Counseling and Development, 75,* 58–63.

Lopez, F. G. (1997). Student–professor relationship styles, childhood attachment bonds and current academic orientations. *Journal of Social and Personal Relationships, 14,* 271–282.

Lopez, F. G., & Brennan, K. A. (2000). Dynamic processes underlying adult attachment organization: Toward an attachment theoretical perspective on the healthy and effective self. *Journal of Counseling Psychology, 47,* 283–300.

MacGregor, A., & Cochran, L. (1988). Work as enactment of family drama. *The Career Development Quarterly, 37,* 139–144.

Maida, C. A., Gordon, N. S., & Faberow, N. L. (1989). *The crisis of competence: Transitional stress and the displaced worker.* New York: Brunner/Mazel.

Main, M. (1990). Cross cultural studies of attachment organization: Recent studies, changing methodologies, and the concept of conditional strategies. *Human Development, 33,* 439–471.

Main, M., Kaplan, N., & Cassidy, J. (1985). Security in infancy, childhood, and adulthood: A move to the level of representation. *Monographs of the Society for Research in Child Development, 50*(1–2), 66–104.

Marris, P. (1982). Attachment and society. In C. M. Parke & J. Stevenson-Hinde (Eds.), *The place of attachment in human behavior* (pp. 31–59). New York: Basic Books.

McGoldrick, M. (1989). Ethnicity and the family life cycle. In B. Carter & M. McGoldrick (Eds.), *The changing family life cycle* (pp. 69–90). Boston: Allyn and Bacon.

Mikulincer, M. (1997). Adult attachment style and information processing: Individual differences in curiosity and cognitive closure. *Journal of Personality and Social Psychology, 72,* 1217–1230.

Mikulincer, M., Florian, V., & Tolmacz, R. (1990). Attachment styles and fear of personal death: A case study of affect regulation. *Journal of Personality and Social Psychology, 58,* 273–280.

Mikulincer, M., Florian, V., & Weller, A. (1993). Attachment styles, coping strategies, and posttraumatic psychological distress: The impact of the Gulf war in Israel. *Journal of Personality and Social Psychology, 64,* 817–826.

Miller, J. B., & Noirot, M. (1999). Attachment memories, models and information processing. *Journal of Social and Personal Relationships, 16*, 147–173.

Murray, B. (1996, April). College youth haunted by increasing pressures. *APA Monitor, 26*(4), 47.

Nelson, D. L., & Quick, J. C. (1991). Social support and newcomer adjustment in organization: Attachment theory at work? *Journal of Organizational Behavior, 12*, 543–554.

Nelson, D. L., Quick, J. C., & Joplin, J. R. (1991). Psychological contracting and newcomer socialization: An attachment theory foundation. *Journal of Social Behavior and Personality, 6*, 55–72.

Orlinsky, D. E., Grawe, K., & Parks, B. K. (1994). Process and outcome in psychotherapy — Noch einmal. In A. E. Bergin & S. L. Garfield (Eds.), *Handbook of psychotherapy and behavior change* (pp. 270–376). New York: Wiley.

Pistole, M. C. (1994). Adult attachment styles: Some thoughts on closeness–distance struggles. *Family Process, 33*, 147–159.

Pistole, M. C. (1995). Adult attachment style and narcissistic vulnerability. *Psychoanalytic Psychology, 12*, 115–126.

Pistole, M. C. (1999). Caregiving: A perspective for counselors. *Journal of Counseling and Development, 77*, 437–446.

Pistole, M. C., & Watkins, C. E., Jr. (1995). Attachment theory, counseling process, and supervision. *The Counseling Psychologist, 23*, 457–478.

Quick, J. C., Joplin, J. R., Nelson, D. L., & Quick, J. D. (1992). Behavioral responses to anxiety: Self-reliance, counterdependence, and overdependence. *Anxiety, Stress, and Coping, 5*, 41–54.

Raskin, P. M., Kummel, P., & Bannister, T. (1998). The relationship between coping styles, attachment, and career salience in partnered working women with children. *Journal of Career Assessment, 6*, 403–416.

Strupp, H. H., & Binder, J. L. (1984). *Psychotherapy in a new key.* New York: Basic Books.

Weinberg, R. B., & Mauksch, L. B. (1991). Examining family-of-origin influences in life at work. *Journal of Marital and Family Therapy, 17*, 233–242.

West, M. L., & Sheldon-Keller, A. E. (1994). *Patterns of relating: An adult attachment perspective.* New York: Guilford Press.

Zimmerman, J., & Cochran, L. (1993). Alignment of family and work roles. *The Career Development Quarterly, 41*, 344–349.

CHAPTER 6

The Systemic Nature of Couple Relationships

An Attachment Perspective

JUDITH A. FEENEY

The conceptualization of romantic love as an attachment process has had a huge impact on the study of adult love relationships, and research in the area has evolved rapidly. Early studies focused on establishing the correlates of individuals' attachment styles, usually using self-report questionnaires and student samples; in contrast, recent studies have explored the processes and outcomes of couple interaction. This chapter highlights the importance of studying adult romantic attachment at the dyadic level. The specific aim, drawing on the principles of systems theory, is to show that an individual's attachment orientation can be played out quite differently, depending on the characteristics of the partner.

ADULT ATTACHMENT THEORY: THE BEGINNINGS

Hazan and Shaver (1987) proposed that romantic love is an attachment process. That is, adult lovers form affectional bonds, analogous in many ways to those formed between infants and their caregivers and reflecting working models of self and social life. This proposition was supported by data from two adult samples: Self-categorization as secure, avoidant, or anxious–ambivalent showed meaningful links with measures assessing early family relationships and "most important" love relationships.

This exploratory research had limitations, as Hazan and Shaver (1987) recognized. For example, the measure of attachment style was extremely simple. Currently, most researchers assess adult attachment security in terms of a four-group model that categorizes respondents as secure, preoccupied, dismissing, or fearful (Bartholomew, 1990), or in terms of the continuous dimensions of comfort with closeness and anxiety over relationships (Feeney & Noller, 1996). An equally important limitation was the focus on individuals' reports of a single ("most important") love relationship. This focus provided a convenient starting point for research, but Hazan and Shaver cautioned that it might seem to overstate the case for attachment style as a trait. They noted that degree of security in a relationship is likely to be a "joint function of attachment style and factors unique to particular partners and circumstances" (Hazan & Shaver, 1987, p. 521).

Despite this cautionary note, studies of romantic attachment have sometimes been seen as implying that attachment style is traitlike and that characteristics of the partner (and of the situation in general) are not very important. In fact, there has been ongoing debate as to whether attachment style is a characteristic of the individual or of a specific relationship, but this question implies something of a false dichotomy. On the one hand, individuals often select environments that confirm their existing views of the world; hence, one's security at a given point in time may reflect *both* the current relationship and prior tendencies (Kirkpatrick & Hazan, 1994). On the other hand, clinicians and researchers agree that relationship experiences can disconfirm existing working models (Rothbard & Shaver, 1994). These points highlight the two-fold importance of partners' characteristics: They can either maintain existing working models or promote change for better or for worse.

Partner Effects and Couple Effects

The notion that an individual's experience of a relationship is affected by partner characteristics is consistent with systems theory but not unique to it. For example, the concept of interdependence, which is central to contemporary thinking about close relationships, places due emphasis on the impact of each partner on the other's thoughts, feelings, and actions. "Partner effects," however, are a useful point of departure in linking attachment and systems theories and highlight the need to move beyond the individual as the unit of analysis.

In one of the first studies of attachment in dating couples, Collins and Read (1990) reported that men's discomfort with closeness and women's anxiety over relationships were associated with negative ratings of the relationship by both partners. These results have received partial support from other studies of dating couples. For example, both Simpson (1990) and Kirkpatrick and Davis (1994) found that men with highly anxious partners rated their relationships as lower in love, satisfaction, and commitment.

Studies of married couples have confirmed the importance of partner's attachment characteristics. In a laboratory study of couple interactions, Kobak and Hazan (1991) found that wives of secure husbands were more rejecting and less supportive during a problem-solving task, and that husbands of secure wives listened more effectively in a confiding task. Subsequent studies have reported partner effects on marital satisfaction (Feeney, 1994) and several aspects of marital communication (Feeney, Noller, & Callan, 1994), with the most consistent finding again being the negative effect of wives' relationship anxiety on husbands' evaluations of the relationship.

Another approach to understanding attachment at the dyadic level involves comparing "couple types," usually defined by each partner's self-categorization as secure or insecure. This approach is more complex in one sense, in that it assesses the unique nature of particular combinations of attachment styles. As such, it also fits more closely with systems theory, which emphasizes that relationship partners mutually influence one another and create a whole that is greater than the sum of its parts (Byng-Hall, 1999).

In terms of adult attachment, "couple type" analyses usually compare three broad types: secure (in which both partners see themselves as secure), insecure (both see themselves as insecure), and mixed (one secure and one insecure partner). Differences between the attitudes and behaviors of secure and insecure couples are typically expected and found, and they do not shed much light on the systemic nature of couple bonds. However, the scores of secure and insecure couples provide an important comparison point for those of "mixed" couples. Overall, then, these analyses evaluate how an individual's security or insecurity is played out in the presence of a partner who is secure or insecure.

In one of the first studies of this kind, Senchak and Leonard (1992) compared couple types in a sample of newlyweds. Secure couples showed better adjustment than other couples, in terms of self-reports of marital intimacy, partner's relationship functioning, and partner's responses to conflict. Mixed couples were generally similar to insecure couples (regardless of whether the secure partner was male or female). Senchak and Leonard concluded that "insecure attachment seems to carry more weight" (p. 61) in influencing relationship quality, but this conclusion has not gone unchallenged.

In a dating sample, insecure couples reported the most negative emotion and the greatest control ("bottling up") of that emotion; secure couples reported the least negative emotion and emotional control, with mixed couples showing intermediate scores (Feeney, 1995). In a small sample of married couples, however, both secure and mixed dyads were rated as lower in conflict and better in overall functioning than insecure dyads (Cohn, Silver, Cowan, Cowan, & Pearson, 1992). (Only mixed dyads with a secure man were studied, as the reverse pairing was uncommon.) This result suggests that a secure (male) partner may buffer the negative effects of insecurity. Couple types were defined in terms of current thinking about childhood relationships, however, and may not be directly comparable to romantic attachment types. Finally, a recent study of marriage points to complex effects of attachment pairings (Sumer, 2000). Mixed couples were closer to secure couples on most measures of interpersonal schemas but closer to insecure couples on hostility. Mixed couples were closer to secure couples when the *wife* was secure; that is, female security buffered the effect of male insecurity, more than the reverse.

Overall, studies of couple types suggest that the functioning of mixed couples may depend on the gender of the secure partner and the nature of the dependent measure. Although these studies are useful in pointing to the dyadic system as an organized whole, they suffer from clear limitations. First, they require large samples, especially if researchers want to compare "male-secure" and "female-secure" mixed couples. Second, they are based on a simple typology and ignore differences between different forms of insecurity. This simplification is a major limitation from the perspective of systems theory, which emphasizes that the attitudes and behaviors of one partner provide the relational context for the other (Minuchin, 1985). After all, an emotionally distant (avoidant) partner will create a very different "context" from a highly dependent (anxious) partner.

Interactive Effects in Hypothetical and Real Relationships

Studies assessing both main and interactive effects of partners' attachment styles provide another way of understanding the couple unit and clearly recognize that such characteristics as avoidance and dependency should be seen in relational terms. This approach fits with Hazan and Shaver's (1987) view that attachment-related feelings are a product of person–situation interactions. For example, a secure individual may feel and act anxious when trying to build a relationship with an avoidant partner. It is also consonant with the principles of systems theory: The couple system involves two mutually regulatory partners, each serving as the other's environment and having an active role in shaping couple interactions (Marvin & Stewart, 1990).

The interactive effects of partners' attachment styles have been studied in both hypothetical and real relationships. In the former approach, researchers manipulate the attachment behavior of the hypothetical partner and assess the joint effects of own and partner's attachment characteristics. Studies in this tradition have yielded conflicting results. In the first use of this method, Pietromonaco and Carnelley (1994) found that some dependent measures showed main effects of own attachment style (e.g., preoccupied participants felt more anxious than secure participants in imagined relationships), and most measures showed main effects of partner's attachment behavior (e.g., participants felt more optimistic about relationships with secure partners). Some interactive effects were also obtained. For example, in terms of positive emotion, only avoidant participants differentiated between avoidant and ambivalent partners, expecting to experience more positive emotion with the latter. Although this result suggests that insecure persons prefer partners with complementary attachment styles, another study using this paradigm found a similarity effect, whereby ambivalent participants preferred ambivalent partners (Frazier, Byer, Fischer, Wright, & DeBord, 1996). Further, a recent study found limited evidence of interactive effects: In general, all types of respondents preferred secure partners, although preoccupied participants expected to experience more positive emotion with preoccupied partners than with other insecure partners (Chappell & Davis, 1998).

Overall, then, most people preferred secure partners, but how insecure individuals react to the different insecure types remains a vexing question. At the same time, we need to keep in mind that the studies just reviewed deal with hypothetical partners; they cannot clarify actual relationship dynamics, unless we assume that people are highly aware of others' attachment characteristics and of their own response patterns. In fact, recent data suggest that people assume more similarity between their own and partners' attachment characteristics than really exists (Ruvolo & Fabin, 1999). In short, studies of intact couples are the only way to assess interactive attachment effects in real life. This method allows us to see whether the effects of one person's attachment security depend on the characteristics of the other, for outcomes as diverse as relationship satisfaction and specific communication patterns. Only a few studies have explored these issues.

Kirkpatrick and Davis (1994) tested the interactive effects of males' and females' attachment on concurrent ratings of dating relationships (commitment, satisfaction, and intimacy) and on later relationship stability. No interactions were found, but their analytic method was equivalent to assessing differences between couple types. Continuous scores on attachment dimensions are likely to provide a more sensitive test (for both main effects and interactions). Although Jones and Cunningham (1996) found no such interactive effect when predicting dating partners' relationship satisfaction, at least two published studies (detailed below) support the moderating role of partners' attachment.

One of these studies assessed the link between attachment security and marital satisfaction in a community sample, in which shorter-term and longer-term marriages were equally represented (Feeney, 1994). For both genders and all lengths of marriage, one's own attachment security (comfort with closeness, low relationship anxiety) predicted greater satisfaction. In addition, wives' security (low relationship anxiety) predicted husbands' satisfaction. Finally, in shorter-term marriages, husbands' comfort and wives' anxiety had interactive effects: Wives' anxiety was related to dissatisfaction for both spouses only when husbands were low in comfort. In other words, the combination of a wife high in anxiety and a husband low in comfort was associated with dissatisfaction.

This result suggests that husbands who are uncomfortable with intimacy (i.e., avoidant) are unable or unwilling to provide the reassurance that anxious wives crave, and conversely, that anxious wives are unable or unwilling to accept the emotional distance desired by avoidant husbands. Interestingly, husbands' anxiety and wives' comfort did *not* interact, suggesting that gender roles may affect the way that attachment behaviors are perceived. The clinging style associated with relationship anxiety is similar to the stereotype of female relationship behavior, and the distant style associated with discomfort with closeness is similar to the stereotype of male behavior. Partners' extreme adherence to these stereotypes may create a dysfunctional system marked by positive feedback loops (Minuchin, 1985). That is, the wife's need for reassurance and the husband's need for distance may trigger each other, further polarizing the partners.

Similarly, Roberts and Noller (1998) reported that physical aggression among cohabiting and married couples was predicted by an interaction between the perpetrator's relationship anxiety and the partner's comfort with closeness. Specifically, relationship anxiety was linked to aggression (both female-to-male and male-to-female) only if the partner was uncomfortable with closeness. As Roberts and Noller suggest, partners in these couples probably struggle to control the emotional climate of their relationships, given their contrasting interpersonal goals and styles. Hence, a self-perpetuating feedback loop is established in which one partner's fear of abandonment and the other's fear of intimacy exacerbate each other. The circular nature of this pattern is highlighted because the "end" result (aggression by the anxious partner) is likely to further increase the other's discomfort with intimacy.

THE COUPLE AS A SYSTEM: NEW FINDINGS

In the remainder of this chapter I present new findings from my own research program, supporting the conceptualization of couple bonds in systems terms. Two methods are reported: assessment of the interactive effects of own and partners' attachment dimensions, and content analysis of unstructured accounts of relationship experiences. Both methods highlight the fact that an individual's attachment orientation can be played out differently depending on the characteristics of the partner.

Interactive Effects of Partners' Attachment Dimensions

This section presents reanalyses of data from three studies of adult attachment. (Previous reports of these studies examined main effects of both partners' attachment dimensions but not interactive effects.) All three studies focused on long-term relationships (dating or marriage), and all three used predominantly community samples. The studies defined attachment security in terms of the dimensions of comfort with closeness (referred to as comfort) and anxiety over relationships (referred to as anxiety).

Interactive effects were tested using hierarchical regression analysis, in which own and partner's comfort and anxiety were entered at Step 1, and the four product terms (man's comfort/woman's comfort, man's comfort/woman's anxiety, man's anxiety/woman's comfort, man's anxiety/woman's anxiety) were entered at Step 2. Consistent with the basic rationale of hierarchical regression analysis, the importance of the product (interaction) terms was gauged by the increase in explained variance at Step 2 (see Feeney, 1994, for a more detailed description of this approach). The methods and findings of the three studies will be outlined, then reviewed in an integrative discussion.

Study 1

Study 1 was designed to test an integrative model of spousal caregiving, which explained willingness to care in terms of partners' attachment and caregiving styles and anticipated burden (Feeney & Hohaus, 2001). In a broad sample of married couples, willingness to care and anticipated burden were assessed by asking respondents to imagine and rate a series of scenarios that might require them to provide spousal care. The reanalysis reported here focused on possible interactive effects in predicting willingness to care and anticipated burden of caregiving.

Husbands' willingness to care was related negatively to partner anxiety, and wives' willingness to care was related positively to own comfort (main effects only). Husbands' sense of burden was unrelated to the attachment dimensions (including product terms), but wives' sense of burden was predicted by the interaction between husbands' anxiety and wives' comfort. Follow-up tests showed that wives' comfort was unrelated to their sense of burden when the partner was low in anxiety, but inversely related to burden when the partner was high in anxiety: Wives anticipated high levels of burden only when they were low in comfort and their husbands were high in anxiety.

As for the interactive effect on marital satisfaction discussed earlier (Feeney, 1994), this finding probably reflects both gender-role and attachment effects. Wives who are comfortable with closeness may feel relatively confident about caring for their spouse, regardless of his security: For these women, caregiving is consistent not only with societal expectations but also with their sense of comfort with intimacy and mutual dependence. In contrast, wives who are uncomfortable with intimacy may be concerned about the particular pressures that are likely to be created by an anxious and demanding spouse.

Study 2

Study 2 was a longitudinal study of communication in early marriage (Feeney et al., 1994; Noller, Feeney, Bonnell, & Callan, 1994). The present reanalysis focused on conflict behavior, using two types of data. First, respondents completed the Communication Patterns Questionnaire (Christensen & Sullaway, 1984), assessing the extent to which conflict interactions are marked by mutuality (mutual discussion and understanding), destructive process (patterns of demand–withdraw and pressure–resist), coercion (threat, verbal and physical aggression), and postconflict distress (guilt and hurt). It is important to note that these scales assess the overall amount of the particular behavior in the relationship (e.g., couple coercion, rather than coercion by husband or by wife). Second, couples took part in two conflict interactions (one issue nominated by each spouse). These interactions were videotaped and replayed for each partner, who identified the influence strategies they used throughout the interactions. Based on these reports, participants received scores reflecting the extent of three conflict styles: positive (reason, assertion, and support), negative (manipulation and threat), and avoidance (physical and emotional retreat).

For husbands, none of the seven conflict measures yielded interactive effects, although main effects of own and partner's attachment dimensions were obtained. (For example, men reported less mutuality when they were highly anxious and more coercion and postconflict distress when their partners were highly anxious.) For women, both main and interactive effects were obtained, with the most consistent effect being the interaction between husbands' anxiety and wives' anxiety. This interaction term predicted coercion, postconflict distress, and avoidance in the laboratory interactions, both for concurrent measures of conflict and for similar measures taken 9 months later.

Interestingly, the form of this effect varied, as shown in Figures 6.1 to

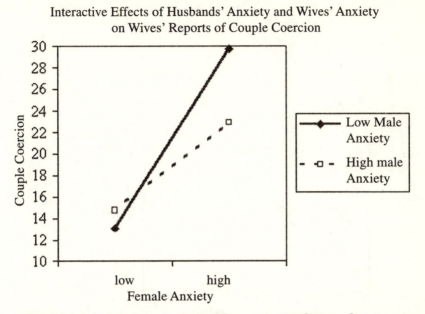

FIGURE 6.1. Scores on Coercion Scale of Communication Patterns Questionnaire.

6.3. Wives' anxiety was more predictive of reports of couple coercion when the husband was *low* in anxiety; that is, anxious wives paired with low-anxious husbands reported even higher levels of couple coercion than those with anxious husbands (see Figure 6.1). This finding is intriguing and suggests the possibility that anxious wives perceive their nonanxious husbands as unable to understand their fears and concerns; this situation may lead to escalating coercion or to misperceptions of partner's intentions as coercive. In addition, wives' anxiety was related positively to their reports of couple distress when husbands were low in anxiety but negatively to their reports of distress when husbands were high in anxiety. As shown in Figure 6.2, then, wives perceived more postconflict distress when only one spouse was high in anxiety. Finally, wives' anxiety was related to their avoidance in the conflict interactions only when husbands were high in anxiety. That is, wives' avoidance was associated specifically with the combination of two anxious spouses (Figure 6.3).

Study 3

The final study employed a sample of long-term dating couples, who took part in standardized interactions involving explicit conflicts of interests

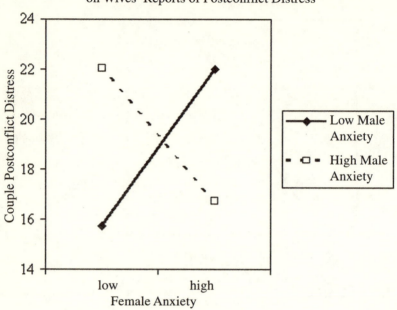

Interactive Effects of Husbands' Anxiety and Wives' Anxiety
on Wives' Reports of Postconflict Distress

FIGURE 6.2. Scores on Postconflict Distress Scale of Communication Patterns
Questionnaire.

(Feeney, 1998). Couples came into the laboratory, and, immediately prior to
each scene, each partner was primed separately to pursue different goals in
the forthcoming interaction (see Raush, Barry, Hertel, & Swain, 1974). The
reanalysis reported here focused on responses to partner's distancing behavior: Either the male or the female was instructed to act in a cold and distant
manner toward the partner, who was instructed to reestablish closeness (the
roles were then reversed in the next interaction). This type of "relationship-
based" conflict is likely to be seen as threatening the relationship, particularly by insecure individuals.

Both verbal and nonverbal responses to partner's distancing were assessed. Verbal behavior was defined in terms of three broad categories, similar to those used by Raush et al. (1974): reason (making suggestions and
rational arguments), power assertion (demanding, threatening, and rejecting), and affiliation (compromising, appealing to fairness, and offering reassurance). Nonverbal behavior was defined in terms of the two factors of
friendly touch (hugging, kissing, and touching partner's face or body) and
avoidance (turning or moving away from partner and averting gaze).

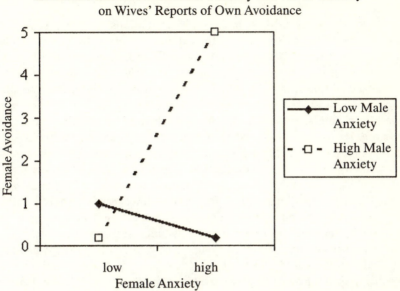

FIGURE 6.3. Number of Self-Reported Instances of Avoidance in the Conflict Interactions

Men's responses to partner's distancing showed only main effect of attachment (own comfort was related negatively to avoidance and positively to touch, and partner's anxiety was related negatively to affiliation). Women's responses to partner's distancing showed that male anxiety and female anxiety interacted to predict three of the dependent variables: power assertion, touch, and avoidance. As in Study 2, this effect took varied forms. For power assertion and avoidance, couples in which both partners were high in anxiety functioned most poorly (as for wives' avoidance in Study 2). Conversely, the highest levels of friendly touch occurred when the man was anxious but the woman was not, suggesting that low-anxious women took account of their partners' insecurities and tried hard to provide support and encouragement.

Integrating the Three Studies

The results of these studies indicate that interactive effects of partners' attachment dimensions are relatively common but that the specific form of the effects varies according to the situational context and the dependent measure. The analyses raise several important points about the couple as a system.

First, the relationship behaviors and evaluations of women seem to be more prone to interactive effects than those of men. Why might this be? Women may be more sensitive to the overall dynamics of relationship situations, including differences in partners' relational concerns and anxieties. The effects of this sensitivity, which probably reflects gender-role socialization, may be positive for the most part. For example, women may be more aware of partners' anxiety and, consequently, more ready to comfort and reassure. Hence, women's relational behavior may serve to minimize some of the potential effects of partner insecurity, except when their own insecurity leads to involvement in destructive interaction cycles. This suggestion fits with Sumer's (2000) data, mentioned earlier, which point to females' greater ability to buffer partner's insecurity. However, there may be situations in which women's sensitivity to relational dynamics colors their perceptions in negative ways. For example, women seem to sense the burden that would be associated with providing care for their insecure partners, especially in the context of their own insecurity. In these situations, they may fail to reap the benefits afforded by "positive illusions" (Murray, Holmes, & Griffin, 1996).

The notion that couple relationships are shaped by partners' sensitivity to each other's concerns fits with systems theory, which regards the individual as an open system that accepts input from outside sources, including the relationship partner. It also fits with Tronick and Weinberg's (1997) claim that dyadic systems involve "dyadic states of consciousness," which range in sophistication from the primary intersubjectivity of the infant through to the empathy of older children and adults. According to Tronick and Weinberg, empathy involves "an awareness of the other's state and a paradoxical awareness of the differentiation between one's own state and the state of the other" (p. 74). Although all adult attachment relationships involve this type of mutual sensitivity and mutual regulation (Marvin & Stewart, 1990), some partners are likely more open to input from the partner than others. In fact, consistent with the present findings, there is some evidence that women show more emotional sensitivity than men, a skill that includes empathizing with the emotional states of others (Guerrero & Reiter, 1998).

Another point raised by these studies is that interactive effects of partners' relationship anxiety may be particularly relevant to conflict interactions and conflict styles. This finding can be understood in terms of the negative mental models associated with relationship anxiety, which are reflected in individuals' feeling misunderstood and underappreciated, being demanding and coercive, and focusing on their own concerns at the expense of those of the partner (Noller et al., 1994). It is easy to see how two partners with these tendencies would construct a dyadic system character-ized by ongoing tension and conflict. Certainly, three of the six interactions in this set singled out the problematic combination of two partners high in anxiety (women in these couples showed high power assertion and nonver-bal avoidance in response to partner's distancing and physical and emo-tional retreat in other laboratory-based conflict interactions).

Women in couples with two anxious partners, however, reported less postconflict distress and less coercion than those in couples with one anx-ious partner. Hence, despite ample evidence that insecurity has negative effects and that insecure couples function poorly, there may be specific mea-sures on which couples who share similar relational concerns fare reason-ably well. For instance, the mutual attack-and-retreat approach to conflict adopted by many high-anxious couples may alleviate some distress in the short-term, although conflict is likely to resurface.

Whereas two anxious partners construct a system marked by complex patterns of conflict, the pairing of an anxious and an avoidant partner seems to have implications for the general emotional climate of the relationship. In Study 1, husbands' anxiety and wives' discomfort jointly predicted wives' anticipated burden of spousal caregiving. Further, in earlier research, wives' anxiety and husbands' discomfort jointly predicted marital satisfaction (Feeney, 1994), and own anxiety and partner discomfort interacted to pre-dict the perpetration of violence (Roberts & Noller, 1998). This problematic pairing can also be understood in terms of circular causality. For example, the fears and concerns of the anxious individual are unlikely to be allayed by the avoidant partner who, as Byng-Hall (1999) neatly expressed it, "sees the only problem with the relationship as the other's discontent" (p. 629).

CONTENT ANALYSIS OF ACCOUNTS OF RELATIONSHIP EXPERIENCES

The analyses reported so far shed light on the couple system, showing that an individual's sense of security or insecurity can be played out differently depending on the attitudes and behaviors of the partner. As noted earlier, this issue can also be addressed by content analysis of relationship accounts. In fact, this method provides a powerful way of investigating the attachment system. It allows researchers to explore spontaneous references to security and insecurity and has the important advantage of minimizing experimenter demand. It can also elicit respondents' views about how the dyadic system is affected by other relationships, both current relationships with friends and family and previous romantic relationships, which shape the templates and repertoires that partners bring to the couple relationship (Minuchin, 1985).

The following section presents further data from the dating couples involved in Study 3. As well as taking part in the conflict interactions, each participant gave an unstructured account of their current relationship and completed a four-group measure of attachment style (Feeney, 1999). The aim here, using these accounts, is to show that the dyad functions as a unit in terms of attachment behavior. In other words, dyadic systems are marked by interactive cycles and feedback loops, and the experiences of the individual must be understood in terms of the relational context. Based on attachment and systems theories, the principles to be illustrated are the following:

- The couple relationship can either foster or erode the sense of security of its members.
- Pursuer–distancer cycles are especially relevant to an understanding of couples' attachment relationships.
- Transition points provide a particular challenge for the couple system, as partners seek either to reestablish familiar interaction patterns or to develop new patterns.
- There is mutual influence between the couple unit and other subsystems of the family.

The Couple Relationship Can Foster the Sense of Security of Its Members

Just as caregivers who show sensitive responsiveness promote secure attachment in infants, romantic partners who consistently acknowledge and meet the other's needs can foster "felt security." If the other already has a sense of security, this experience of warm and responsive interaction confirms existing models. Conversely, if he or she is insecure, the experience disconfirms existing models and may gradually reshape them. This process of change is consistent with attachment theory; after all, if working models reflect experiences, it must be possible (though perhaps difficult) to accommodate those models to a changing reality (Rothbard & Shaver, 1994).

From this perspective, insecurity is not a fixed "trait," even though individuals sometimes select situations that perpetuate their insecurity. In fact, when people discuss their relationships, they often note a shift in their attitudes and behaviors, attributing this change to the relational context. For example, in this study of 72 dating couples, almost one quarter of the sample spontaneously mentioned their negative models of close relationships, linking these to previous experiences with family members or romantic partners. Of these respondents, almost two thirds stated that the current relationship had afforded them the opportunity to revise those models for the better. In the following extract, for instance, a woman notes that she feels more secure in her current relationship than in previous ones because of her partner's acceptance and dependability.

> In my previous long-term relationships, I haven't felt the security and trust that I feel with S. So I definitely have something to compare it to, and I know that with S, he truly loves me and I truly am special to him. He lets me fulfil my needs, and accepts me completely. So I feel quite emotionally secure and comfortable. And for that reason, I trust him completely, and that's a really special feeling for me.

This woman and her partner both endorsed the secure description of the measure of attachment style (although she implies that she may have responded differently in the past). The next extract is from a woman who saw herself as dismissing but in the process of change. Her tendency to downplay relationships and limit intimacy is evident, but it seems to be lessening in response to her (secure) partner's consistent affection. In other words, her insecurity is played out differently with this partner, a difference that she attributes to his unusually caring and loving nature. These partner characteristics result in more positive behavior from the respondent, as well as a more positive attitude to intimacy.

> I've never been one to get deeply into relationships. I never have with any partner before, even if they wanted to. But my current partner has always been especially keen, and showed a lot of interest, a lot of affection, a lot of love, and would do anything for me. So some months down the track, I started to respond to all this; I tried reciprocating the positive feelings coming from him, and opening up to him.

The next extract is somewhat different, in that the respondent describes his partner's past relationship difficulties, rather than his own (he saw himself as securely attached, whereas his partner described herself as fearful). In other respects, however, the message is similar: When one partner consistently encourages openness and mutual expression, the other can modify the maladaptive behaviors associated with insecurity. Again, we see that the woman's tendency toward insecurity is played out differently now that she has a partner who responds constructively to her particular relational style.

> From what she's told me of the other men she's been involved with, there's always been this anxiety and this communication problem; she just clams up. And I can see that her last breakup came about because her partner would also clam up and not bring things out in the open, so they just

brewed. But I don't let this happen. I say "There's a problem, let's talk," and so far, we've always managed to solve things.

The Couple Relationship Can Erode the Sense of Security of Its Members

Whereas partners who provide ongoing love and support can foster a sense of security, the reverse is also true: Insecurities in one individual can be perpetuated or even exacerbated by responses of the partner. Hence, individuals can struggle much more in one relational context than in another. The next examples illustrate this phenomenon, and, because we are now considering relationship problems and how they escalate in the face of certain responses, it is informative to look at the reports of both partners. In the first case, a woman who saw herself as fearfully attached discusses how the negative effects of her own "natural insecurity" are exacerbated by her current partner's nonresponsiveness.

> During this relationship, especially, I've often felt separate from my partner. He doesn't tell me how he feels about me and I'm naturally insecure, so I worry about it. Often, when I've felt this sort of anxiety, he hasn't even realized. Sometimes he's self-absorbed, and doesn't seem to care what I want. I feel bad when he doesn't listen to me or take an active interest in my life. But I don't open up about it very much, because I don't like conflict.

Of course, one could argue that this woman's insecurity causes her to see self-absorption in the partner where it does not exist; after all, negative working models can lead individuals to see even benign relationship events in a negative light. However, she describes this relationship as especially difficult, supporting the role of the relational context. Moreover, comments from her fearful partner support her claim that he is unresponsive to her concerns. His unresponsiveness probably stems, in part, from her reluctance to express those concerns; regardless, it seems to fuel her anxiety: "As far as relationship problems go, well I haven't had to deal with any. Everything's OK. Or I think it is; I guess I can't speak for my partner."

The importance of relational context is also seen in the next extract, which highlights how the respondent's actions and the partner's response circle back to affect her. Specifically, this preoccupied woman describes how her attempts to discuss her relationship anxieties tend to be met with a "cool response," which fuels further anxiety.

> We don't spend that much time together, which worries me. I feel like I'm always wanting to see him, and sometimes I feel like he doesn't feel the same way. I wish that I could feel secure about his need to be with

me, on a day-to-day basis, but when I raise this, he doesn't show much enthusiasm. He's quite cool in response, which makes me worry more.

The dynamics of this relationship are clarified by her partner's comments. The partner, who described himself as fearful in attachment style, talked about his desire to have "breaks" in the relationship, despite the difficulty it caused for his partner.

It's important to have a break in your relationship every now and again; that way, you get to realize whether you really love the person or not, and whether you really want to stay with them. She finds this idea a bit tough.

Interestingly, as he expresses these doubts about his own love and commitment, his comments are strikingly similar to Hazan and Shaver's (1987) description of anxious–ambivalent attachment, although that description adopts the perspective of the other (*anxious*) party ("I often worry that my partner doesn't really love me, or won't want to stay with me"). Not surprisingly, then, these breaks in the relationship exacerbate his partner's doubts and anxieties. The concepts of interactive cycles and feedback loops are also relevant to the next case, in which a secure female discusses the negative effects of her partner's previous experience. She suggests that this hurtful experience causes him to set limits on intimacy in the current relationship; further, this behavior adversely affects her own interaction style, as she acts to protect herself against hurt and rejection.

My partner has been hurt before. I take that into consideration all the time, and as time goes on he seems to get closer to me. I'd like it to be closer, but then I don't want to get hurt either, and I don't say too much because I don't want to push him into something he's not ready for. So I'm just working on it and waiting for him. If it doesn't work out, well I'm not going in too far so that I won't get very hurt.

If we assume the validity of self-reported attachment, this case suggests that even secure individuals can become anxious about loss and rejection in the face of emotionally distant partners. (Similarly, as mentioned earlier, Hazan and Shaver (1987) noted that an avoidant partner might prompt a secure person to feel and act anxious.) This woman's partner talked at length about his previous hurtful experience but showed little sympathy for his current partner. In fact, his comments reflected his dismissing attachment style. For example, he admitted that he often failed to phone his partner or include her in his activities, but in comparing his behavior with that of friends who invested more energy in their relationships, dismissed their actions as "maybe just the result of a guilty conscience."

Pursuer–Distancer Cycles

The examples presented so far show that each partner provides the context for the other's behavior. As Byng-Hall (1999) suggests, the interactive cycles that form in this way are illustrated most vividly by the pursuer–distancer struggle, which centers on issues of closeness and distance. Regulating proximity is a key attachment issue, and one that is played out differently in different types of couples (Feeney, 1999). In some couples, and especially where at least one partner is secure, these issues are negotiated without too much distress. For example, a preoccupied male with a secure partner commented:

> Sometimes, one or the other of us feels a need to push the other away a bit, because we're spending too much time together and getting too enmeshed. And this can lead to quarrels, which neither of us enjoys or wants. So if this happens, I try not to see her as much over a period of a few days, or she tries not to see me for a few days, and things settle down.

His partner seemed to agree with this assessment of the situation, noting quite independently: "Sometimes one of us feels pushed away emotionally, and that can make you feel hurt or upset. But those feelings soon die down—you realize that there's always a reason, and that it's probably half your fault."

Conversely, when both partners are insecure, and especially if they differ markedly in their preferences for closeness and distance, interaction cycles can become increasingly dysfunctional. A preoccupied respondent with a dismissing partner described this kind of "push–pull" cycle to which both partners clearly contributed.

> He used to buy me things all the time and make me feel so special. But when I became more deeply involved, he eased back. I didn't like that, so I eased back too. The moment I did that, it became intense again. But as soon as I start becoming interested, he doesn't show the same keenness as he does at other times. Maybe he's only after the challenge.

As this example illustrates, the couple system has homeostatic features that tend to maintain a relatively stable state; when behavior departs from the expected range, it is controlled via corrective feedback loops. Comments made by her dismissing partner indicate that he is very aware of their differing approaches to intimacy:

> My partner's much more emotional about the whole issue of closeness. She needs more emotion than I do and she gets more emotional than I do—well, she reacts a *lot* more emotionally than I do. My feelings are

more like stone. She tells me how she feels lonely sometimes—very lonely.
I wouldn't say that type of thing—I would never bring it up.

These comments suggest that he perceives their differing approaches to
closeness–distance (his "stony" style and her "emotional" style) as rather
immutable. Here we see that the process of corrective feedback loops, although usually adaptive, can involve rigid patterns and considerable distress in the case of dysfunctional couples. As Byng-Hall (1999) has noted,
pursuer–distancer cycles are maintained in part by negative perceptions of
intention; in the above example, the woman seems to attribute her partner's
"easing back" to his lack of interest in her. Similarly, in the next example, a
dismissing man and his fearful partner seem set on a recurring collision
course, as his need for distance and her need for reassurance exacerbate
each other.

> We just don't see eye-to-eye on the whole issue of being together. She
> feels that being together all the time brings two people closer; I think it
> smothers you. She resents time apart, even when I'm at work. I don't
> count that as time apart; it's not my time to do as I please, without being
> nagged. I don't know if it's immature, but at times I just take time for
> myself. She gets very uneasy, but then we sort it out for a while, till it
> happens again.

Again, this couple is clearly involved in a circular interaction pattern
that affects them as a unit. The ongoing cycle of closeness–distance struggle
is also evident in his partner's comments:

> Sometimes I've felt hurt, because it's seemed as though he'd rather spend
> time alone than with me, and didn't care about me as much as I care
> about him. We had a long talk about it, and came to a sort of compro-
> mise. It didn't affect our relationship once we sorted it out. Though I still
> can't understand [crying]—I'm still hurt by it.

Note the marked inconsistency between this woman's initial verbal
message (it doesn't affect our relationship now) and the intense emotionality displayed immediately after. This inconsistency may reflect the presence
of contradictory working models or a tension between the respondent's own
view of the relationship and her desire to portray it favorably to "outsiders."

Transitions Affect the Whole System

According to systems theory, both homeostatis and change are important
features of systems. That is, although couples (and other systems) usually

try to maintain a relatively steady state of functioning, they sometimes require a major reorganization of interaction patterns. This process is likely to be particularly difficult when partners are insecure and hence prone to interpret challenge and change as threats to the relationship. In the next extract, a dismissing male acknowledges his tendency to avoid intimacy, especially when feeling anxious or afraid. Faced with major changes (relocating, embarking on a new course of study, and being separated from his partner), his avoidant behavior impacted the couple system. However, his secure partner's response helped promote a more adaptive pattern of relating.

> When I was leaving, I felt very scared and alone, so I naturally did what I've always done when I'm afraid—push people away. My partner was there for me and trying to comfort me, so when I pushed her away she was very hurt, though I didn't see it at the time. But she kept trying to help me and explained to me why we needed to tackle things together. Eventually we worked through my feelings and problems.

Conversely, when partners are prone to different forms of insecurity, major changes (such as living together) can involve a real struggle to develop new and effective interaction patterns. As in the previous example, the next respondent (self-categorized as fearful) notes that his relationship behavior has changed recently. However, in this case, the change is for the worse, and he attributes his domineering behavior to the related factors of cohabitation and his preoccupied partner's pressure for more intimacy.

> Another reason I want time alone is that I live with my partner. And I don't think you should live with someone at such a young age, but she disagrees. It's caused me a lot of stress and unease. I've been living with her for nine months now, and it hasn't got any easier. It's created many arguments between us. I seem to want more time to myself than I have in past relationships, maybe because this is the first partner I've lived with. It seems to have caused me to play a domineering role.

Again, this man's partner acknowledged their ongoing struggle over issues of closeness and distance, describing the problems as follows:

> He's made it very clear to me that he needs his time and his space and his own area to move. And I've finally realized that I've got to give him that space. So I've begun to do that, but by shutting him out a bit. He's responded quite aggressively to this. So it's all a vicious circle. It's even got to the stage where we've discussed one of us moving out, just to keep the relationship going.

The Couple Unit as a Subsystem

Although this chapter focuses on the *couple* as a unit, it is important to acknowledge the mutual influence that exists between that unit and other subsystems of the family. Although several subsystems, including siblings, are relevant (e.g., Feeney, 1999), parents are particularly central to the bond between young dating partners. In the next extract, a secure male describes the negative interaction patterns between his insecure partner and her parents. In particular, he notes that his partner's submissiveness toward her parents makes him doubt her authenticity in their couple interactions.

> I felt she didn't want to see me, but then I saw that her parents were manipulating her. Her Mum is the queen of manipulating, and my partner falls for it every time. Her parents make her feel guilty or afraid, and she doesn't stand up to them and say how she feels. It affects us as a couple, in that I often wonder whether she's honest with *me*. I think the only way we'll get around it is to get married and leave.

Unfortunately, this proposed "solution" may result in partners forging a premature commitment; given the mutual influence between family subsystems, it may also escalate conflict within the young woman's family and between the family and the couple.

Sometimes, difficulties are created by differences in partners' family styles, or "family scripts" (Byng-Hall, 1999). Comments by another young woman again illustrate the individual's simultaneous membership in several subsystems: She suggests that the differing family styles make it difficult for her to cross the "boundary" that would bring her into her partner's family.

> I don't go to see his family very often because they aren't as close and friendly as mine. They treat me nicely, but it's all very formal and rigid and just not like my parents at all, so I'm not comfortable there. I don't feel part of the family, whereas when he's at my place he feels exactly like he's part of our family. It's almost as though I'm competing for him and I'm an enemy of the family, rather than a friend.

CONCLUSIONS

The couple relationship is a complex construction, reflecting partners' prior experiences and expectations, the unique interaction patterns to which each actively contributes, and the broader family system. A key concept is that each partner provides the context for the other's behavior. Both quantitative and qualitative data, for example, point to negative interaction cycles in couples involving an anxious and an avoidant partner. The pursuer–distancer cycle represents a struggle to regulate proximity and control the emotional climate of the relationship. As such, it is driven by goals and concerns that are highly affect-laden, reminding us that the dyadic system must be understood in terms of emotion as well as behavior (Caffery & Erdman, 2000). This point is further highlighted by the dissatisfaction and the sense of burden that can arise in couples with an anxious and an avoidant partner. The mutual influence that characterizes dyadic systems is also clear in these couples: The anxious individual may respond to the partner's avoidance with threats or violence, which are likely to trigger further avoidance.

Quantitative data also point to the joint effects of partners' relationship anxiety, especially with regard to conflict interactions. On the one hand, couples with two anxious partners tend to avoid conflict or engage in power plays, both of which serve to maintain or exacerbate friction. On the other hand, a secure partner may not always provide a context that "brings out the best" in the anxious individual; anxious women with nonanxious partners see their conflicts as coercive and distressing, perhaps because they feel that their concerns are not shared or understood.

At this stage, little is known about the dynamics occurring between two avoidant partners. It seems that relatively few such couples maintain long-term relationships, or at least volunteer for relationships research (Kirkpatrick & Davis, 1994). Those who survive the courtship period may develop interaction patterns that fit their particular needs. In Fitzpatrick's (1988) marital typology, separate couples (who, like avoidants, limit emotional involvement), develop relationships marked by low interdependence, avoidance of open conflict, and consensus on many issues. Similarly, avoidant couples may construct a system that is fairly stable, at least until challenged by major transitions.

As Stevenson-Hinde (1990) noted, both attachment and systems theories seek to describe adaptive and maladaptive relationship functioning and recognize the key role of such variables as affect, communication, conflict, and dominance. Despite (or because of) this common ground, each contributes to our understanding of couple bonds. Attachment theory has a particular strength in addressing the emotions and motivations associated with intimate relating, whereas systems theory highlights the need to consider the broader context in which individuals and relationships are embedded.

REFERENCES

Bartholomew, K. (1990). Avoidance of intimacy: An attachment perspective. *Journal of Social and Personal Relationships, 7,* 147–178.

Byng-Hall, J. (1999). Family and couple therapy: Toward greater security. In J. Cassidy & P. R. Shaver (Eds.), *Handbook of attachment: Theory, research, and clinical applications* (pp. 625–645). New York: Guilford Press.

Caffery, T., & Erdman, P. (2000). Conceptualizing parent–adolescent conflict: Applications from systems and attachment theories. *Family Journal: Counseling and Therapy for Couples and Families, 8,* 14–21.

Chappell, K. D., & Davis, K. E. (1998). Attachment, partner choice, and perception of romantic partners: An experimental test of the attachment-security hypothesis. *Personal Relationships, 5,* 327–342.

Christensen, A., & Sullaway, M. (1984). *Communication Patterns Questionnaire.* Unpublished manuscript, University of California, Los Angeles.

Cohn, D. A., Silver, D. H., Cowan, C. P., Cowan, P. A., & Pearson, J. (1992). Working models of childhood attachment and couple relationships. *Journal of Family Issues, 13,* 432–449.

Collins, N. L., & Read, S. J. (1990). Adult attachment, working models, and relationship quality in dating couples. *Journal of Personality and Social Psychology, 58,* 644–663.

Feeney, J. A. (1994). Attachment style, communication patterns, and satisfaction across the life cycle of marriage. *Personal Relationships, 1,* 333–348.

Feeney, J. A. (1995). Adult attachment and emotional control. *Personal Relationships, 2,* 143–159.

Feeney, J. A. (1998). Adult attachment and relationship-centered anxiety: Responses to physical and emotional distancing. In Simpson, J. A., & Rholes, W. S. (Eds.), *Attachment theory and close relationships* (pp. 189–218). New York: Guilford Press.

Feeney, J. A. (1999). Issues of closeness and distance in dating relationships: Effects of sex and attachment style. *Journal of Social and Personal Relationships, 16,* 571–590.

Feeney, J. A., & Hohaus, L. (2001). Attachment and spousal caregiving. *Personal Relationships, 8,* 21–39.

Feeney, J. A., & Noller, P. (1996). *Adult attachment.* Thousand Oaks, CA: Sage.

Feeney, J. A., Noller, P., & Callan, V. J. (1994). Attachment style, communication and satisfaction in the early years of marriage. In K. Bartholomew & D. Perlman (Eds.), *Advances in personal relationships: Vol.5. Attachment processes in adulthood* (pp. 269–308). London: Jessica Kingsley.

Fitzpatrick, M. A. (1988). A typological approach to marital interaction. In P. Noller & M. A. Fitzpatrick (Eds.), *Perspectives on marital interaction* (pp. 98–120). Clevedon, England: Multilingual Matters.

Frazier, P. A., Byer, A. L., Fischer, A. R., Wright, D. M., & DeBord, K. A. (1996). Adult attachment style and partner choice: Correlational and experimental findings. *Personal Relationships, 3,* 117–136.

Guerrero, L. K., & Reiter, R. L. (1998). Expressing emotion: Sex differences in social skills and communicative responses to anger, sadness, and jealousy. In D. J. Canary & K. Dindia (Eds.), *Sex differences and similarities in communication* (pp. 321–350). Mahwah, NJ: Erlbaum.

Hazan, C., & Shaver, P. R. (1987). Romantic love conceptualized as an attachment process. *Journal of Personality and Social Psychology, 52*, 511–524.

Jones, J. T., & Cunningham, J. D. (1996). Attachment styles and other predictors of relationship satisfaction in dating couples. *Personal Relationships, 3*, 387–399.

Kirkpatrick, L. E., & Davis, K. E. (1994). Attachment style, gender, and relationship stability: A longitudinal analysis. *Journal of Personality and Social Psychology, 66*, 502–512.

Kirkpatrick, L. E., & Hazan, C. (1994). Attachment styles and close relationships: A four-year prospective study. *Personal Relationships, 1*, 123–142.

Kobak, R. R., & Hazan, C. (1991). Attachment in marriage: Effects of security and accuracy of working models. *Journal of Personality and Social Psychology, 60*, 861–869.

Marvin, R. S., & Stewart, R. B. (1990). A family systems framework for the study of attachment. In M. T. Greenberg, D. Cicchetti, & E. M. Cummings (Eds.), *Attachment in the preschool years: Theory, research, and intervention* (pp. 51–86). Chicago: University of Chicago Press.

Minuchin, P. (1985). Families and individual development: Provocations from the field of family therapy. *Child Development, 56*, 289–302.

Murray, S. L., Holmes, J. G., & Griffin, D. W. (1996). The benefits of positive illusions: Idealization and the construction of satisfaction in close relationships. *Journal of Personality and Social Psychology, 70*, 79–98.

Noller, P., Feeney, J. A., Bonnell, D., & Callan, V. J. (1994). A longitudinal study of conflict in early marriage. *Journal of Social and Personal Relationships, 11*, 233–252.

Pietromonaco, P. R., & Carnelley, K. B. (1994). Gender and working models of attachment: Consequences for perceptions of self and romantic relationships. *Personal Relationships, 1*, 63–82.

Raush, H. L., Barry, W. A., Hertel, R. K., & Swain, M. A. (1974). *Communication, conflict and marriage*. San Fransisco: Jossey-Bass.

Roberts, N., & Noller, P. (1998). The associations between adult attachment and couple violence: The role of communication patterns and relationship satisfaction. In J. A. Simpson & W. S. Rholes (Eds.), *Attachment theory and close relationships* (pp. 317–350). New York: Guilford Press.

Rothbard, J. C., & Shaver, P. R. (1994). Continuity of attachment across the life span. In M. B. Sperling & W. H. Berman (Eds.), *Attachment in adults: Theory, assessment, and treatment* (pp. 31–71). New York: Guilford Press.

Ruvolo, A. P., & Fabin, L. A. (1999). Two of a kind: Perceptions of own and partner's attachment characteristics. *Personal Relationships, 6*, 57–79.

Senchak, M., & Leonard, K. E. (1992). Attachment styles and marital adjustment among newlywed couples. *Journal of Social and Personal Relationships, 9*, 51–64.

Simpson, J. A. (1990). Influence of attachment styles on romantic relationships. *Journal of Personality and Social Psychology, 59*, 971–980.

Stevenson-Hinde, J. (1990). Attachment within family systems: An overview. *Infant Mental Health Journal, 11*, 218–227.

Sumer, N. (2000, June). *The interplay between attachment mental models and inter-personal schemas among married couples.* Paper presented at Second Joint Conference of ISSPR and INPR, Brisbane, Australia.

Tronick, E. Z., & Weinberg, M. K. (1997). Depressed mothers and infants: Failure to form dyadic states of consciousness. In L. Murray & P. J. Cooper (Eds.), *Postpartum depression and child development* (pp. 54–81). New York: Guilford Press.

CHAPTER 7

A Systemic Approach to Restructuring Adult Attachment

The EFT Model of Couples Therapy

SUSAN M. JOHNSON
MARLENE BEST

Emotionally focused couples therapy (EFT) is a brief, empirically validated intervention that enables couples to redefine and repair their attachment bond (S. Johnson, 1996; Johnson, Hunsley, Greenberg, & Schindler, 1999). EFT views close relationships from the perspective of attachment theory and integrates systemic and experiential interventions to de-escalate negative interactional patterns and foster new bonding events that increase the security of the bond between partners. The name, emotionally focused, was given to this model of intervention to stress the primary significance of emotion and emotional communication in the organization of the reciprocally determining system of responses that constitute an attachment relationship (Johnson, 1998a).

From the EFT perspective, attachment theory is best viewed as a transactional, systemic theory. This theory offers the couples therapist a map to the topography of close relationships and the habitual forms of engagement that define a particular attachment relationship. In contrast to what is outlined in this chapter, one can view attachment, not so much in transactional, systemic terms, but rather in more intrapsychic terms, as a series of representations, or ways of coping with emotion, that reside inside the skin of the person who is attached. This more intrapsychic thread in attachment theory tends to focus on attachment as a state of mind about attachment relationships (as measured by the Adult Attachment Interview: AAI; George, Kaplan, & Main, 1996) and on attachment responses and inner working models as traitlike personality variables. This chapter, however, views habitual attachment responses in more systemic terms, as strategies that are influenced by the dance, or the patterns, of interactions in particular relationships.

Like Kobak (1999), we see attachment as essentially transactional and systemic. An attachment relationship is a dance in which *within* elements, such as models of self and other and ways of regulating emotion, are defined in a reciprocally determining way by the *between* elements, the steps in the interactional dance with those on whom we depend. The essence of systems theory is to look at a whole system and how elements in a system organize and maintain each other. Bowlby (1973, p. 180) spoke of the relationship between an individual and his environment (including others) as the "outer ring" of a system, and of this outer ring as being complementary to the "inner ring" that maintains "homeostasis" within a person's skin.

The recognition of the systemic nature of attachment theory, along with the explicit integration of systems theory and attachment, elucidates both of these theories and makes each more relevant for the couple and family therapist. A system is a "set of objects, together with relationships between the objects and their attributes" (Hall & Fagan, 1956, p. 18). For our purposes, the "objects" in the system are people, however, and the relationships between them have a specific nature and significance that the systemic perspective has not always taken into account. Systemic therapies have tended to focus on patterns of interaction and how they evolve or become constrained and constraining, rather than on the lived experience of dancers in the dance (Merkel & Searight, 1992). These therapies have then sometimes been labeled as impersonal and mechanistic. Attachment theory fosters the inclusion of experiential variables, such as "felt security" and emotional responses to separation and loss, into the general consideration of systemic patterns in relationship interactions and the social context. Emotional experience and communication are the essential fabric of an attachment relationship and organize the pattern of interactions that constitute an interactional "system."

The systemic perspective also keeps attachment concepts grounded in the process of interaction in specific relationships. As Shaver and Hazan (1993) point out, the patterns of interaction between current attachment figures ongoingly confirm and maintain an individual's construction of an attachment relationship, rather than simply internal models from the past biasing present perceptions. Attachment responses and models are also being linked more and more to specific relationships rather than being seen as global tendencies that are formed in childhood and then become self-reinforcing (Bretherton & Munholland, 1999). In general, internal representational models of attachment are proving to be more fluid and changeable than was once imagined. Research suggests that a significant percentage of people change their attachment style, or ways of engaging others, over time (Davila, Karney, & Bradbury, 1999).

RELEVANT LINKS BETWEEN ATTACHMENT AND SYSTEMS THEORY

Let us first consider the links between attachment and systems theory that are most pertinent to the couples therapist. First, both theories use the concept of circular causality to explain how intimates interact and create stable patterns in that interaction. Bowlby (1969) spoke of goal corrected behavior where feedback loops allow participants to modify responses that deviate from mutual goals, such as secure connectedness. Both theories direct the couples therapist to look at chain-linked sequences (Bowlby), that is, at the process of interaction in which each partner evokes responses from the other and in which organization itself conveys stability and sometimes constrains new and different responses. Bowlby used traditional systemic language to express how a behavioral system maintained stability; he spoke continually of creating and maintaining homeostasis. Rather than simply view this stability as reflecting the inherent self-reinforcing nature of patterned interactions, Bowlby suggested that an internal state of felt security or anxiety, and ways of regulating such anxiety, organized such interactional patterns (Cassidy, 1999).

Second, both theories share a similar view of dysfunction. In both systems and attachment theory, flexibility and the ability to update ways of seeing and responding constitute health, whereas rigid, constricted ways of processing information and responding are problematic. Both theories focus then on process rather than on static, linear models of causality. The systemic principle of equifinality states that process, the how of things, determines outcome. Many beginnings can then lead to the same outcome, or the same beginnings can lead to different outcomes.

Third, both theories are, at their best, nonpathologizing. Bowlby (1979) maintains, for example, that negative working models of attachment that define the self as unlovable or as unworthy and others as untrustworthy are not projections but are "perfectly reasonable constructions" (p. 23) that were adaptive in a particular context. The problem is then viewed as the narrow patterns of interactions or inner processing that people become caught in and cannot revise, not the people themselves.

Fourth, both theories are able to integrate inner and outer, intrapsychic and interpersonal, into a wholistic perspective. Emotionally loaded communication patterns form and maintain specific ways of constructing inner and outer worlds. Systems theory has been criticized for ignoring its own maxims about wholeness and ignoring such factors as emotion. However, nothing inherent in this theory precludes a focus on emotion, and some have argued that emotion is a primary signaling system that constitutes a leading or organizing element in a relational family system (S. Johnson, 1998a). Both theories offer a "reality regulating, reality creating not just reality reflecting" system (Bretherton & Munholland, 1999, p. 98). Both are able to incorporate how interactions reflect and create inner experience and how inner experience then reflects and creates interactional responses. Both, at best, link dancer and dance into a holistic, evolving picture.

ATTACHMENT THEORY EXTENDS
THE SYSTEMIC PERSPECTIVE

In some ways, attachment theory goes beyond the systemic perspective. Attachment informs us as to the critical "leading" elements and defining events in an attachment system and offers us specific goals, tasks, and pathways to change. Systems theory offers basic principles for understanding any system. Attachment theory tells us more about the specific system that is an intimate relationship between family members and spouses. It also tells us that such emotions as fear will have control precedence (Tronick, 1989) over other elements at particular times and that particular interactions are especially crucial and relationship defining. For example, being able to reach for and offer comfort appears to predict relationship quality in adult partners (Pasch & Bradbury, 1998).

Couples therapy has long been viewed as a technique in search of a theory. As Roberts (1992) has pointed out, this modality developed without a theory of relationship or a theory of love to guide it. For a while, exchange theory appeared to offer a coherent perspective on close relationships; however, it became clear that its applicability to intimate relationships was severely limited (S. Johnson, 1986). People in happy, close relationships do not operate on a contingent exchange basis; this behavior is typical only of unhappy couples. Attachment theory tells us that the interactional patterns that confront a couples therapist are best understood in the context of needs for contact, comfort, and security that have been laid down in the process of evolution and have protected men and women from the dangers and trauma of isolation. Attachment figures offer us a safe haven in a dangerous world and a secure base from which to venture out and explore and learn about our world. Proximity to an attachment figure offers a way of regulating emotion and achieving an internal homeostasis, in that it "tranquillizes the nervous system" (Schnore, 1994, p. 244) and tames fear. A secure connection with others promotes flexibility and adaptation to the environment. Specifically, such a connection helps individuals to deal with their emotions in a constructive way, to process information effectively and consider alternative perspectives, and to communicate in an open, direct, coherent way with others (S. Johnson & Whiffen, 1999). The systemic ideal of flexibility and open, congruent communication can be made more specific here. For example, research on attachment theory tells us when such communication is important: At moments of uncertainty, ambiguity, anxiety, and loss, these specific attachment needs arise. Whether such needs are met at these times will disproportionately influence the response patterns and the definition of attachment relationships (Simpson & Rholes, 1994). This focus on the pivotal importance of soothing and comforting responses at such times parallels recent research results that stress the importance of such responses in the definition of close relationships (Gottman, Coan, Carrere, & Swanson, 1998).

Attachment theory also tells us that emotional accessibility and responsiveness are crucial, defining features of attachment relationships. Research has also found that emotional engagement and the nature of this engagement are predictive of the future status of a couple's relationship (Gottman, 1994), rather than the number of conflicts or the resolution of conflict issues. Emotional signals and how they are responded to appear to organize the system of interactions in attachment relationships (Pasch & Bradbury, 1998; Johnson & Denton, in press). The ability to recognize and acknowledge the other's affective state and modify one's emotional response in the face of the other's need makes the difference in couples' satisfaction (M. Johnson & Bradbury, 1999). Attachment theory moves affect into primary place and designates it as a leading element in close relational systems.

Attachment theory and the kinds of research results summarized above also give us a way to understand and explain the findings that specific patterns in close relationships, such as critical, contemptuous pursuit followed by defended distancing or stonewalling, are corrosive to the stability and viability of these relationships. These patterns may be viewed as the enactment of separation distress (Bowlby, 1969), where angry protest at loss of connection, then clinging and seeking, depression and despair, and finally detachment, follow on the perceived loss of connection with a valued and irreplaceable other. Distressed partners become more and more coercive as a way of defending against loss and the anxiety of abandonment and rejection. Unfortunately, the more one partner pushes and demands a response, the more threatening they appear to the other partner, who then withdraws further. This reciprocally determining feedback loop perpetuates both partners' insecurity and negative emotional states.

The relatively limited patterns of interaction found in distressed couple relationships also reflect the specific nature of this attachment system. There are only so many ways of dealing with a threat to the security of the connection with an attachment figure (Main, Kaplan, & Cassidy, 1985). Attachment responses will be hyperactivated or minimized and denied. Those who minimize attachment needs and interactions will tend to withdraw precisely when they or their partners feel vulnerable and need contact comfort (Simpson et al., 1992). The more easily stimulated or rigidly applied these forms of engagement (Sroufe, Carlson, & Shulman, 1993) with inner experience and attachment figures are, the more rapidly negative cycles will occur and the more difficult it will be to create new kinds of interactions in couples therapy (S. Johnson & Whiffen, 1999). Those who have been violated in attachment relationships will tend to engage others for support and protection with intensity and then, just as intensely, become afraid of depending on them and withdraw. Others are at once the source of and the solution to danger (Main & Hesse, 1990). This pattern of fearful avoidant interactions with intimates is associated with trauma survivors (S. Johnson & Williams Keeler, 1998). Posttraumatic stress disorder and clinical depression are the two most frequent emotional problems associated with marital distress (Whisman, 1999). Attachment theory can give us an understanding as to why this is so. Depression is a naturally occurring part of separation distress and a model of self as unlovable (Whiffen & Johnson, 1997), and the effects of trauma make it more difficult to trust and connect with others and also make isolation more overwhelming and toxic.

Attachment theory, and all systemic perspectives, also stress how models of self and other are constantly defined in interactions with others. The confirmation process in interactions maintains the stability of self concepts rather than simply the conservative nature of existing internal models. Attachment focuses the lens on internal representations concerning the lovable nature of self and the trustworthy nature of others in particular. The more secure and connected I am with those I love, the more clear and congruent the communication between us and the more I can be myself (Minuchin & Fishman, 1981). As Mikulincer (1995) suggests, flexible, open systems of interaction with loved ones tend to foster a more complex, articulated, and coherent sense of self. New interactional patterns can then lead to a new sense of self.

COUPLE INTERVENTIONS BASED ON ATTACHMENT THEORY

A couples therapy that is systemic and also conceptualizes intimate relational systems in terms of attachment will then do the following:

1. Focus on the process of interaction, where attachment needs and dilemmas are enacted. The therapist will focus on the process of de-escalating negative cycles of separation distress, rather than on general skill building or finding solutions to pragmatic content issues. The therapist will also validate attachment needs and processes and frame such needs as adaptive.
2. Privilege emotional communication and explicate how such communication evokes the steps in the interactional dance. The therapist will pay particular attention to the deconstruction and soothing of fear and attachment anxiety, which tend to organize negative responses to the partner.
3. Shape new bonding cycles and create pivotal attachment events, such as the resolution of attachment injuries and violations (S. Johnson, 1996; S. Johnson, Makinen, & Millikin, 2001). Attachment theory tells us which new patterns of interaction have the potential to redefine the dance and create not just a modification of elements but level-two systemic change (Watzlawick, Weakland, & Fisch, 1974), that is to transform and rapidly reorganize the system as a whole.
4. Actively foster the creation of a secure base and a safe haven in the therapy session. Safety and support enable clients to explore their inner world, assert their needs and wants, tolerate differences, and risk new steps in the dance with their spouse. The security of the session offers partners a platform to stand on in the shifting sand of their relationship. This platform allows them to regulate their emotions and process information in a different way. In secure interactions, individuals are more likely to rely on new information when making social judgments, to be able to deal with ambiguity, and to allow themselves to be more curious (Mikulincer, 1997). The therapist must then be accessible and responsive in a collaborative way with each partner throughout the therapy process.
5. Recognize the powerful process of self-definition that is implicit in any attachment interaction and actively use new interactions to revise negative models of self that inhibit emotional engagement with the spouse. For example, shame that arises from a sense that the self is somehow unlovable, and therefore not entitled to care and attention, primes withdrawal and lack of open communication about one's needs and wants in a close relationship.
6. Address specific pivotal moments in interactions that define the relationship as insecure, constrain the steps in the couple's dance, and, more specifically, focus on attachment injuries that block relationship repair.
7. View key aspects of adult relationships through an attachment lens. Adult attachment differs from child attachment in that it is more reciprocal, is more representational, and plays a key role in sexual interactions. Male

partners can often express their need for sexual contact but cannot express their need to "cuddle and cling" (Hazan & Zeifman, 1994). Framing sexual behavior in the context of attachment can change the way partners view and communicate about their sexual relationship.

EFT: A COUPLES THERAPY THAT INTEGRATES ATTACHMENT AND SYSTEMS THEORIES

What does a couples therapy that integrates systemic and attachment perspectives look like in practice?

The process of change in EFT takes place in nine steps. The first four involve assessment and the de-escalation of problematic interactional cycles. The middle steps (5 to 7) emphasize the creation of specific change events where interactional positions shift and new bonding events occur. In these steps, new cycles are shaped that provide an alternative and antidote to the negative cycle. The last two steps of therapy (8 and 9) address the consolidation of change and the integration of these changes into the everyday life of the couple. These steps, although described in linear form, occur in a spiral fashion, where each step incorporates and adds to the next. In a mildly distressed, securely attached couple, the partners work quickly through the steps at a parallel rate. In more distressed couples, the more passive or withdrawn partner is usually invited to go through the steps slightly ahead of the other. The increased emotional engagement of this partner then helps the other, more critical partner shift into a more trusting stance.

The Nine Steps of EFT

Stage 1. Cycle De-escalation

Step 1. Assessment. Creating an alliance and articulating the core conflicts and attachment issues:

Step 2. Identifying the problematic cycle, such as critical pursuit–defensive withdrawal, that maintains attachment insecurity and marital distress.

Step 3. Accessing the unacknowledged emotions that organize interactional positions and placing these in an attachment frame.

Step 4. Reframing the problem in terms of the systemic cycle and the underlying attachment emotions and needs.

Stage 2. Changing Interactional Positions

Step 5. Promoting identification with disowned attachment needs and aspects of self, and integrating these into relationship patterns.
Step 6. Promoting the other's acceptance of these needs and aspects of self.
Step 7. Facilitating the expression of specific needs and wants, and creating emotional engagement.

Key change events—withdrawer reengagement and blamer softening—evolve here. These events are completed in Step 7. When both partners complete this step, a prototypical bonding event occurs, either at home or in the session. In such an event, a previously unresponsive partner will reach out and offer comfort and reassurance, and the other, more critical, spouse will ask for their attachment needs to be met from a position of vulnerability. This event is called a "softening" and is associated with clinically significant change in EFT. The relationship is then redefined by this interaction as a safe haven and a secure base.

Stage 3. Consolidation and Integration

Step 8. Facilitating the emergence of new solutions to old problematic relationship issues in an atmosphere of collaboration and safety.
Step 9. Consolidating new positions characterized by accessibility and responsiveness and new cycles of attachment behaviors.

In all of these steps, the therapist moves between helping partners crystallize their emotional experience in the present and setting interactional tasks that add new elements to the interactional cycle. The therapist will track, reflect, and expand the inner experience of an individual partner and then use the expression of this experience to create a new dialogue in order to reorganize the interactional cycle. The therapist might first help a withdrawn, avoidant spouse formulate his sense of shame that primes his withdrawal, then help his partner to hear his experience, and finally move to restructuring an interaction around this shameful sense of self. An example could be, "So can you tell her please, I feel so small. Like a eunuch. I don't want you to see me. So, I just want to numb out and turn away." The content of this comment is about taking distance. However, the process of confiding represents a move away from avoidant withdrawal and the beginning of active engagement. This partner is then more engaged with his own attachment needs and longings and in the interaction with his spouse.

In terms of the EFT change process, the first shift, which occurs at the end of Step 4, constitutes a first-order change (Watzlawick et al., 1974). Reactive emotional responses that heighten each partner's attachment insecurities are still in place, but they are less extreme. Partners begin to risk more emotional engagement and to view the cycle or dance, rather than the other spouse, as the enemy. This shift sets the stage for the work of second-order change, reorganizing the interactional dance in the direction of safe attachment. In the middle stage of therapy (Steps 5–7), there are two change events that are crucial turning points in EFT. The first is withdrawer's reengagement, where this partner becomes more active in defining the relationship and more accessible to the other partner. The second change event, a softening, occurs when a previously critical spouse is able to risk expressing attachment needs and fears and to begin to trustingly engage with his or her partner. Research on the process of change has found that this event predicts recovery from marital distress in EFT (S. Johnson & Greenberg, 1988). If there is only partial engagement in these change events or if the couple reaches an impasse here, the relationship may still improve, but the impact of therapy will be less forceful. Transcripts and detailed descriptions of a softening, which often ends in a prototypical bonding event in which one partner asks for comfort from a responsive other, can be found in the literature (S. Johnson & Greenberg, 1995; S. Johnson, 1996).

The bonding event that usually occurs in the final stages of a softening initiates a new cycle of confiding, emotional engagement and responsiveness. This kind of event has the potential, because of its emotional salience in meeting basic attachment needs, to heal longstanding wounds in the relationship and to redefine the nature of the bond. When, for example, a critical, aggressive partner, who is in the protest-and-pursue stages of separation distress, is able to share her deep fears of abandonment and receive comfort and reassurance from her partner, the bond changes. She experiences a shift from isolation to connectedness and from frustration to a sense of efficacy in her ability to create a new kind of relationship. Once this kind of change event has occurred, the couple moves naturally into consolidating this positive cycle. Once partners can create this kind of safe emotional engagement, they are then able to solve practical issues that have been fueling the conflict between them.

Who Benefits From Attachment-Oriented Interventions?

For whom is an attachment-oriented, systemic intervention, such as EFT, best suited? First, EFT is not used for couples where abuse is an ongoing part of the relationship. Abusive partners are referred to group or individual therapy to help them deal with their anger and abusive behavior. They are offered EFT only after this therapy is completed and their partner no longer feels at risk. Secondly, EFT is used only in an abbreviated form for couples who are separating. Research on success in EFT (S. Johnson & Talitman, 1997) also allows specific predictions to be made regarding who will benefit from EFT. As with most psychotherapies, the alliance with the therapist seems to predict outcome. However, the perceived relevance of the tasks of therapy appears to be the most important aspect of this alliance. Task relevance may then be more central to treatment success than a positive bond with the therapist or a sense of shared goals. In general, the couples who do well in EFT are those for whom the focus on attachment needs and the creation of trust and emotional connection make sense. The positive outcomes and the large effect sizes associated with EFT (S. Johnson et al., 1999) suggest that this perspective resonates with the couples who come for couples therapy. The collaborative nature of the alliance with the therapist, which provides the couple with a secure base in therapy, generally promotes active engagement in the therapy process. Interestingly, this alliance, and, by implication, this engagement, appears to be a much more potent predictor of success than initial distress level. Such distress levels only accounted for 4% of the variance in outcome in a recent study (S. Johnson & Talitman, 1997). This result is interesting in light of the fact that initial distress has been found to account for up to 46% of the outcome variance in other marital therapies (Whisman & Jacobson, 1990).

EFT appears to work well with male partners who are described by their partners as inexpressive. This suggests that EFT may provide such partners with a safe base from which to explore and express their experience of the relationship. It was also more effective with older men (over 35), who may be more receptive to a focus on intimacy and attachment. As feminist writers have suggested, it is often positive to challenge typical gender styles and assume that both sexes have basically the same needs, albeit that they may express them differently (Knudson-Martin & Mahoney, 1999; Vatcher & Bogo, 2001). Traditionality, which is associated with men being oriented toward independence and their partners being oriented toward affiliation, does not seem to hamper progress in EFT. A recent study also found that clients possessing lower levels of cognitive complexity and education seem to do well with this model (Denton, Burleson, Clark, Rodriguez, & Hobbes, 2000). The most powerful predictor of success may be a particular kind of trust on the part of the female partner, namely, her faith that her spouse cares for her, in spite of all the difficulties in the relationship (S. Johnson & Talitman, 1997). In western cultures, the female partner tends to monitor the quality of the bond and take responsibility for maintaining closeness. It may be then that once this partner loses hope in her spouse's caring, a positive redefinition of the marital bond becomes impossible. The end point of

Bowlby's model of separation distress is detachment, an unwillingness to risk and invest in the relationship. The research on marital distress similarly finds that emotional disengagement is more predictive of marital dissolution than such factors as the ability to resolve disagreements (Gottman, 1994). An unwillingness to emotionally engage in therapy and with the partner may be a key negative prognostic indicator in any therapy that focuses upon the creation of a more secure bond.

EFT INTERVENTIONS

The therapist focuses on two tasks, the accessing and reformulating of emotional responses and the shaping of new interactions based on these responses. In the first task, the therapist focuses upon the emotion that is most poignant and salient in the client's experience and in terms of attachment needs and fears, or that plays a central role in organizing patterns of negative interaction. The therapist stays close to the "leading edge" of the client's experience and uses experiential interventions (Rogers, 1951; Greenberg, Rice, & Elliott, 1993), reflection, evocative questions, validation, heightening, and empathic interpretation to expand that experience. Reactive responses, such as anger, evolve into more primary emotions, such as a sense of grief or fear. In the second task, the therapist tracks and reflects the patterns of interaction, identifying the negative cycle that constrains and narrows the responses of the partners to each other. The therapist uses structural techniques, such as reframing, and creates new enactments (Minuchin & Fishman, 1981; Nichols & Fellenberg, 2000). He or she slowly, step by step, gives interactional tasks that shape new kinds of relationship events. Problems are reframed in terms of cycles and patterns and in terms of attachment needs and fears. So, for instance, the therapist will ask a partner to share specific fears with his or her partner, thus creating a new kind of dialogue that fosters secure attachment. These tasks and interventions are outlined in detail elsewhere, together with transcripts of therapy sessions (Johnson, 1996, 1998b, 1999, 2000).

Impasses in the therapy process most often occur in Stage 2, particularly when previously hostile partners are asked to risk placing themselves in the hands of their partner. The EFT therapist may then, in systemic fashion, reflect the process or create a narrative of therapy up to the impasse and elucidate the patterns that now appear to be immovable, as well as the dilemmas this impasse presents to the partners. Once partners actively articulate their stuck position in the dance of distress, they feel the constraining effect of this position more acutely and are often more willing to take a new step. The therapist may also conduct individual sessions to examine the specific elements in the interaction (his stonewalling or her inability to trust) that block positive shifts. This intervention is less traditionally systemic in that it intervenes on an individual level; however, it is still focused on the patterns of interaction and the blocks to new steps in the dance. The therapist may also address key, defining attachment events, such as attachment injuries, that block the creation of trust and reconciliation.

Attachment theorists have pointed out that incidents in which one partner responds or fails to respond at times of urgent need seem to disproportionately influence the quality of an attachment relationship (Simpson & Rholes, 1994). Such incidents either shatter or confirm a partner's assumptions about attachment relationships and the dependability of the partner. Negative attachment-related events, particularly abandonments and betrayals, often then cause seemingly irreparable damage to close relationships. Many partners enter therapy not only in general distress but also with the goal of bringing closure to such events and so restoring lost intimacy and trust. During the therapy process, these events, even if they are long past, often reemerge in an alive and intensely emotional manner, much like a traumatic flashback, and overwhelm the injured partner. These incidents, usually occurring in the context of life transitions, loss, physical danger, or uncertainty, can be considered relationship traumas and, if unresolved, tend to block the creation of trust and undermine relationship repair (S. Johnson et al., 2001). In systemic fashion, the patterns of interaction that occur around such injuries tend to compound them. When the other partner then fails to respond in a reparative, reassuring manner or when the injured spouse cannot accept such reassurance, the injury is aggravated. As the couple experience failure in their attempts to move beyond such injuries and repair the bond between them, their despair and alienation deepen. So, a partner's withdrawal from his wife while she suffers a miscarriage, as well as his subsequent unwillingness to discuss this incident, becomes a recurring focus of the couple's dialogue and blocks the development of new, more positive interactions.

Attachment has been called a theory of trauma (Atkinson, 1997) in that it emphasizes the extreme emotional adversity of isolation and separation, particularly at times of increased vulnerability. The trauma literature emphasizes how emotional responses to fear, such as fight, flight, and freeze, can limit and constrict interactions with others. This theoretical framework offers an explanation of why certain painful events become pivotal in a relationship, as well as an understanding of what the key features of such events will be, how they will impact a particular couple's relationship, and how such events can be optimally resolved and new patterns of interaction developed.

Once the attachment injury is resolved, the therapist can more effectively foster the growth of trust, softening events, and the beginning of positive cycles of bonding and connection.

A Change Event

It may be useful to consider a key change event in EFT, in this case a softening, in terms of systemic change and a transformation of the attachment relationship. As a previously critical husband is confronted by his now more assertive wife and told she will no longer tolerate his tirades and demeaning comments, he then begins to reach beyond his need to control his wife and access his considerable anxiety that arises when she becomes depressed and withdraws from him. As he gradually is able to tolerate and articulate his fear and insecurity, he begins to reach out to his wife for reassurance, in spite of the fact that he despises this "weakness." His wife then accepts, comforts, and reassures him, and he weeps in her arms and releases a torrent of fears and longings that he has never confided in her or anyone.

There are many levels of change in this drama. On a systemic interactional level, the following changes occur: (a) His position in the dance changes both in terms of hierarchy and in terms of closeness and boundaries (he moves to a more equal footing and allows a new kind of contact to occur). (b) Her position also then changes to a more equal and less withdrawn one. (c) One patterned interaction is replaced by another; attack–withdraw is replaced by reach and express needs and fears, followed by reassure and comfort. (d) This new interaction element reorganizes the dance between the couple. It provides an antidote for and undermines the power of the negative cycle they brought into therapy. The pattern of the dance is less constrained and more flexible.

From the perspective of attachment, the changes above are, of course, crucial. Interactions are characterized by more mutuality, equality, and intimate contact. Some of the levels of change on which a systemic therapist might not focus, however, are crucial for the attachment-oriented clinician. These are the following:

1. The husband organizes his emotional experience differently, in terms of vulnerability and fear rather than in terms of anger. This emotion moves him, or in more academic language, activates an action tendency to seek comfort rather than dominate.
2. This then opens new ways for him to regulate his emotions in this relationship, ways that pull his wife closer to him and foster secure bonding interactions rather than push her away.
3. This event potentially affects cognitions in both partners, that is, specific models of the self (she accepts my "weakness" and finds me lovable, so I

can revise this sense of myself as having to stay dominant to be accepted), the other (she is someone I can turn to), and the relationship (this is a place where I can reveal myself and feel secure).

4. This event also potentially affects not just the content of such models but *how* the husband thinks of and processes attachment information. As he grows less concerned with regulating his negative emotions and controlling his wife, he becomes more curious, more able to construct coherent narratives about his relationship, and more able to find meaning in such narratives that empower him and help him problem solve.

5. Once this pattern of interactions is established, an attachment theorist would assume that the husband would become less depressed and more resilient in his everyday life, because he now has created a safe haven and a secure base with his partner.

The above sequence includes interactional and intrapsychic changes on the levels of behavior, emotion, and cognition. They can all be viewed as systemic changes (if the whole within and between system is considered), and they can all be considered as changes in the nature of the attachment bond between the partners (if this bond is seen in transactional terms).

The Clinical Efficacy of EFT

Evidence indicates that viewing distressed couples and families from a systemic perspective and then refining this perspective by understanding these relationships within an attachment context enables the couples therapist to foster relatively stable and significant changes in 10 to 12 sessions. In a summary article of EFT outcome research, the effect size from the best clinical trials of EFT was calculated at 1.3 (S. Johnson et al., 1999). This effect size indicates that the average person treated with EFT is better off than 90% of untreated persons. This significantly exceeds published estimates for the effect sizes of couples therapy interventions that do not use an attachment perspective. Follow-up results suggest that treatment effects are stable or improve over time. In terms of the percentage of couples recovered (not simply improved but scoring as nondistressed on a measure of marital satisfaction), studies of EFT found rates of 70% to 75% recovery from relationship distress, in 8 to 12 sessions. There is also some evidence that this approach is effective with families who are dealing with disturbed adolescents (Johnson, Maddeaux, & Blouin, 1998). Furthermore, a number of small studies on the process of change in EFT supports the notion that engagement with emotional experience and interactional shifts are the active ingredients of change in this approach (S. Johnson et.al., 1999).

A CASE STUDY

Rick and Suzannne were in their early 30s and had been married for 5 years when they began couples therapy. They described their relationship as one between "roommates," in which they lived uncomfortably, barely talking to each other. Rick had just recently begun a new career as an electrician, a transition which he found stressful, and he devoted a lot of time to his job, just trying to make ends meet. Suzanne worked in office administration in a government department and cared for their two young children, 4 years old and 1 year old. Either one of the children regularly slept with Suzanne in the couple's bed, while Rick was relegated to the living room sofa. The couple agreed that they argued constantly and were caught in a pattern of defensively blaming each other for their unhappiness in the marriage.

Rick complained that when he came home from work all he heard was Suzanne's complaints and problems. He missed the fun they used to have together pursuing their shared interests. Since the children were born, he experienced life with Suzanne as "a drag," he criticized her "bad attitude," and he resented the fact that "she never wanted to do anything (with him) anymore." He proposed that they needed a break from the children, that he would like to go out more and have fun, but that Suzanne was reluctant to get a babysitter. Rick described feeling frustrated in his relationship and not understanding why they were not happy together because they shared a lot of interests and used to have fun together before they had children. He said that he was happy to have become a father but felt disappointed that having children seemed to have completely changed Suzanne. He described feeling pushed aside by Suzanne when the children were born and feeling she no longer gave him any time. He acknowledged that a lot of their difficulties stemmed from the fact that he had not been active in taking care of the children, but that he was not really interested in doing so. He praised Suzanne's ability as a mother and indicated that she should continue to tend to the children because he really had no idea what to do.

Suzanne reacted to Rick's description of their lives together as "a drag." For her "it hurts." She complained that since the birth of her second child, things had not gone well in the relationship. The baby had been colicky, and Suzanne found herself alone, with no support from her husband. She talked about feeling resentful of Rick because he did not take care of the children but only played with them. She described wanting Rick to help care for the children, not send them away for someone else to mind. She also expressed displeasure at what she described as Rick's excessive drinking, the "mean and hurtful" things he said to her when they argued, and the fact that he frequently left the house during an argument. In fact, they both experienced their arguments as never being resolved, their disagreements as perpetual, and the clashes between them as being easily triggered by Suzanne's complaints or Rick's avoiding behavior.

Suzanne and Rick's situation was typical of many marriages facing a transition to parenthood. New priorities, roles, and ways of working and being together as a team, as well as romantic partners, needed to be defined. They were searching for ways of depending on one another and supporting each other during a period in which each of them felt insecure and vulnerable in their sense of competence as parents. Therapy focused on helping them see how their individual reactions contributed to the cycle they found themselves in, where Suzanne pursued Rick for support and Rick withdrew from her because he felt overwhelmed and incompetent. Suzanne, in turn, would feel alone and abandoned by Rick and become more critical of his behavior, and he would withdraw further by drinking more, which drew further criticism from Suzanne. Couples therapy helped each of them to go beyond the angry blaming and defensive withdrawal, to express their fears and hear and respond to each other's anxieties about how inadequate and unloved they felt in their relationship, and finally to turn toward each other for comfort and support.

Over the first few sessions, Rick became more able to describe how no matter what he did to help Suzanne or show tenderness toward her, it never seemed enough. He felt that she constantly rejected both his affection and his sexual advances. He felt that there was never any "reward" for the effort he was making to be more helpful. Suzanne replied that he had always pursued her for "just sex," and that she was not interested. Although she affirmed that she still found him physically attractive, she perceived "a wall" around her that she had constructed to protect herself from the pain of feeling "desperately alone" and unsupported by Rick when her infant daughter had been colicky. Every time Rick pursued her for intimacy, she touched back to the pain of this attachment injury, characterized by his failure to respond to her need for comfort and support when she was feeling particularly vulnerable. Suzanne did not then trust that any change that Rick had made would be enduring, and that to take down "the wall" would be to expose her to the risk of feeling that pain again. Rick was anxious for Suzanne to just "let go" of what happened over a year before. Although he was "sorry" that she had been so miserable, he really didn't see how he could do anything about it now. Hearing her describe her sense of "abandonment" and "desolation" made him "shut down." He found it hard to tolerate her distress and admitted that at times like these, when he felt "overwhelmed" and "unable," he would tell Suzanne that she was "crazy" and head out to the bar to join his buddies. Suzanne said that she had begun to think that maybe she was "crazy." She just couldn't "get beyond" her feeling of "resentment" and "rage" toward Rick. When asked whether she ever had felt supported and taken care of by Rick, she replied that she was always the one "who did the looking after," that she had to take care of herself. Now that they had children, she had to take care of them too, and there "wasn't enough of her to go around." She said Rick acted like "an immature teenager" and she could never count on him to be there when she needed him. She felt last on his list of priorities, after his own self-interest and his friends. Rick vehemently denied this assertion and said he was upset by his wife's "constant disapproval" and her "complete lack of trust," no matter what he did. He said that he felt like "a failure" and that their situation was "hopeless." In the above description, it is easy to see outer rings (as Bowlby would describe it) of negative interactions, inner rings of attachment insecurity and negative models of self and other, and how each confirm the other and narrow the partner's experience of the relationship. More specifically, Suzanne's sense of injury was confirmed, and the comfort and connection needed to resolve such an injury was impossible to find.

The therapist reflected the cycle and how it left both of them feeling diminished and alone and also probed for the emotions underlying the steps in the dance. Neither Suzanne's critical defensiveness nor Rick's drinking behavior were viewed as pathologies. Rather, these behaviors were understood as responses that each partner had developed to survive their negative relationship cycle. Gradually both partners began to feel more comfortable in therapy, as the therapist allowed each of them a chance to express their feelings and as these feelings were understood in the context of the cycle. They both admitted how afraid they were of losing their marriage, and each began to make more effort day to day. Rick began to help out more around the house and with the children, and he cut down significantly on his drinking. He became more verbally open and more easily expressed some of his hurts and fears. Suzanne acknowledged Rick's help and expressed appreciation for the changes he was making. After eight sessions, de-escalation of the tension seemed to have occurred. From a systemic point of view, the system became less rigid and constrained. From an attachment point of view, the couple began to create a secure base from which to learn about their relationship.

The therapist had to work persistently to get Rick to interact directly with Suzanne during the sessions. Although initially he could not see the point of talking to her in front of the therapist, he began to realize that sessions with the therapist provided an opportunity to talk to Suzanne about his experience in a new way. He described how he felt like "a loser" when Suzanne criticized him all the time, especially when he was trying so hard, and how when she rebuffed him sexually he felt "unlovable." He began to express his feelings and needs more and more clearly to Suzanne. For example, he said to Suzanne:

I try to be affectionate to you, I want to give you hugs, but you never hug me back. It's not just about sex, it's that I want you to recognize me, I want to feel I'm somebody important in your life, not just for what I can do, for the chores I perform correctly, but because I'm a good guy, that you love me. I know you're angry and that you're behind your wall, but I'm waiting for you. I will wait for you, but I also need something back from you. I want to be with you. I'm starving out here alone.

Suzanne seemed to need to hear that Rick was suffering too. From behind her "wall" she wanted to see him "pay" for all the hurt she had felt when she was alone with her colicky child. She accused him of "not seeing my pain," of being "tuned out" and "selfish." For example, she told him:

I am never going to let you hurt me again. I don't trust you to put me first, to care about my feelings, to look after me. I don't care if you don't know how to help. I don't know what to do either lots of times, but I want you with me, beside me. I don't want to be alone anymore. But I'd rather be alone behind my wall than trust you and get so hurt again.

Suzanne's ambivalence about letting Rick back in became clearer as the sessions progressed, and she became angrier and angrier at Rick the more he continued to stay reengaged in the relationship, by spending more time with her and the children and letting her know about how frustrating it was for him to still be shut out of emotional and physical intimacy. She collected "proof" to bring to every session to justify her reluctance to risk "letting the wall down." Although the couple argued less because Rick was now more engaged in household and family activities and he had become more aware of and expressed his own feelings, Suzanne did not feel he could respond to her.

One week the couple arrived for the session in stony silence. Suzanne had been sick over the weekend, and Rick had gone out on Sunday afternoon to help a friend at a food fair booth. Suzanne was livid. She said that the relationship was "hopeless," "finished," and that she had been right to never trust that Rick would be there for her when she needed him. The therapist realized the incident had triggered the earlier attachment injury for Suzanne, in which she had felt vulnerable, scared, insecure, and alone, and helped her to connect the emotions of "helplessness," "desperation," and "abandonment" to both situations. Suzanne curled forward, trembling and weeping:

Suzanne: You can't hear what I am saying—you're like a brick—you don't understand how much I hurt inside, how much you hurt me.

Therapist: Suzanne, you don't feel Rick knows how much you needed him and how desperate you felt when you were so very alone, feeling sick, or like before, trying so hard to comfort your baby, who just wouldn't calm down . . .

Suzanne: She just kept crying and crying—nothing I did worked. He just wanted to take her to his mother's. I felt so useless, so ashamed.

Rick: I was just trying to help you. I didn't know what to do. I thought my mother could help you because I sure couldn't.

Suzanne: But I didn't want your mother. (She points her finger at him.) I wanted YOU. I wanted you to be there with me, not desert me like I didn't matter, like you didn't care how I felt. I wanted you right there with me so I wouldn't feel so bad. I wanted you to tell me that I was a good mother.

Therapist: (In a soft voice) What's that like Rick, for you to hear how much Suzanne wanted you then, wants you now, and then blockades herself behind her wall so you won't see how much she needs you?

Rick: (He puts his head down and stares at his hands.) I hate it when she pushes me away, but it's good to know she does need me. I never knew she needed me. She gets so angry that it's hard to know that somewhere in there she really does care about me.

Therapist: And Suzanne, it's so hard for you to feel how much you need Rick because it brings back how abandoned and scared you were when you were all alone.

Rick: But I want to be with her now. I just don't know how she wants me to be, how to please her.

Therapist: You're not really sure about how to reach Suzanne, and you're afraid you'll do it wrong and she'll push you away again. (Rick nods.) Can you tell her how much you want to be with her, but that you need her to help you to know what she wants? (Rick does this; Suzanne crosses her arms over her belly, looks out the window, and says nothing.)

Therapist: What's happening, Suzanne, when Rick says that he'd really like to be there with you?

Suzanne: (Set mouth, quiet tone.) I don't believe it.

Therapist: You're scared? You feel somehow vulnerable and little that it's you that needs comforting, that you don't always have it all together on your own, that if you let down your wall a little you'll be so exposed ? (She nods and cries.) And maybe Rick won't be there (She nods again.)

Rick: But I don't want her to hurt anymore. Now I know she just wants me to be with her, that I'm important.

Therapist: Can you tell her "I see how much you're hurting—I know I've hurt you so much in the past, but I want to be there with you now, comfort you." (He does.)

Suzanne: I don't know. I'm just confused. I don't know how to feel. He says that he wants to be with me now, but so many times he just left me. I don't know what to think. He can say anything he wants, but I don't believe he'll be there.

Therapist: Can you tell him how scared and vulnerable you feel right now and how hard it is for you to come out from behind your wall to meet him? How hard it is to risk that he'll really be there, that's it's safe to come out.

Suzanne: (Very quietly) I want to . . . but I can't. It doesn't feel safe yet.

Over the next several sessions, the therapist worked at helping the couple express their attachment needs and fears, framing their responses in terms of the cycle of angry protest and defensive withdrawal that kept them from connecting with each other. The processing of intrapsychic issues in the context of the interpersonal conflict was key to the shifting of their interactional dynamic. Suzanne's anger seemed to soften a little as she began to see more clearly how each time Rick "let her down," the old attachment injury was replayed and how this pattern had become an integral part of their relationship cycle. She described that touching those feelings of "isolation" and "incompetence" made her feel "worried for her sanity," and she went "wild with rage inside," just to survive. Rick began to see that despite the fact that Suzanne seemed "in control of everything" all the time, she really did feel vulnerable, and that she needed and wanted him to be there to comfort her and reassure her.

As she became more able to allow him to comfort her, Rick became more confident and stronger. "I don't feel like I'm on probation anymore. I'm a free man. I feel acknowledged and recognized that I can have a good impact on how she feels." Suzanne still struggled with "giving up the control" that she had had behind her wall, but she began to appreciate the benefits of the rediscovered connectedness she felt with Rick as she was able to allow him to come closer emotionally and physically. He became more gentle and patient in the ways her pursued her for intimacy, reassuring her that he'd be there for as long as she needed. As he repeatedly reassured her through his actions and new expressed awareness of her sensitivities, she began to trust that she could "come out and play" with less risk of hurt. The more Rick was able to be there for Suzanne, the more confident and competent he felt as "a man and as a parent." He still went out and spent time with friends, but not for reason of escaping the relationship.

At the end of therapy, Suzanne and Rick said that they still had arguments, but they didn't last as long and they were able to reconnect much more quickly. Suzanne described Rick as "more mature and reliable." I see that "the way he *is* has changed, not just what he *does*." Rick saw Suzanne as less of a "control freak." "I have a place in this family now. It's both of us, not just Suzanne, with the kids." "I have something to offer, something to contribute to our family besides a pay check." Working on the attachment injury was key to interrupting the destructive cycle in which the couple had been caught. The creation of new interactions helped them begin to rebuild a productive cycle in which they could rely on the relationship as a secure base and a safe haven. The rigid processing style of their destructive cycle had become more flexible and responsive to their changing needs and circumstances. They were then better able to address some of the more practical day-to-day issues in their lives, like financial challenges and parenting their children as a team. Rick and Suzanne again shared the couple's bed, and together they were able to gradually train their children to sleep in their own beds. This couple expanded their interaction patterns to include cycles of comfort and emotional connection and updated their working models of self and other.

CONCLUSION

Couple and family therapy is becoming more integrative as a field (S. Johnson & Lebow, 2000). Systems theory is being seen in a broader light; as being able to incorporate such variables as emotion rather than just focusing on interactions per se. We have suggested that attachment theory is best viewed as a transactional systemic theory, because it focuses on patterns of ongoing communication and how those patterns become the raw material from which models of self, other, and relationships are constructed. Attachment can also be viewed as an internalized aspect of personality or style and used in a more linear, nonsystemic manner to predict future attachments and internal models from past attachments (Kobak, 2000). We have also suggested that an attachment perspective expands the traditional systemic view. Attachment theory adds a more explicit focus on individuals in a relational system and views emotional states as key organizers of interactions. It also informs us in a more explicit manner about the nature of the system that involves our most intimate relationships. It can then help therapists who seek to change the complex drama of interactions in families to know what patterns are especially important in relationship definition, how particular patterns will affect relationships and the individuals within them, how to most effectively reorganize a relational system, and what charges will really make a difference in the long term.

REFERENCES

Atkinson, L. (1997). Attachment and psychopathology: From laboratory to clinic. In L. Atkinson & K. Zucker (Eds.), *Attachment and psychopathology* (pp. 3–16). New York: Guilford Press.

Bowlby, J. (1969). *Attachment and loss: Vol. 1. Attachment.* New York: Basic Books.

Bowlby, J. (1979). *The making and breaking of affectional bonds.* London: Tavistock.

Bowlby, J. (1973). *Attachment: Vol. 2. Separation.* New York: Basic Books.

Bretherton, I., &. Munholland, K. A. (1999). Internal working models in attachment relationships. In J. Cassidy & P. Shaver (Eds.), *Handbook of attachment: Theory, research, and clinical applications* (pp. 89–111). New York: Guilford Press.

Cassidy, J. (1999). The nature of the child's ties. In J. Cassidy & P. Shaver (Eds.), *Handbook of attachment: Theory, research and clinical applications* (pp. 3–20). New York: Guilford Press.

Davila, J., Karney, B. R., & Bradbury, T. N. (1999). Attachment change processes in the early years of marriage. *Journal of Personality and Social Psychology, 76,* 783-802.

Denton, W. H., Burleson, B. R., Clark, T. E., Rodriguez, C. P., & Hobbs, B. V. (2000). A randomized trial of emotion focused therapy for couples in a training clinic. *Journal of Marital and Family Therapy, 26,* 65–78.

George, C., Kaplan, N., & Main, M. (1996). Adult attachment interview. Unpublished manuscript, University of California, Berkeley.

Gottman, J. (1994). *What predicts divorce?* Hillsdale, NJ: Erlbaum.

Gottman, J. M., Coan, J., Carrere, S., & Swanson, C. (1998). Predicting marital happiness and stability from newlywed interactions. *Journal of Marriage and the Family, 60,* 5–22.

Greenberg, L. S., Rice, L., & Elliott, R. (1993). *Facilitating emotional change: The moment by moment process.* New York: Guilford Press.

Hall, A. D., & Fagan, R. E. (1956). Definition of a system. *General Systems Yearbook, I,* 18–28.

Hazan, C., & Zeifman, D. (1994). Sex and the psychological tether. In K. Bartholomew & D. Perlman (Eds.), *Attachment Processes in Adulthood* (pp. 151–180). London, PA: Jessica Kingsley.

Johnson, M., & Bradbury, T. (1999). The topography of distress. *Personal Relationships, 6,* 19–40.

Johnson, S. M. (1986). Bonds or bargains: Relationship paradigms and their significance for marital therapy. *Journal of Marital and Family Therapy, 12,* 259–267.

Johnson, S. (1996). *The practice of emotionally focused marital therapy: Creating connection.* New York: Brunner/Mazel.

Johnson, S. (1998a). Emotionally focused marital therapy: Using the power of emotion. In F. D'Attilio (Ed.), *The integrative casebook of couples therapy* (pp. 450–472). New York: Guilford Press.

Johnson, S. (1998b). Listening to the music: Emotion as a natural part of systems theory. *Journal of Systemic Therapies: Special Edition on the Use of Emotion in Couples and Family Therapy, 1,* 1–17.

Johnson, S. (1999). Emotionally focused couples therapy: Straight to the heart. In J. Donovan (Ed.), *Short term couples therapy*. New York: Guilford Press.

Johnson, S. M. (2000). Emotionally focused couples therapy. In F. Dattilio & L. J. Bevilacqua (Eds.), *Comparative treatments for relationship dysfunction* (pp. 163–185). New York: Springer.

Johnson, S. M., & Denton, W. (in press). Emotionally focused couples therapy: Changing the music: Changing the dance. In A. S. Gurman (Ed.), *The clinical handbook of couples therapy* (3rd ed.). New York: Guilford Press.

Johnson, S., & Greenberg, L. (1988). Relating process to outcome in marital therapy. *Journal of Marital and Family Therapy*, *14*, 175–183.

Johnson, S., & Greenberg, L. (1995). The emotionally focused approach to problems in adult attachment. In N. S. Jacobson & A. S. Gurman (Eds.), *The clinical handbook of marital therapy* (2nd ed., pp. 121–141). New York: Guilford Press.

Johnson, S., Hunsley, J., Greenberg, L., & Schlinder, D. (1999). Emotionally focused couples therapy: Status and challenges. *Journal of Clinical Psychology: Science and Practice*, *6*, 67–79.

Johnson, S. M., & Lebow, J. (2000). The "Coming of Age" of couple therapy: A decade review. *Journal of Marriage and Family Counseling*, *26*, 23–38.

Johnson, S. M., Maddeaux, C., & Blouin, J. (1998). Emotionally focused family therapy for bulimia: Changing attachment patterns. *Psychotherapy*, *35*, 238–247.

Johnson, S. M., Makinen, J., & Millikin, J. (2001). Attachment injuries in couple relationships: A new perspective on impasses in couples therapy. *Journal of Marital and Family Therapy*,

Johnson, S., & Talitman, E. (1997). Predictors of success in emotionally focused marital therapy. *Journal of Marital & Family Therapy*, *23*, 135–152.

Johnson, S., & Whiffen, V. (1999). Made to measure: Adapting emotionally focused couple therapy to partners' attachment styles. *Clinical Psychology: Science and Practice*, *6*, 366–381.

Johnson, S., & Williams-Keeler, L. (1998). Creating healing relationships for couples dealing with trauma: The use of emotionally focused marital therapy. *Journal of Marital and Family Therapy*, *24*, 227–236.

Knudson-Martin, C., & Mahoney, A. (1999). Beyond different worlds: A post gender approach to relationship development. *Family Process*, *38*, 325–340.

Kobak, R. (2000). The emotional dynamics of disruptions in attachment relationships: Implications for theory, research and clinical intervention. In J. Cassidy & P. Shaver (Eds.), *Handbook of attachment: Theory, research, and practice* (pp. 21–43). New York: Guilford Press.

Main, M., & Hesse, E. (1990). Parents' unresolved traumatic experiences are related to infant disorganized attachment status. In M. Greenberg, & D. Cicchetti (Eds.), *Attachment in the pre-school years*. Chicago: University of Chicago Press.

Main, M., Kaplan, N., & Cassidy, J. (1985). Security in infancy, childhood and adulthood: A move to the level of representation. In I. Bretherton & E. Waters (Eds.), *Growing points of attachment theory and research. Monographs of the Society for Research in Child Development*, *50*, 66–104.

Merkel, W., & Seawright, H. (1992). Why families are not like swamps, solar systems, or thermostats: Some limits of systems theory as applied to family therapy. *Contemporary Family Therapy, 14*, 33–50.

Mikulincer, M. (1995). Attachment style and the mental representation of self. *Journal of Personality and Social Psychology, 69*, 1203–1215.

Mikulincer, M. (1997). Adult attachment style and information processing: Individual differences in curiosity and cognitive closure. *Journal of Personality and Social Psychology, 72*, 1217–1230.

Minuchin, S., & Fishman, H. C. (1981). *Family therapy techniques*. Cambridge, MA: Harvard University Press.

Nichols, M. P., & Fellenburg, S. (2000). The effective use of enactments in family therapy. *Journal of Marital and Family Therapy, 26*, 143–152.

Pasch, L. A., & Bradbury, T. (1998). Social support, conflict and the development of marital dysfunction. *Journal of Consulting & Clinical Psychology, 66*, 219–230.

Roberts, T. W. (1992). Sexual attraction and romantic love: Forgotten variables in marital therapy. *Journal of Marital and Family Therapy, 18*, 357–364.

Rogers, C. (1951). *Client centered therapy*. Boston: Houghton-Mifflin.

Schnore, A. N. (1994). *Affect regulation and the organization of self*. Hillsdale, NJ: Erlbaum.

Shaver, P., & Hazan, C. (1993). Adult romantic attachment: Theory and evidence. In D. Perlman & W. Jones (Eds.), *Advances in personal relationships: Vol. 4* (pp. 29–70). London, PA: Kingsley.

Simpson, J. A., Rholes, W. S., & Nelligan, J. S. (1992). Support seeking and support giving within couples in an anxiety provoking situation: The role of attachment styles. *Journal of Personality and Social Psychology, 62*, 434–446.

Simpson, J., & Rholes, W. (1994). Stress and secure base relationships in adulthood. In K. Bartholomew & D. Perlman (Eds.), *Attachment processes in adulthood* (pp. 181–204). London, PA: Jessica Kingsley.

Sroufe, L. A., Carlson, E., & Shulman, S. (1993). Individuals in relationships. In D. C. Funder, R. Parke, C. Tomlinson-Keasey, & K. Widman (Eds.), *Studying lives through time* (pp. 315–342). Washington, DC: APA Press.

Tronick, E. Z. (1989). Emotions and emotional communication in infants. *American Psychologist, 44*, 112–119.

Vatcher, C., & Bogo, M. (2001). The feminist/emotionally focused therapy practice model: An integrated approach for couple therapy. *Journal of Marital and Family Therapy, 27*, 69–84.

Watzlawick, P., Weakland, J. H., & Fisch, R. (1974). *Change: Principles of problem formation and problem resolution*. New York: Norton.

Whiffen, V., & Johnson, S. M. (1998). An attachment theory framework for the treatment of child bearing depression. *Clinical Psychology: Science and Practice, 5*, 478–492.

Whisman, M. (1999). Marital dissatisfaction and psychiatric disorders: Results from a National co-morbidity survey. *Journal of Abnormal Psychology, 108*, 701–706.

Whisman, M., & Jacobson, N. S. (1990). Power, marital satisfaction and response to marital therapy. *Journal of Family Psychology, 4*, 202–212.

PART V

Specific Clinical Issues

CHAPTER 8

Linking Systems and Attachment Theory

A Conceptual Framework for Marital Violence

CLAIRE WORRELL HASLEM
PHYLLIS ERDMAN

Attachment theory has proven to be a clinically valuable way to assess and conceptualize adult romantic relationships (Crowell & Waters, 1994; Feeney & Noller, 1990; Griffin & Bartholomew, 1994; Hazan & Shaver, 1994; West & Sheldon-Keller, 1992) as well as abusive relationships (Bowlby, 1979; Dutton & Painter, 1993; Dutton, Saunders, Starzomski, & Bartholomew, 1994; Holtzworth-Munroe, Stuart, & Hutchinson, 1997; Mayseless, 1991; Roberts & Noller, 1998). However, much of the research applying attachment theory to abusive relationships has focused on individual partners or on specific characteristics of the spousal relationship rather than looking at both partners in the relationship. Additionally, Strouse (1973) has proposed that attachment relationships and spousal violence occur within the context of larger systems.

This chapter presents a conceptual framework for linking attachment theory and systems theory in explaining the interactional dynamics of violent couples, thus addressing the issues of both partners, as well as their interaction, and the contextual nature of the violence. In fact, numerous authors have supported the integration of the two approaches, emphasizing how such an integration would increase recognition of how family interactions affect the attachment process. We include in this chapter the results of a qualitative study of six violent couples (Haslam, 2000) that document the

systemic nature of the attachment-related concepts revealed in the participants' responses.

CONCEPTUALIZING VIOLENCE

Numerous theories attempt to explain heterosexual partner violence. Most
of these regard the goals and characteristics of male and female partners
separately; for example, several researchers have developed various batterer
typologies based on the severity and purpose of abuse behavior and degree
of psychopathology (Gondolf, 1988; Holtzworth-Munroe & Stuart, 1994).
Researchers have used other theories to explain the women's reasons for
staying in abusive relationships (Rusbult & Martz, 1995; Strube, 1988;
Walker, 1984) or have used social learning theory to explain how violence
is a product of behaviors learned by both partners during their childhoods
(Corvo, 1993; Henning, Leitenberg, & Coffey, 1996). Family systems theorists explain spousal violence as the result of rigid rules, roles, and interactions between partners (Giles-Sims, 1983; Strauss, 1973) or as the interaction
of positive and negative spousal bonds (Goldner, 1999; Goldner, Penn,
Sheinberg, & Walker, 1990).

   Another explanation that is conceptually linked with family systems
uses attachment theory. Proponents of attachment theory suggest that spousal violence is the result of both partners' negative working models of attachment. Bowlby (1973) theorized that children internalize experiences
with caregivers into mental representations of self and others, referred to as
internal working models. These models then guide the formation of subsequent relationships, not as new constructions, but rather as models by which
new relationships are selected and recreated in the image of those previously experienced (Sroufe & Fleeson, 1986). As we develop into adults,
attachment changes from the childhood asymmetrical, complementary relationship with a caregiver into reciprocal relationships in adulthood (Waters, 1997). Thus, the primary position given to a childhood caregiver sets
the stage for attachment in adulthood and potentially influences lasting bonds
with a sexual partner (Hazan & Zeifman, 1994).

LINKING ATTACHMENT THEORY AND FAMILY SYSTEMS

Theoretically, there is an inherent conceptual link between attachment theory
and family systems. Many authors suggest that the study of attachment within
a systemic framework would provide an increased and broader understanding of the relational dynamics (Byng-Hall, 1990, 1991a, 1991b, 1995a, 1995b;

Byng-Hall & Stevenson-Hinde, 1991; Donley, 1993; Emde, 1991; Giblin, 1994; Heard, 1982; Minuchin, 1985; Quadrio & Levy, 1988; Stevenson-Hinde, 1990). The attachment relationship between a parent and child, as well as between intimate partners, reveals the same characteristics of other systemic relationships (Goldenberg & Goldenberg, 1991). Viewed in systemic terms, the attachment relationship may be perceived as a feedback system wherein behaviors of one serve as stimulus and feedback for the other. In the same way that infants' attachment behaviors serve as stimuli to their caretakers regarding their availability, adults' attachment behaviors also serve as stimuli to their partners regarding their availability. So whereas such infant behaviors as clinging, anxiety, and crying serve to reestablish proximity to a caregiver, which in infancy is a parent or parent-substitute, similar forms of these behaviors may be exhibited by adults in adulthood to establish proximity to a marital partner. In fact, marital relationships may be viewed as attachment relationships between adults (Johnson, 1986), which is consistent with Bowlby's (1988) contention that attachment relationships occur throughout the span of one's life.

Additionally, it is important to understand the context in which relationships occur—another systemic concept that contributes to the understanding of attachment relationships (Donley, 1993). Several researchers have addressed the importance of intergenerational transmission of working models of intimacy (Cowan, Cohn, Cowan, & Pearson, 1996; Dutton, Saunders, Starzomski, & Bartholomew, 1994) as well as the influence of family-of-origin dynamics on each partner (Byng-Hall, 1990, 1995a, 1995b; Byng-Hall & Stevenson-Hinde, 1991; Gullette, 1988; Holtzworth-Munroe et al., 1997; Marvin & Stewart, 1990; Mayseless, 1991).

Explaining Violence Within an Attachment Theory and Systems Framework

According to Bowlby (1969, 1973), interpersonal anger frequently develops from frustrated attachment needs and functions as an attempt to regain proximity with an attachment figure. Threats or separations from an attachment figure result in emotional responses, such as terror, grief, or rage. Children who experience continued separations or threats of separations during childhood may carry such frustration into adulthood, where it manifests itself as extreme anger, or "intimacy anger." Consequently, violent outbursts in male adults may be viewed as protests toward the marital partners predicated by perceived threats of separation and/or abandonment (Dutton et al., 1994). In fact, Bowlby (1988) stated that "maladaptive violence met within families can be understood as the distorted and exaggerated versions of behavior that is potentially functional, especially attachment behavior" (p. 81), and that the violence that emanates from the dread and fear of losing a spouse may be "designed to control the other and to keep him or her from departing" (p. 95). Such behaviors may be viewed as risk factors for increased abusiveness in intimate relationships and are theoretically linked with how anxious–ambivalent children have been described in returning to their caregivers—simultaneously seeking contact and pulling away (Ainsworth, Blehar, Waters, & Wall, 1978). Hence, violence may be intergenerational, linking the anxiously attached behaviors learned during infancy to those manifested in adult intimate relationships as anger, jealousy, anxiety, and abusiveness. Violence between partners may be viewed as a way to equalize the relationship. For avoidant partners, violent behavior serves as a distancing tool when closeness is too frightening, and for anxious–ambivalent partners, it serves as a way to assert power and prevent the partner from leaving (Mayseless, 1991).

Attachment researchers have examined how childhood working models operate in adulthood. Categorizing parents as either secure, dismissing, preoccupied, or unresolved–ambivalent (due to childhood trauma), Main, Kaplan, and Cassidy (1985) found a strong association between parents' recalled childhood experiences and their relationships with their own children. Hazan and Shaver (1987) found corresponding attachment patterns in adult romantic relationships and noted that individuals with different attachment patterns described their experiences and expectations about love relationships very differently. It is important to remember that Bowlby held that strong bonds form even when proximity to caregivers is threatened, as evidenced by findings that abused children continue to be attached, albeit insecurely, to abusive caregivers (Cichetti & Barnett, 1991; Cowan et al., 1996; Crittendon, 1992). Attachment behavior not only withstands maltreatment but also actively maintains strong attachment bonds. Bowlby (1969) noted that a caregiver's rejection of a child's attempts to gain proximity often evokes the opposite effect of what was intended—the child becomes more clinging and anxious. These behaviors are most commonly associated with anxious–preoccupied attachment in adults (Bowlby, 1969). The intensely ambivalent attachment of violent partners leads to loneliness and fear of losing one's mate, resulting in extreme controlling behaviors (Bowlby, 1988). The aggressive outbursts of a violent partner may, therefore, be precipitated by threats, or perceived threats, of abandonment and may actually be attempts to prevent the separation. The resulting reciprocal interaction then looks something like this: The victim feels unworthy of her abusive partner, and although she fears remaining with him, she also fears leaving him, both emotionally and physically. Her partner, who also views himself negatively and fears the threat of losing his partner then takes physical and/or psychological advantage of his partner's low sense of worthiness to regain illusory power and to assure against losing her. The abused remains in the relationship; the abuser, then realizing he is not losing his partner, apologizes and becomes warm and loving. The abused then forgives (Walker, 1984), and the cycle repeats, thus preserving the homeostasis of the system.

RESULTS OF HASLAM'S STUDY

Haslam (2000) conducted a qualitative study with six violent couples in which she attempted to examine the perceived influence of childhood attachment bonds on the couples' spousal bonds. All the couples were heterosexual partners who had experienced male-to-female violence in their relationship. Specifically, her study was designed to answer the following questions: How do battered wives and their battering husbands describe their childhood attachment experiences and their attachment to each other? What meaning do battered wives and their battering husbands give to childhood experiences as influencing their spousal relationship?

The ages of the couples interviewed ranged from late 20s to early 60s, with four couples in the range from 30 to 40 years of age. Three of the couples were Anglo-American, one was African-American, one couple included a Native American with an Anglo-American partner, and one included a Mexican with an Anglo-American partner. All six couples interviewed had either been told of, or witnessed, violence in their parents' families. Eight of these individuals described violence between extended family members of both parents as the norm. Three wives and two husbands had been told that one or both of their parents had been sexually abused as a child, and three of these five were also sexually abused by close relatives as children. These same three individuals also experienced severe physical and emotional abuse in childhood. Every individual had childhood experiences with a parent who abused alcohol: Ten of the twelve indicated their fathers abused alcohol, and two others described their fathers as "closet drinkers." Seven of the individuals indicated their mothers also abused alcohol, and almost all of the individuals described alcohol or drug abuse as a problem in their own lives as well. Nine of the individuals were raised in same-parent families, and seven of these were cared for primarily by people other than their parents (e.g., grandparents, neighbors, older siblings, or foster parents). Three were raised primarily by multiple, temporary caregivers.

Attachment-Related Findings

The following six themes emerged from the interviews with these six couples: abandonment and fear of being alone; comfortlessness, uncertainty, and lack of safety; powerlessness and an inability to manage or change life circumstances; confusion about rules, roles, and behavior; unworthiness and shame; and hopelessness and helplessness. Before presenting a summary of the findings within each of the above themes, we would like to explain these themes from an attachment–systemic perspective.

An advantage of looking at spousal abuse via attachment theory is that it provides a means to connect childhood experiences to adult consequences. Another advantage is that attachment concepts are applied across the lifespan, in stages of development, thereby allowing close examination of significant experiences and with whom they occurred, of the reasons some experiences were more critical than others, and of the consequences of those experiences across the lifespan.

From a systemic perspective, looking at the context in which behaviors exist provides meaningful information. For example, the majority of the individuals interviewed described their childhood families as violent toward wives and children across several generations: For these individuals, violence was endorsed by their families. A significant portion of the individuals also pointed out that their families were considered outsiders (e.g., hippies, good-for-nothings, or white trash) by their communities. So for these individuals, family endorsement of spousal violence was clear and open, but community attitudes would be described as "turning a blind eye." Three of the wives indicated that violence and trouble in their homes was a closely guarded secret. In these situations, these wives perceived their fathers' violence as tacitly endorsed by the church and society at large. All of the individuals struggled to understand their relationships in the context of childhood and family history.

Abandonment and Fear of Being Alone

The human need for reliable connectedness is a basic concept of attachment theory, and similar to the concept of differentiation proposed by Bowen (1985). One of the participants in Haslam's (2000) study grew up in an extremely violent and abusive environment, never certain who would be in his house or in his life. How he perceived that experience as a child, and the impact it had on his adult life, is expressed in the following statement:

> Mama always said she'd come back for us. She did, until I was about six, when she dressed all up to leave, and I knew that she was off again. She

took us to school that day, and we never saw her again. . . . Every time my wife threatened to leave me, I'd feel like that little boy sitting on the curb, just waiting in the dark. (p. 132)

Other participants related similar experiences, as indicated in the following statements:

Somehow, I always found a lost kitten to hold. I guess they reminded me of myself, unwanted and thrown away. They were so warm and safe. They needed me just like I needed them, and they purred to show me. . . . Even after I'd grown up, seeing a thrown away kitten or lost child reminded me of how I felt as a kid. (p. 133)

The worst thing about my growing up was the fact that every fight meant somebody I loved left me. Just like every fight with my husband felt like he was leaving. I would hang on to him, begging, promising, and putting up with anything to keep him from leaving. (pp. 134–135)

Another participant revealed how exposure to such an environment influenced his relationship with his wife:

My wife didn't know what to do with all my carrying on, I couldn't have explained myself then if I'd tried. When I couldn't make her see how I needed her to be those things [I needed] . . . I'd be ready for war. Now I know that, until I understood my history . . . nothing my wife could have done or said would have been enough. (p. 135)

One participant recalled pleading with his father over how to make his mother more available to him. He commented on how these experiences were repeated in his marriage as follows:

I was willing to do anything—beg, cry . . . to protect myself from being left again. See, I was so afraid of having to deal with not just the world but with my own fears and doubts all by myself for the rest of my days. (p. 139)

Comfortlessness, Uncertainty, and Lack of Safety

Children have a fundamental need for comfort during times of distress, and the degree to which they are provided safety, comfort, and encouragement contributes to how they view themselves and how they relate to others as adults (Bowlby, 1969). One of the participants in Haslam's (2000) study indicated how her early remembrances influenced her relationships:

> I grew up hearing and watching my family fight. . . . Nobody ever laughed. I don't know whether anybody else cried, but I did. And I cried alone. . . . I never remember going to sleep without my pillow wet from tears. . . . I learned to comfort myself with sex. I didn't know how to let anybody into my heart, to trust that, if they hurt me, I could survive. So I would take on a lot of different lovers for a while and then either bail out or start a fight to make them leave. (p. 140)

Another interviewee indicated that she never had anyone she could count on being there in the morning, and she described how this affected her marriage as follows:

> As a child, there was nobody to help me. . . . In my marriage, I was so insecure that I would call my so-called family or friends . . . to tell me what to do. . . . I still couldn't take a stand on anything. He [my husband] complained because he was the only one working and complained when I went to work. . . . I couldn't do anything right, and so I just gave up and iced over. Even after the beatings were over, I'd just be frozen on the floor, waiting for somebody to save me. (p. 141)

One participant discussed how he lived with random strangers and a "now-and-then so-called mother" and how this affected his relationship with his wife:

> Before my mother left for good, her brother would show up now and then and chew her out about how we were living. He'd ask me questions and tease around and leave on his motorcycle . . . begging him to take me too. After mama left, there was a little kid who lived next door who'd smuggle food to us when his mom wasn't home. Sometimes we'd talk and he'd even cry with me. Maybe that's one of the reasons it's so important to me to have my say. Used to, my mind would just race with doubts about my wife, like she was running around on me or leaving me and taking my kids. (pp. 144–145)

A quote from another participant described how she was taught to deal with a cold, demanding father by a meek mother and how these experiences led to her isolation in her own marriage. She stated,

> I grew up watching my meek mother be wiped out by a cold, demanding father. She was so intent on him and getting me to be like he wanted me to be that she never noticed I needed her help and her love. I just tried to stay out of their way. . . . When my own marriage came along . . . little did I know that coldness wasn't the worst way to be mean and demanding. So, I tried being and doing what he wanted, but that didn't help

because my husband only got more demanding and violent. Finally, I'd slipped back into my old ways so totally and my voice had gotten so small that it took the neighbors calling the law to stop what was happening. (pp. 146–147)

Powerlessness and an Inability to Manage or Change Life's Circumstances

Children's ability to manage their environment, including their caregivers, is significant to their sense of themselves as worthy and of others as being reliable and caring (Ainsworth, 1985, 1989). Participants in Haslam's (2000) study frequently spoke of using desperate means to distract their caregivers from fighting and of giving in to their abusers as a way to survive.

> As a kid, I was powerless to change anything that went on at home. Outside that house, I was determined to take charge and not let go. I'd figured that survival meant doing whatever you've go to do . . . use people, lie to them . . . hide out inside when all else failed, even tell myself that they couldn't get to me. (pp. 148–149)

One participant talked about how she was abandoned by her mother and gave up on herself and how that influenced her marriage:

> Moms are supposed to care . . . so I eventually gave up on myself. Like, if mama thought I wasn't worth sticking around and standing up for , maybe I wasn't. . . . I learned to withhold my feelings . . . then nobody would have power over me. In my marriage, I held back my feelings as a way to get even for the beatings. . . . Sad to say, the old behavior worked pretty well until I saw my children's faces. They hadn't learned to hide their feelings yet. (p. 150)

Another example of powerlessness by this wife, and how her husband responded to his own childhood trauma, was given by this participant:

> When the fights were over, mama would try to make up for what had happened, but by then I had learned that she wasn't able to do anything about it. I knew I couldn't do anything about her or him or my life. . . . I married later than most primarily because I didn't want to have to count on someone and I thought marrying a man younger than I would let me be in charge. . . . I found out the hard way that my husband was even more determined to be in charge because of his own childhood hurts. The difference was that he backed up his determination with force. (p. 152)

Confusion About Rules, Roles, and Behavior

The basis for security in children is having caregivers who are reliably and predictably caring. Secure children are able to form goal-directed partnerships with their caregivers by becoming aware of their parents' intentions and either adjusting to them or amending them to meet their own needs (Ainsworth et al., 1978). From this secure base, Bowlby (1969) proposed that children form a mental template of rules for dealing with others and for expecting others to deal with them. The participants in Haslam's (2000) study described being confused about what it took to survive in life, about how to handle themselves and others, and about how to be men, women, lovers, partners, and parents. Survival, rather than success, became their priority as children. One participant described how he interpreted his lot in life by stating,

> I started studying what was going on around me and finally figured out that Daddy got his way by dictating the rules and enforcing them . . . so, I decided that when I got grown, I'd make the rules. That was a big problem in my marriage because I made the rules, but I still wasn't measuring up. Then I'd get defensive and have to beat my way into feeling right. (p. 158)

One male participant spoke of how he desperately looked for a model for a strong, respectable man and how his thinking bound him to behave within his family's rules for manhood:

> I saw other men who were respected and didn't act like my daddy. I just didn't know how to get to be their way. I thought I was doomed to be either long-suffering like the women or hard like the men. I watched and tried to figure it out on my own. I didn't know how to ask anybody for help. (p. 159)

Other comments from participants also addressed confusion over who they were and how to act to get what they needed. Examples from some of their statements are as follows:

> So, I decided if I was so good at being bad, then bad enough was what I'd do. (p. 160)

> In my marriage, I deal with the confusion every day, how to be and not to be. (p. 160)

> I had no idea of talking things through without a fight. Never saw anybody do it, and everything was worth a fight. (p. 160)

The only way we didn't fight each other was when somebody outside got involved, and then we'd fight the outsiders back to back. That's what I took family loyalty to mean. (p. 161)

I didn't know what love and respect was like between husbands and wives. Didn't know how to ask for or give what was needed and wanted. I didn't even know what to ask for or give. It was hard to change the destructive things I was doing because I didn't know what they were and was too afraid to look inside to find out. (p. 163)

Unworthiness and Shame

Bowlby (1973, 1988) pointed out when children's experiences with important caregivers are reliably caring and reassuring, children are able to trust themselves and others as worthy. However, when attachment figures are unreliable or punitive, children adjust their views of self and others accordingly. Several of the participants in Haslam's study connected feelings of unworthiness and shame as children to their being sexually abused. One indicated that "My heart always hurt when I remember my childhood, especially the shame. . . . In my marriage, I've hid the real me, the one who felt so ashamed and dirty" (p. 165). Another stated,

Any way I looked, I was the one at fault and I wore the shame. Added to that was the fact that nobody wanted to be around my family or let their kids be around us. After I married, I decided my wife had to be crazy or worthless to love somebody like me and set out to prove it to both of us. (p. 166)

Other comments that clearly reveal how individuals' shame ended up influencing their relationships with their marriage partners are as follows:

In all my love relationships and especially in my marriage, when I feel close to being hurt, I could get to be that camera, watching and waiting to be used. . . . I kept choosing people to love who would play the abuser for my camera, my life. (p. 167)

I gave up on myself real early in life. Best I can remember, it was after holding on to my daddy's pant leg, begging him not to hurt my mama and being shaken until my teeth hurt . . . when I realized mama was just as tied into the fighting as daddy, I knew that it made no difference what I said or did . . . so, I gave up on expecting anything for myself. (p. 168)

Hopelessness and Helplessness

Children who have no hope of comfort and no sense of what to expect from parents become disorganized and disoriented regarding their own attachment, and they are currently believed to suffer the most pronounced risk for mental disorders (Main & Solomon, 1990).

> I'll never forget the day Child Protective Services came out to pick me up. That time, I'd finally given up on things ever changing for me. . . . I just went wherever they took me or sent me, from foster home to relatives and back to another foster home. It didn't matter anymore. (p. 174)

> I just breathed and drank and walked and worked . . . kind of like a zombie. My wife tried so hard to get me to feel again, but I guess I'd worn out my ability to feel so long ago that I couldn't get where she wanted me to be. (p. 175)

> When he [my husband] got bored and gave up on me and started going out, I did nothing and don't quite know when the realization soaked in. . . . It wouldn't have mattered because I was staying in my hollow life. . . . When my husband brought one of his women into our home, fully expecting that I wouldn't care, I just lost it . . . throwing around words . . . the fight was pretty rough that night. In some ways, he did me a favor because he broke through my shell and there was more strength than I ever imagined.

One participant acknowledged how he gradually lost hope for both his family and himself.

> I never went back . . . and dropped out of school shortly after, started drinking hard and living hard—maybe to cut off any way to leave them [parents], maybe to prove that I was no different. I'm still not sure, but I am sure that I lost any hope I ever had of changing our lives.

Discussion of Findings

Cohn, Cowan, Cowan, and Pearson, (1992) distinguished between attachment styles and attachment behaviors. Attachment styles are based on working models that are established in childhood and persist over time; they include perceptions of self and others and preferred ways of behaving and interacting. Attachment behaviors are specific functions of working models, activated in times of perceived stress and insecurity, and are intended to restore equilibrium.

Participants in Haslam's study described themselves in childhood as unsure and doubtful of their safety, confused about what to expect, and powerless over how to modify their caregivers' behavior. As adults, their fear of being abandoned served as the driving force behind their attempts to maintain, at any costs, intimacy with and the availability of their spouses. The more they feared the potential loss of their partner, the harder they tried to gain reassurance of that partner's closeness. Lacking the skills and emotional security to express their fears, they instead exhibited their fear through violence and control. Their partners, who were experiencing their own fears of loss and also lacked the skills to express it, reacted the only way they knew—withdrawing emotionally and/or submitting. To do otherwise—to challenge the violence—might risk losing their partners. Both partners then became intertwined in circular patterns, reinforcing their own fears and worthlessness yet unable to break the pattern, thereby restoring the equilibrium.

The literature provides clinical accounts documenting that abusive men tend to be anxious and ambivalent about intimacy, possess the desire for emotional closeness while simultaneously avoiding it, and find separateness or autonomy of their spouses to be intolerable. These men fear being abandoned, possess low self-confidence, and struggle with making decisions on their own. Murphy, Meyer, and O'Leary (1994) assessed the characteristics of assaultive men and found them to be more dependent on their spouses, as indicated by a tendency to focus on that primary relationship to the exclusion of others; to be lower in self-esteem and social confidence; and to maintain a higher perceived inadequacy. Although these men were highly dissatisfied with the relationship, they possessed a strong emotional investment in it.

Bowlby described violence in attachment relationships as a maladaptive version of functional anger. Its description as dysfunctional is based on internal representations of others as unavailable and untrustworthy; however, it is not dysfunctional in that it serves an adaptive means of attaining proximity to others or withdrawing to avoid proximity. In other words, these behaviors serve a purpose in the particular system or context in which they occur. Anxiously attached adults are far more likely to perceive themselves as threatened and thus more likely to use attachment behaviors that are dependent on others—clinging, demanding, and insatiably needing reassurance and availability. Insecure adult relationships are also typified by inaccuracy in receiving, sending, interpreting, and responding to requests for reassurance. Based on the self-reports from the participants in Haslam's study, these couples were not so much reluctant to give support as they were just unsure of their partners' needs and lacked knowledge of how to respond. Although the will to love was in place, the knowledge of how to carry it out was impaired.

Murphy et al. (1994) suggested a similar pursue–withdraw pattern as that described above in a study they conducted to identify the dependency characteristics of assaultive men. They proposed that dependency needs, evolving from the batterer's emotional vulnerabilities, may contribute to an escalating cycle of coercive control regulated by changes in emotional distance. The coercive behaviors may result in short-term behavioral compliance or emotional reunion but ultimately end up with the partner increasingly withdrawing.

Pistole, Clark, and Tubbs (1995) and Rusbult and Martz (1995) present further support for conceptualizing abusive relationships by describing the interactions in terms of an investment model. They describe how satisfaction in a relationship, which refers to the extent to which one evaluates a relationship positively, and dependence, which refers to the extent that one relies on the relationship for positive outcomes and for meeting the intimacy needs of that partner, are actually related phenomena. Increases in rewards over time in a relationship result in increased satisfaction, which then results in a decrease in perceived quality of alternatives. Therefore, the level of investment in the relationship, for instance in terms of time and emotional effort, increases and the commitment to the relationship increases. The opposite can be expected to occur with a decrease in rewards. However, they suggest that this is not a linear process, and that satisfaction and dependency can be contradictory and the relationship can still remain intact. For instance, one person can be dissatisfied with the relationship but strongly committed to preserving it if the investments are high and the alternatives are limited or nonexistent. In a relationship in which one partner is anxiously attached and the attention is focused more on the costs (i.e., fear of absence of the person) than the positives, the rewards may be very low; however, the investment is high and the perceived alternatives are low, keeping the two partners involved but very dissatisfied.

CONCLUSION

Some feminist researchers dispute the appropriateness of applying a systems approach to conceptualizing couple violence. Roberts and Noller (1998) summarized some of that criticism and stated, "Central to the feminist position is the belief that the systemic approach relieves the perpetrator of responsibility for his violence, by viewing violence as a product of the family system" (p. 319). However, as they point out, in many violent relationships both partners exhibit violent behaviors, not just the male. In Haslam's (2000) study, violence was present not only in both partners in some of the relationships but also occurred in both mothers and fathers of the participants.

This evidence shifts the view of violence as a gender-specific attribute to one of a contextual response to system dynamics.

Caffery (1999) gave additional support for applying systems theory to the study of attachment; he examined six dimensions of family functioning, as identified by the McMaster Model of Family Functioning, to determine how they affect security of attachment in college-age students. His results were consistent with theoretical assumptions regarding attachment and family functioning (Byng-Hall, 1990, 1991b; Byng-Hall & Stevenson-Hinde, 1991; Donley, 1993; Marvin & Stewart, 1990; Stevenson-Hinde, 1990). Caffery found affective responsiveness to be the best predictor of attachment style in his study. The absence of emotional support and nurturance can lead family members to experience anxiety over the lack of consistent acceptance, which drives members to seek approval and acceptance from others outside.

A finding in Caffery's (1999) study that is particularly relevant to Haslam's (2000) results was the effect that role functioning within the family had on attachment security. Caffery described role functioning as the presence of established procedures for accomplishing and maintaining family tasks (Epstein, Baldwin, & Bishop, 1983), including establishing and maintaining procedures for meeting the emotional needs of family members (Epstein, Bishop, Ryan, Miller, & Keitner, 1993). Byng-Hall (1990, 1991b) explained a similar process, which he described as an interconnected network of relationships that work together to provide the emotional needs of family members: Security occurs when members know that their needs will be met by other family members. A lack of consistent and predictable procedures for carrying out and maintaining family tasks contributes to a lack of safety and security for the individual. As noted in Haslam's study, one of the key themes in the participants' responses was confusion about rules, roles, and behavior. These participants lacked the knowledge about how to handle themselves in various roles, such as lovers, partners, and parents. They reported an absence of role models from whom they could learn how to navigate through life, and they learned that survival, at any cost, was frequently the most important lesson. As children, they never experienced affective support from a consistent and reliable source, and therefore, as adults and marital partners, did not know how to provide or receive support from their spouses. Caffery's and Haslam's studies both provide empirical support for the use of family therapy in the treatment of attachment issues.

Further verifying the relatedness of attachment theory and systems theory would contribute both research value and clinical significance. Systemic-based interventions, such as the use of genograms, could provide valuable information that would address both the attachment concerns and the systemic dynamics. These two approaches together could provide an enhanced understanding of client issues that would potentially benefit both the therapist and the client.

REFERENCES

Ainsworth, M. (1985). Attachment across the lifespan. *Bulletin of the New York Academy of Medicine, 61,* 792–812.

Ainsworth, M. D. S. (1989). Attachment beyond infancy. *American Psychologist, 44,* 709–716.

Ainsworth, M. D. S., Blehar, M. C., Waters, E., & Wall, S. (1978). *Patterns of attachment: A psychological study of the Strange Situation.* Hillsdale, NJ: Erlbaum.

Bowen, M. (1985). *Family therapy in clinical practice.* Northvale, NJ: Aronson.

Bowlby, J. (1969). *Attachment and loss: Vol. 1. Attachment.* New York: Basic Books.

Bowlby, J. (1973). *Attachment and loss: Vol. 2. Separation, anxiety, and anger.* New York: Basic Books.

Bowlby, J. (1979). *The making and breaking of affectional bonds.* London: Tavistock.

Bowlby, J. (1988). *A secure base: Parent–child attachment and healthy human development.* New York: Basic Books.

Byng-Hall, J. (1990). Attachment theory and family therapy: A clinical view. *Infant Mental Health Journal, 11,* 228–236.

Byng-Hall, J. (1991a). The application of attachment theory to understanding and treatment in family therapy. In C. M. Parks, J. Stevenson-Hinde, & P. Marris (Eds.), *Attachment across the life cycle* (pp. 199–215). New York: Tavistock/ Routledge.

Byng-Hall, J. (1991b). An appreciation of John Bowlby: His significance for family therapy. *Journal of Family Therapy, 13,* 5–16.

Byng-Hall, J. (1995a). Creating a secure family base: Some implications of attachment theory for therapy. *Family Process, 34*(1), 45–58.

Byng-Hall, J. (1995b). *Rewriting family scripts: Improvisations and systems change.* New York: Guilford Press.

Byng-Hall, J., & Stevenson-Hinde, J. (1991). Attachment relationships within a family system. *Infant Mental Health Journal, 12,* 187–200.

Caffery, T. E. (1999). A study of the effects of family functioning on attachment security in college students. (Doctoral Dissertation, Texas A&M University–Commerce, 1999). *Abstracts International, 60,* 5241.

Cichetti, D., & Barnett, D. (1991). Attachment organization in maltreated preschoolers. *Development and Psychopathology, 3*(4), 397–411.

Cohn, D., Cowan, P., Cowan, C., & Pearson, J. (1992). Working models of childhood attachment and couples' relationships. *Journal of Family Issues, 13,* 432–449.

Corvo, K. (1993). *Attachment and violence in the families of origin of domestically violent men.* Unpublished manuscript.

Cowan, P., Cohn, D., Cowan, C., & Pearson, J. (1996). Parents' attachment histories and children's externalizing and internalizing behaviors: Exploring family systems models of linkage. *Journal of Consulting and Clinical Psychology, 64,* 53–63.

Crittendon, P. (1992). Children's strategies for coping with adverse home environments: An interpretation using attachment theory. *Child Abuse and Neglect, 16,* 127–140.

Crowell, J., & Waters, E. (1994). Bowlby's theory grown up: The role of attachment in adult love relations. *Psychological Inquiry, 5,* 31–34.

Donley, M. G. (1993). Attachment and the emotional unit. *Family Process, 32,* 3-20.

Dutton, D., & Painter, S. L. (1993). Emotional attachments in abusive relationships: A test of traumatic bonding theory. *Violence and Victims, 8,* 105–120.

Dutton, D., Saunders, K., Starzomski, A., & Bartholomew, K. (1994). Intimacy-anger and insecure attachment as precursors of abuse in intimate relationships. *Journal of Applied Social Psychology, 24,* 1367–1386.

Emde, R. N. (1991). The wonders of our complex enterprise: Steps enabled by attachment and the effects of relationships on relationships. *Infant Mental Health Journal, 12,* 164–173.

Epstein, N. B., Baldwin, L. M., & Bishop, D. S. (1983). The McMaster family assessment device. *Journal of Marital Therapy, 9,* 171–180.

Epstein, N. B., Bishop, D., Ryan, C., Miller, I., & Keitner, G. (1993). The McMaster model view of health family functioning. In F. Walsh (Ed.), *Normal family processes* (2nd ed., pp. 138–160). New York: Guilford Press.

Feeney, J., & Noller, P. (1990). Attachment style as a predictor of adult romantic relationships. *Journal of Personality and Social Psychology, 56,* 281–291.

Giblin, P. (1994). Attachment: A concept that connects. *The Family Journal: Counseling and Therapy for Couples and Families, 2,* 349–353.

Giles-Sims, J. (1983). *Wife-beating: A systems theory approach.* New York: Guilford Press.

Goldenberg, I., & Goldenberg, H. (1991). *Family therapy: An overview.* Pacific Grove, CA: Brooks/Cole.

Goldner, V. (1999). Morality and multiplicity: Perspectives on the treatment of violence in intimate life. *Journal of Marital and Family Therapy, 25,* 325–363.

Goldner, V., Penn, P., Sheinberg, M., & Walker, G. (1990). Love and violence: Gender paradoxes in volatile relationships. *Family Process, 29,* 343–364.

Gondolf, E. (1988). *Battered women as survivors: An alternative to treating learned helplessness.* Lexington, MA: Lexington Books.

Griffin, D., & Bartholomew, K. (1994). Models of the self and other: Fundamental dimensions underlying measures of adult attachment. *Journal of Personality and Social Psychology, 67,* 430–445.

Gullette, L. (1988). *Children in maritially violent families: A look at family dynamics, 19,* 119–131.

Haslam, C. (2000). *A phenomenological study of the childhood and spousal attachment experiences of couples who have experienced violence in their relationships.* (Doctoral Dissertation, Texas A&M University–Commerce, 2000). *Dissertation Abstracts International, 61,* 1307.

Hazan, C., & Shaver, P. (1987). Romantic love conceptualized as an attachment process. *Journal of Personality and Social Psychology, 52,* 511–524.

Hazan, C., & Shaver, P. (1994). Attachment as an organizational framework for research on close relationships. *Psychological Inquiry, 5,* 1–22.

Hazan, C., & Zeifman, D. (1994). Sex and the psychological tether. In K. Bartholomew & D. Perlman (Eds.), *Advances in personal relationships: Vol. 5.* (pp. 511–524). London: Jessica Kingsley.

Heard, D. (1982). Family systems and the attachment dynamic. *Journal of Family Therapy, 4,* 99–116.

Henning, K., Leitenberg, H., & Coffey, P. (1996). Long-term psychological and social impact of witnessing physical conflict between parents. *Journal of Interpersonal Violence, 11,* 35–51.

Holtzworth-Munroe, A., & Stuart, G. (1994). Typologies of male batterers: Three subtypes and differences among them. *Psychological Bulletin, 116,* 476–497.

Holtzworth-Munroe, A, Stuart, G., & Hutchinson, G. (1997). Violent versus nonviolent husbands: Differences in attachment patterns, dependency, and jealousy. *Journal of Family Psychology, 11,* 314–331.

Johnson, S. (1986). Bonds or bargains: Relationship paradigms and their significance for marital therapy. *Journal of Marital and Family Therapy, 12,* 256–267.

Main, M., Kaplan, N., & Cassidy, J. (1985). Security in infancy, childhood, and adulthood: A move to the level of representation. In I. Bretherton & E. Waters (Eds.), *Growing points of attachment theory and research, Monographs of the Society for Research in Child Development, 50*(1-2, Serial No. 209), 66–104.

Main, M., & Solomon, J. (1990). Procedures for identifying infants as disorganized/disoriented during the Ainsworth Strange Situation. In M. T. Greenberg, D. Cichetti, & E. M. Cummings (Eds.), *Attachment in the preschool years: Theory, research, and intervention* (pp. 121–160). Chicago: University of Chicago Press.

Marvin, R. S., & Stewart, R. B. (1990). A family systems framework for the study of attachment. In M. T. Greenberg, D. Cicchetti, & E. M. Cummings (Eds.), *Attachment in the preschool years: Theory, research and intervention* (pp. 51–86). Chicago: University of Chicago Press.

Mayseless, O. (1991). Adult attachment patterns and courtship violence. *Family Relations, 40,* 21–28.

Minuchin, P. (1985). Families and individual development: Provocations from the field of family therapy. *Child Development, 56,* 289–302.

Murphy, C., Meyer, S., & O'Leary, D. (1994). Dependency characteristics of partner assaultive men. *Journal of Abnormal Psychology, 103,* 729–735.

Pistole, M. C., Clark, E. M., & Tubbs, A. L. (1995). Love relationships: Attachment style and the investment model. *Journal of Mental Health Counseling, 17,* 199–209.

Quadrio, C., & Levy, F. (1988). Separation crises in over-attached families. *Australian and New Zealand Journal of Family Therapy, 9,* 123–130.

Roberts, N., & Noller, P. (1998). The associations between adult attachment and couple violence. In J. A. Simpson & W. S. Rholes (Eds.), *Attachment theory and close relationships* (pp. 317–350). New York: Guilford Press.

Rusbult, C., & Martz, J. (1995). Remaining in an abusive relationship: An investment model of nonvoluntary dependence. *Personality and Social Psychology Bulletin, 21,* 558–571.

Sroufe, L., & Fleeson, J. (1986). Attachment and the construction of relationships. In W. Hartup & Z. Rubin (Eds.), *Relationships and development* (pp. 51–71). Hillsdale, NJ: Erlbaum.

Stevenson-Hinde, J. (1990). Attachment within family systems: An overview. *Infant Mental Health Journal, 11*, 218–227.

Strauss, M. (1973). A general systems theory approach to a theory of violence between family members. *Social Science Information, 12*, 105–125.

Strube, M. (1988). The decision to leave an abusive relationship: Empirical evidence and theoretical issues. *Psychological Bulletin, 104*, 236–250.

Walker, L. (1984). *The battered woman syndrome.* New York: Springer.

Waters, E. (1997). *Measures of adult attachment.* Retrieved from: Attachment: Theory and Research @ Stony Brook, http://www.psy.sunysb.edu/ewaters/aairev/aai5.htm

West, M., & Sheldon-Keller, A. (1992). The assessment of dimensions relevant to adult reciprocal attachment. *Canadian Journal of Psychiatry, 37*, 600–606.

CHAPTER 9

An Approach to Treatment of Attachment Issues in the Adult and Child Subsystems Through the Use of Thematic Play Therapy in Conjunction with Couples Therapy

MICHAEL R. CARNS
ROBIN ENGLISH
LESLIE HULING
ANN CARNS

This chapter presents a description of a counseling intervention for treating families with attachment issues within two subsystems—the parent–child and the marital. A case study is presented in which a mother and her two-year-old son both presented with characteristics consistent with attachment-related concerns. Individual thematic play therapy, which is a form of play therapy currently used with young children who display symptoms of insecure attachment, was used with the male child. Conjoint couple therapy was used with the parents. In spite of the child's young age, positive results in the family system were achieved within ten sessions through these combined therapeutic approaches. To preserve anonymity, fictitious names are used in the case example.

SIMILARITIES AND DIFFERENCES BETWEEN ATTACHMENT THEORY AND FAMILY THERAPY

Until the second half of the twentieth century the opinion was widely held that the need for physical and emotional bonding was secondary to the infant drives of hunger and thirst (Sears, Maccoby, & Lewin, 1957). Harlow (1958) found convincing evidence that emotional nurturance takes precedence over other infant needs. Using this evidence as a basis, Bowlby (1969/1982) formulated his attachment theory. The foundation of the theory is that a child has an innate tendency to emotionally bond with a caregiver. The theory states that through the security of this attachment, fundamental emotional needs of the infant are met, which allows the child to develop a healthy balance between attachment (affinity) and the desire to explore the surrounding environment (individuation; Bowlby). This attachment to a caregiver and the variations of how the caregiver responds to the infant form a blueprint for future relationships that influences the capacity of an individual to form intimate relationships and to become autonomous.

The psychodynamic family theorist Murray Bowen (1978) used similar terminology, specifically differentiation and fusion, in describing family relational patterns. He described the differentiated person as one who is more flexible and self-sufficient and has a flexible balance between the needs for togetherness and those for individual autonomy. Conversely, the undifferentiated individual tends to be less flexible and overly dependent on others (Bowen).

Although the language and concepts used to discuss and define attachment issues are clearly similar to those used for family therapy, the tendency is to view attachment-related issues as an intrapsychic rather than an interpsychic phenomenon. Kaslow (1996) stated that "He (Bowlby) was clear in stating that attachment behavior is the property of an individual rather than a relationship" (p. 86). However, Kaslow makes the point that attachment behaviors are a function of multiple relationships and of multiple systems of relationships. That is, attachment behaviors evolve from relationships the individual has to family, school, and community. She also views attachment behaviors as variant, according to the type of attachment the individual has with various systems. That is, attachment behavior of an individual may vary with the system (family, school, or community) in which the individual is viewed.

In other words, whereas Bowlby (1969/1982) concentrated on the behavior of the individual when considering treatment formats, Kaslow (1996) suggested that the relational context of the individual must be assessed when considering treatment modalities. This diversity of focus may be the result of differences in philosophical approaches. Bowlby, due to his philosophy of counseling, expected that the primary relational experiences of early child-hood would form more or less a constant set of behavioral responses to intimacy and initiative over the life span. Kaslow, however, considered the developmental aspects of the individual as continuous rather than noncon-tinuous. She contended that attachment difficulties in early childhood can be, and often are, modified through relationships over time within the fam-ily system.

This chapter examines the attachment issues of the child with a focus on the developmental stage of autonomy and individuation. A closer examina-tion of these two issues in this particular case indicates a problem between the parents and the child in establishing an internalized sense of security for the child's entry and completion of the tasks in this stage of development.

CHARACTERISTICS OF ATTACHMENT ISSUES IN EARLY CHILDHOOD FROM A TRANSGENERATIONAL PERSPECTIVE

Attachment issues in children may be seen as the observable behaviors of unresolved parental attachment issues of the parents' family of origin. Based on these unresolved issues, the parent either consciously or unconsciously follows one of two courses of parenting. The parents may replicate the par-ent–child experiences from their own childhood or may attempt to avoid repeating these experiences (Byng-Hall, 1990).

Terry M. Levy (2000), in his book *Handbook of Attachment Interventions* appeared to support the need for family therapy intervention when he stated the following: "Thus, disorganized attachment is transmitted intergener-ationally; parents raised in violent, frightening, and maltreating families trans-mit their fear and unresolved losses to their children through insensitive or abusive care, depression, and lack of love and affection" (p. 11). He further stated that, "effective treatment must address the various social systems in the life of the child and family" (p. 17).

In the present case, a focus on couples' therapy seemed the most appli-cable family therapy emphasis. Levy (2000) wrote the following concerning attachment theory interventions in conjoint therapy: "Distressed couples often come to the martial therapist with tales of specific attachment injuries that have not been healed and are undermining the security of the bond between the partners" (p. 173). One partner may present with insecure at-tachment while the other may be securely attached. This situation arises when the partner with unresolved attachment issues seeks out a partner to supply his or her unfulfilled attachment needs, or, stated simply, the needy seek out the nurturers.

Levy (2000) indicated that there are two central types of dysfunctional attachment themes in couples' therapy. The first is characterized by distancing and avoidant behavior, and the other is characterized by anxious and reactive behavior. In the case presented here, the authors determined that this couple constituted an anxious attached partnership. Levy therapeutically responds to such a partnership by stating:

> Therapy with a couple containing an anxiously attached partner requires interventions, which accommodate to this way of being. The tendency of anxious partners to be reactive and interpret relationship events negatively requires the therapist to validate secondary reactive affect and help differentiate and expand this affect until primary attachment emotions can be stated coherently. (p. 181)

Thus, the authors were challenged with helping the mother in this case realize that when she intervened in her husband's attempts to discipline their son, she was reacting to her own issues with her stepfather. The goal of therapy then was to help the mother support and contribute to the structuring and discipline of their son, instead of sabotaging the efforts of the father.

CASE STUDY

The presenting problem was the behavior of Evan, a 2-year-old white male who was having severe difficulty both at home and at the day care center. The day care center reported to the parents that in response to discipline or adult directives, Evan engaged in aggressive behaviors toward adults and children. These behaviors included biting, kicking, scratching, and throwing tantrums. According to the parents, Mr. and Mrs. Martin, who were in their early 20s, Evan was a social outcast in the neighborhood because of his aggressive behaviors and had even injured children in the neighborhood. While in the waiting room, Evan was also observed displaying aggressive behavior toward his parents. Evan bit his father on the cheek on one occasion and hit both his mother and father on several occasions. He also displayed difficulty separating from his parents when it came time for the parents to go to their session and him to go to his.

Conjoint Therapy

The parents entered therapy clearly disagreeing about how to deal with their child's aggressive behavior. Mrs. Martin, who was in her first trimester of pregnancy with a second child, was quite verbal and had strong beliefs about wanting to be patient and tolerant with Evan and trying to avoid conflicts with him. Mr. Martin was much more reserved and, although he did not agree with this approach, yielded to Mrs. Martin's strong opinions.

Mrs. Martin described herself as being highly knowledgeable about child development because of training she had received in conjunction with a part-time job as a childcare provider. In addition, she reported having a "keen interest" in the subject, along with "reading about it all of the time." She clearly conveyed to all present that she had much more expertise in these matters than her husband. From the therapist's perspective, it appeared that Mrs. Martin was in the habit of wielding her expertise much like a club and that she used it frequently against her husband.

Mrs. Martin acknowledged Evan's behavior problems but saw herself as "standing between" Evan and those who would discipline him inappropriately due to their lack of knowledge of appropriate child development, including Mr. Martin and teachers at Evan's school. She reluctantly acknowledged that his behavior was outside acceptable norms, but was also reluctant to allow any type of intervention for Evan because of his young age. She seemed to have little concept of any type of parental structuring that might occur between the ends of the continuum of total tolerance on one end and physical punishment on the other end. At this point, the therapist made the decision to further explore the origins of these parenting views.

A family history was collected on both Mr. and Mrs. Martin's families of origin to help identify how their specific parenting values originated. A genogram (Bowen, 1978) was conducted with both Mr. and Mrs. Martin. Mrs. Martin revealed that she lived alone with her mother until the age of five, at which time her mother remarried. Until this point, Mrs. Martin had slept with her mother. According to Mrs. Martin, her mother's new husband demanded that Mrs. Martin sleep in her own bedroom. Mrs. Martin related this story with great anger and obvious unresolved resentment concerning the intrusion of this new husband between her and her mother. In our opinion as the therapists, this story and Mrs. Martin's anger at her stepfather were consistent with preoccupied attachment style and suggested evidence of an intergenerational conflict (Bowen). It appeared that prior to her remarriage, Mrs. Martin's mother may have been overly permissive (possibly as a result of her own unresolved attachment difficulties). When the stepfather entered the picture and was overly harsh, Mrs. Martin's mother was unable or unwilling to mediate in favor of a more mutually acceptable solution. We hypothesized that this dynamic was not an isolated event but rather a pattern of interaction within the family. Furthermore, the dynamic contributed to Mrs. Martin's view that good parents are permissive and bad parents are harsh and that good mothers should, in fact, protect their children from the harsh interactions of others. Her own childhood experiences were shaping her polarized views of parenting as being a choice between extreme permissiveness and extreme harshness, without a middle ground.

Mr. Martin's history reflected a pattern of female domination in his life. He was the youngest of three children: He had two older sisters who, according to Mr. Martin, "bossed and babied me." Mrs. Martin seemed to be particularly intrigued by the notion of her husband's family of origin having an impact on his parenting of Evan. It was the first time she acknowledged how her husband's experiences prepared him for parenting. This awareness initiated a discussion between Mr. and Mrs. Martin concerning their discrepant views on discipline and structure with Evan. At one point, Mr. Martin indicated that Evan slept with him and his wife, and he acknowledged that there might be a connection between this and his wife's childhood experiences. The mother's insistence that Evan sleep in the couple's bed was seen by the therapists as a projection of her own unresolved attachment issues from childhood. This information and observation seemed to further affirm that Mrs. Martin's difficulties were due to insecure attachment issues.

In the continuing work with Evan's parents, it became clear that there were underlying marital difficulties. In a family systems theory analysis, Mrs. Martin's overfunctioning was "balanced" by Mr. Martin's underfunctioning. From this viewpoint, Evan was likely expressing the couple's unexpressed anger and hostility through his aggressive play activity. In the therapists' opinion, Mrs. Martin, through her parenting behavior, was acting out her childhood attachment issues. Therefore, the goals for treating the attachment concerns of the couple included helping both Mr. and Mrs. Martin understand the significance of the events of her childhood and how those events contributed to the presenting concern. Through this understanding we hoped to help Mr. Martin gain a more sympathetic view of the significance of his wife's parenting skills, while helping Mrs. Martin gain insight into the purposes of her parenting behaviors and the extent to which these behaviors hindered the goals of therapy.

To prevent placing Mrs. Martin in the role of identified patient, in addition to helping Mr. Martin see his part in the problem maintenance, an exploration of Mr. Martin's family-of-origin issues were important. Mr. Martin became aware of the domination by females in his family-of-origin, which led to his compliance and lack of assertiveness within the marital relationship. To insure that Mr. Martin could express his suppressed negative feelings and attitudes toward his wife without threatening Mrs. Martin's attachment concerns, we suggested that these issues be brought to therapy and not discussed outside of therapy. Therapy then began to focus on the couple's communication process.

This part of the therapy process began with the couple sharing concerns and feelings about the marital relationship and about parenting. One partner was coached to reflect what he or she heard from the partner, and the first partner was then given the opportunity to clarify any miscommunications. After several rounds of this, the roles were switched so that the other partner had the opportunity to express concerns and feelings. This process allowed each partner to better understand the position and views of the other and also to hear what the other partner appreciated about the marriage and the contribution each was making.

As the communication skills improved between the couple, we introduced parenting skills from the Early Childhood S.T.E.P. program (Dinkmeyer, McKay, & Dinkmeyer, 1989). One of the major interventions used with the parents was involving Evan in decision making regarding decisions that affected him by giving him choices between alternatives that were acceptable to the parents. One example was giving Evan the choice of walking on his own to the playroom or being carried to the playroom. Another example was giving him a choice of playing in the tub without excessive splashing or ending the bath. A second skill that was introduced was explaining to Evan in advance what could be expected. For example, he was told "we have five more minutes to play and then we are going to put on our shoes and leave" as opposed to a long, drawn-out departure in which Mrs. Martin tried to obtain Evan's agreement before leaving.

Thematic Play Therapy

In the initial session, the play therapist interacted with Evan and developed an understanding of his typical problem-solving patterns, responses to stress, common frustrations, and usual responses to adult limit setting. Evan required many behavioral limits in the playroom, and the therapist's limit-setting statements were met with defiance, such as Evan yelling "No," continuing the behavior, and crying for his parents. Evan demonstrated a variety of aggressive behaviors, such as biting his father's cheek, throwing sand and toys, biting toys, pulling puppets' ears and tails, ripping loose wallpaper off the walls, as well as running out of the playroom.

In subsequent play therapy sessions, Evan became increasingly difficult, as he refused to separate from his parents, especially his mother, whose pregnancy was becoming increasingly obvious. He experienced heightened anxiety when his parents brought him to the playroom and frequently cried and had tantrums for up to an hour. It became apparent that traditional reflective play therapy techniques that promote catharsis of suppressed anger only allowed Evan to continue repetition of this maladaptive play. Our estimation was that Evan's increasingly out-of-control behavior stemmed from lack of structure in the playroom. To provide more structure, and therefore more safety, we decided to focus future therapy sessions on involving

Evan in sandtray therapy. According to Homeyer and Sweeney (1998), sandtray provides boundaries, limits, and safety for the child.

Patterns of behaviors indicating aggressive attachment issues were evident in Evan's escalating aggressive play toward dolls and figures in the sandbox over several play therapy sessions. In conjunction with these increasing aggressive themes, there was an increase in helpless and hopeless behavior. For example, more powerful figures in the sandbox repeatedly overpowered the less powerful "baby" character.

Meanwhile, the play therapist noticed several general themes in Evan's play. These themes included safety, anger, nurturance, and constancy. The treatment team was concerned because these play themes are frequently present in children who are subsequently diagnosed with attachment disorder. Evan spent much of each session burying and retrieving figures in the sandbox that he identified as "Mommy, Daddy, and Baby." Themes in play therapy may offer insight into the child's unresolved issues. These issues often hamper a child's ability to establish a secure attachment with an adult figure. In addition, as a result of these issues, the child fails to perceive the self as worthy (Benedict & Mongoven, 1997).

Evan compulsively and repeatedly acted out scenes in which the baby was being injured by the adult figures. In the sandbox, Evan frequently toppled over cups of sand that he indicated was "food for the baby lion." Using figures of a cub lion and adult lions, he hit the cub using the parent lion figures. This play indicated a theme of failed nurturance.

The play therapist also observed Evan's need for constancy. Evan would exhibit considerable anxiety when entering the playroom if he discovered that toys were missing or were in a different location from the previous play session. If the therapist did not supply this constancy, Evan would make repeated reference to the omission or moved object with escalating anxiety.

The therapist also noticed that regardless of his emotional state, Evan often looked at the clock on the wall of the room. She decided to design a ritual involving the clock to structure the session and help provide Evan with a sense of safety and security in the playroom. Upon entering the room, the therapist actively encouraged Evan to climb on a chair to look at the clock while she showed him the time his parents would return. As Evan climbed up, the therapist stood right behind him providing physical safety. She reinforced this protection with the statement: "Everyone has to be safe in the playroom." The play therapist asked Evan's parents to bring a picture of their family for Evan to place by the clock at the beginning of each session. This photograph began to be a transitional object to help Evan reduce his separation anxiety. Placing his picture and talking about where the hands on the clock would be when his parents returned became a source of security for Evan. The therapist felt that Evan was beginning to develop a secure base when he purposefully wobbled the chair to get the therapist to steady him.

Concurrently, the therapist became active in attempting to alter Evan's experiences of failed nurturance. For example, the therapist began stating, "Good mommies don't hurt their babies" whenever Evan prevented the baby figures in the sandbox from receiving food. To reinforce the concept of nurturance, the therapist brought in other toys, such as the ambulance car or medical kit and doctored the baby with Band-Aids, shots, and medicines to "make the baby well again." Evan began to model this play by putting two Band-Aids on his face at the beginning of every play session and two Band-Aids in the same place on the therapist's face. He also asked for some Band-Aids to keep in his pockets and take home. These actions were a first step toward nurturance and away from destructive play and were the first time that he attempted to repair rather than destroy.

Another significant technique in reducing Evan's separation anxiety was the use of a book entitled *Will You Come Back for Me?* (Tompert, 1992). This book explores a preschool child's anxiety over whether her mother will return for her after school. Evan would occasionally sit with the therapist while they looked at the pictures together and read portions of the book. Over time, Evan asked for the book rather than throwing a tantrum when he became anxious about the separation from his mother. As the therapist and Evan discussed the story and its pictures, Evan visibly calmed down and his anxiety lessened. He was able to remain in the playroom for the entire session from that point on.

Evan's play became less mechanical and ritualized. He began to have a spontaneous quality that the therapist had not seen before. The therapist began to see Evan playing with more age-appropriate games like hide-and-seek, and he began to laugh and smile occasionally.

Termination

Evan's parents were reporting that his behavior had improved significantly and that they were working more as a team in parenting. They were understandably apprehensive about the impending arrival of the new baby and their ability to cope with the demands of two children. They voiced commitment to combine the most adaptive values of both of their families of origin using the guidelines and insights they had gained in counseling.

By this time, Evan eagerly entered the playroom and wanted to stay longer than the allotted time. Termination began about a month before Evan's last session. Play therapy termination activities were structured according to Benedict and Mongovan's (1997) thematic play therapy suggestions. To ensure that Evan did not equate termination with the negative experiences of social isolation, which was a factor in his family, the therapist began focusing on the various positive experiences in play therapy. Evan was given permission to discuss his feelings, and the therapist shared her own feelings of loss as she modeled appropriate emotional expression.

Each week, the therapist assisted Evan in drawing an "X" through boxes on a sheet of paper to indicate how many more times they would be together in the playroom. Evan practiced drawing "X's" on the white erase board and then angrily erased them, indicating clearly that he was unhappy that the number of sessions remaining was few. The next to the last session, Evan bit the therapist with the rubber alligator, something he had never done before, to express his anger about leaving. He immediately "fixed" the therapist with Band-Aids and shots and told her, "You'll be OK now." This indicated a reversal in his ability to nurture rather than simply be the recipient of nurturance. During the last session, Evan's therapist told him a story about their special times together in the playroom, and his final departure from the playroom was without anxiety or apprehension.

CONCLUSION

The success of this case is due in large part to the therapeutic focuses that occurred from investigating attachment theory. The therapy team was able to construct interventions with each subsystem of the family, using interventions suggested in attachment theory literature, which were highly successful. Using thematic play therapy techniques with Evan and family of origin and behavioral contracting with the parents enhanced both the individual therapy of Evan and the couples work of his parents.

The success of these techniques is especially intriguing when considering both the young age of the child and the brief time frame of one semester in which these changes occurred. The parents presented themselves for therapy with great reticence. This posture is not unusual, because parents often are reluctant to examine parenting styles in which they are ego involved. The success of the thematic play therapy techniques provided encouragement for the parents to examine their own parenting styles and their own family-of-origin issues contributing to their parenting styles. The success of the couple's therapy with the parents resulted in more consistent and adaptive parenting, which further enhanced Evan's security and, thus, his emotional growth in the play therapy process.

There were no intergenerational sessions with the family. However, as the parents observed the successes occurring in play therapy and modeled what they observed occurring between therapist and child in the waiting room, they were encouraged to attempt at home the parenting strategies suggested in conjoint therapy.

We believe that significant factors in improving Evan's hostile attitude and behavior were the mother's decreased negative intensity toward both her husband and Evan, and the husband's more assertive attitude with his wife and his son. This change apparently resulted from the parents' improved communication with each other and their understanding, awareness, and acceptance of the underlying family-of-origin issues concerning the attachment concerns of Evan's mother with her own mother and the learned passivity of Evan's father.

We encourage other clinicians serving children with similar presenting concerns to consider using a comparative prescriptive therapy format of play therapy techniques in conjunction with separate parent therapy. Our hope is that this strategy can be helpful in treating the myriad problems brought to therapy that stem from attachment issues.

REFERENCES

Benedict, H. & Mongoven, L. (1997). In H. Kaduson, & D. Angelosi (Eds.), *The playing cure: Individualized play therapy for specific childhood problems*. Northvale, NJ: Jason Aronson.

Bowen, M. (1978). *Family therapy in clinical practice*. Northvale, NJ: Jason Aronson.

Bowlby, J. (1969/1982). *Attachment and loss: Vol 1. Attachment*. New York: Basic Books.

Byng-Hall, J. (1990). The effects of relationships on relationships. In World Association for Infant Psychiatry and Allied Disciplines (Eds.), *Special issue in memory of John Bowlby: Based on papers presented at the regional meeting of the World Association of Infant Psychiatry and Allied Disciplines* (pp. 148–268). Brandon, VT: Clinical Psychology.

Dinkmeyer, D., McKay, G., & Dinkmeyer, J. (1989). *Early childhood STEP*. Circle Pines, MN: American Guidance Service.

Harlow, H. F. (1958). The nature of love. *American Psychologist, 13,* 673.

Homeyer, L., & Sweeney D. (1998). *Sandtray: A practical manual*. Canyon Lake, TX: Lindan Press.

Kaslow, F. (1996). *Handbook of relational diagnosis and dysfuctional family patterns*. New York: John Wiley & Sons.

Levy, T. (2000). *Handbook of attachment interventions*. San Diego, CA: Academic Press.

Sears, R., Maccoby, E., & Lewin, H. (1957). *Patterns of child rearing*. Evanston, IL: Row, Peterson.

Tompert, A. (1992). *Will you come back for me?* Morton Grove, IL: Albert Whitman.

CHAPTER 10

Integrative Systemic Approaches to Attachment-Related Trauma[1]

SYLVIA A. MAROTTA

In the last two decades, a considerable body of literature has accumulated on attachment and family systems theories. This literature includes conceptual, empirical, and applied formulations on how human beings, individually and in their families, develop the social bonds that sustain human life. Throughout history, human beings have had to adapt to tragic life experiences that have taxed coping mechanisms even for highly adaptable human beings (Van der Kolk & McFarlane, 1996). Paralleling the time frame when attachment and family systems theorists were coalescing their understandings, traumatology was developing as a field of study following the inclusion of traumatic stress disorders as a diagnostic category in 1980. I attempt in this chapter to bring the three fields of study together, as a way of catalyzing the next 20 years of research and practice. This chapter has three purposes. The first is to propose an integrated model for understanding how individuals and their families build attachment bonds. The second is to develop the model by using case study material to conceptualize three family systems in which attachments have been affected by a particular type of traumatic experience, that of childhood sexual abuse (CSA). The third purpose is to provide five strategies for implementing the model with individuals with a history of CSA, with the goal of building resilient attachments.

---

1. I thank Seth Gillihan for his considerable skill at computer-generated images and for the time he took to transform my pencil drawing of the model to a finished figure.

TOWARD AN INTEGRATIVE THEORY

Development in context is a theoretical model described by Bronfenbrenner (1979) in which the developing human being adapts to, and in turn is shaped by, four levels of embedded environmental systems, beginning at a dyadic or micro level and progressing up to the macro level of social policy, cultural values, and social norms. In between, the mesosystem level relates two or more microsystems to each other, and the exosystem level includes systems that may affect the person indirectly, such as employment settings with over-time policies that restrict parental hours at home. This exosystemic influence, though indirect, may have consequences to the developing person in terms of limiting adequate access to parental caregivers. Bronfenbrenner and Ceci (1994) developed the model further by proposing mechanisms called proximal processes, which may mediate the interface between person and environment. Skill development, knowledge acquisition, and strategizing are examples of these processes, which must be bidirectional and must develop over a period of time. Neither the person nor the environment is passive in this model: Circular causality applies as persons influence their environment and the environment exerts pressure to shape the individual's life trajectory. By describing the family as an environmental system, the dynamic nature of the interactions between individuals and environments might be made more explicit.

To integrate the development-in-context model with attachment theory, I propose borrowing an image from the most basic biology of the organism, the double helix structure of human DNA. This proposed configuration addresses concerns that the development in context model lacks—dynamic linkages between and among system levels (Kasambira & Edwards, 2000; Moen, 1996). Figure 10.1 shows the components of the posited model. People and environments exist in contexts that include time, settings, and geographical locations; developmental processes are context specific. Both attachment and individuation may be separate developmental pathways (Franz & White, 1985) between an adapting person and a dynamic environment consisting of multiple system levels, one of which is the family. Family systems represent micro-level components of the environmental side of the model. The importance of family systems was implicit in Freud's (1949) theoretical emphasis on early family experiences as shaping development and later in Bowlby's (1988) and Ainsworth's (1989) exploration of caregiving behaviors that influence early and late interpersonal attachments. By now, an impressive body of evidence describing the role of family systems in fostering or impeding attachments in individuals has accumulated (Alexander, 1992; Byng-Hall, 1999; Cowan, Cohn, Cowan, & Pearson, 1996; Lopez, Melendez, & Rice, 2000). The development-in-context model requires at-

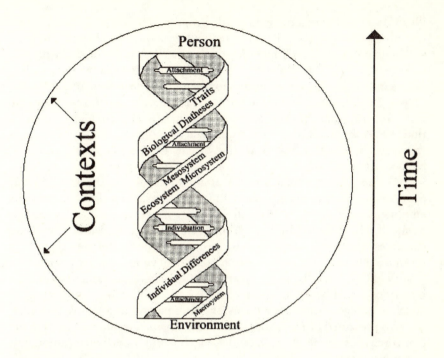

FIGURE 10.1. Development in context: A proposed model for integrating attachment and systems theories.

tention to the environmental side of the equation as a dynamic, lifelong influence on the developing person. Previous emphasis in the literature on the personological side of the model may reflect the difficulty of operationalizing environmental components as elements for research, a difficulty I will be develop further below.

With environment as a focus, inclusion of trauma into this conceptual framework of person–environment interactions linked by attachment processes follows naturally. Attachment-related consequences of traumatic exposures have been well described in the literature (e.g., Courtois, 1988; Gusman et al., 1996; Herman, 1992; Marotta & Asner, 1997) and include failures of trust and disruptions in intimacy across the lifespan. These attachment-related consequences can have positive valences as well, being associated with increased autonomy, a drive for social status, and high achievement needs (Elliott, 1994; Marotta & Asner, 1997). Traumatic stressors that have interpersonal etiologies, such as those associated with abusing or deficit environments, are ubiquitous (Emery & Laumann-Billings, 1998), which provides an unfortunate justification for including these as illustrations of the components of the proposed model. Indeed, it appears that physical neglect occurs more frequently than either physical abuse or sexual abuse, with developmental sequelae that are only recently beginning to be understood. Finally, the presence of an environmental stressor is a necessary if not sufficient condition for diagnosing posttraumatic stress disorders (PTSD), a diagnostic category that is the only one in the *Diagnostic and Statistical Manual of Mental Disorders* (American Psychological Association, 1994) that requires an environmental analysis over and above the intrapsychic characteristics of an individual. In this diagnostic category, biological, psychological, and environmental systems converge.

The specific traumatic stressor of childhood sexual abuse (CSA) will provide the content to be discussed in the sections that follow. Its choice as an illustrative example is warranted because it occurs across all socioeconomic levels, racial and ethnic groups, and geographical locations. Case examples used to illustrate the components of the model are composites taken from both clinical and research samples of young adult women with a history of CSA from diverse racial and ethnic backgrounds and whose abuse history occurred between ages 6 and 10. I adapted family classification of attachment status from a synthesis of child, parent, and family relational patterns presented by Byng-Hall (1999). Family socioeconomic status in the case material is middle class, and individual functioning is high on autonomy, initiative, and achievement.

ATTACHMENT PROCESSES IN AN ADAPTIVE FAMILY SYSTEM

Consider an 8-year-old girl, sexually abused by a neighboring adolescent boy more than 5 years older. The child reports the abuse, the report is taken seriously, and further abuse is prevented. At the mesosystem level, the settings of home, school, and neighborhood communicate effectively, and protective mechanisms are put in place to prevent further abuse. At the macrosystem level, families in this community value intellectual achievement. The school environment is a rich one and includes counseling services in sufficient quantity and quality to promote processing of the traumatic experience. Protective measures at home include enrolling the child in educationally enriching activities that remove her from family, neighborhood, and school as often as possible. The child excels and receives recognition for the additional educational opportunities. Extrapolating from Bowlby's (1988) framework of the secure base, the family system in this scenario promotes healthy development by encouraging open communication of dysfunctional experiences, both inside and outside the home. Parenting style may be authoritative, with clear boundaries, flexible rules, and avenues for repair when rules are breached. Note that from the development-in-context perspective, adults and children alike are actively developing, and perfection is neither expected nor required. Mistakes will be made, but they become vehicles for learning rather than for shaming. Proximal processes, such as strategizing to manage problems, promote effective information processing, and the traumatic experience is accommodated into family schemata. Such a family environment may help explain the proportion of adults with a history of CSA who do not go on to develop symptoms (Grand & Alpert, 1993), though that is a hypothesis that has not been tested. The individual's attachment style may be autonomous–secure, even in the presence of the traumatic experience of CSA.

Less benign consequences to an individual can ensue in that same family system, even as it remains adaptively secure. For example, an unintended consequence of protective removal of a child following reported abuse may be that the child interprets her ongoing isolation as indicative of a self that is so different that she must be isolated from the rest of her family. The more she excels in activities that remove her from family and neighborhood, the less likely she is to have time available to discuss the trauma with her family. Family members may misconstrue the distance-induced silence as healing and be reluctant to open a subject that appears to be resolved. In this scenario, although the base remains secure, shared meaning-making is precluded, and the traumatic material may manifest itself in adulthood as an impaired self-reference. From an information processing perspective, the system maintains its homeostasis, but the traumatic material is disconnected from the family's narrative. In this scenario, the individual's experience of CSA may result in a preoccupied attachment style.

ATTACHMENT PROCESSES
IN A DISENGAGED FAMILY SYSTEM

In a disengaged family system, high anxiety predominates and avoidance becomes the chief coping mechanism. An adult woman, sexually abused by a sibling, comes from an Irish family of origin that traveled extensively for a worldwide employer. This exosystemic influence prevents acquisition of close attachments outside the family. Given the number of moves this family experienced, long-term attachments are implicitly discouraged and family privacy is encouraged. The incest is never reported within the family, and the four siblings are described as distant from each other and from the parental subsystem. The incestuous experience impedes both protective and affectionate family functioning, and the entire microsystem becomes anxious. The family is a matriarchy, the father being emotionally unavailable and preoccupied with work. The parental subsystem is fragile as a consequence. Mesosystems are only minimally linked, reflecting the ethnic family value of keeping family business within its walls. At the macro level, the family's having been exposed to ideologies and social policies in many countries reinforces the closing off of the family system to social norms that may be perceived as contradictory. This family's parenting style is authoritarian, with rules that take precedence over people, and open communication is infrequent. Proximal processes cannot be bidirectional in this system, interfering with both personal and systemic information processing. Trauma cannot be metabolized. When the woman is 13, the family settles in the United States. Faced with the need to acculturate once again, the teenager's developmentally congruent wish to fit in is complicated by the secrecy of abuse and the lack of a secure cultural base, and avoidance mechanisms solidify. An avoidant attachment style in the individual is a possible outcome of traumatic experiences within this disengaged system.

ATTACHMENT PROCESSES IN A CHAOTIC FAMILY SYSTEM

A chaotic family system is characterized by conflict between the parental subsystem, between older and younger siblings, and between the parental and child subsystems. Emotional expressiveness in the form of angry confrontations is normative but unpredictable. Divorce is a frequent topic of conversation, though this family's religious practice precludes its actualization. The perpetrator of the sexual abuse in this case is a paternal uncle who remained in contact with the family until his death. The client revealed the abuse in her teenage years during the course of an angry encounter with her mother over the daughter's sexual acting out. The report was greeted with angry disbelief, followed by resentful acceptance of one more family problem with which the family must cope. Parenting style is mostly laissez-faire, characterized by inconsistent and ineffective attempts to enforce family norms. Role reversal in the form of parentification of children and blurred boundaries are the proximal processes. The family's religiosity promotes mesosystem ties with extended family and with a faith community. At the macrosystem level, however, social norms are perceived to be contrary to the family's religious ideology. The outcome of this family's chaos may be a disorganized individual attachment style.

ASSESSMENT AND MEASUREMENT ISSUES

Up to this point, I've held constant the adult developmental level, socioeconomic status, gender of the developing person, and the age at onset of the traumatic stressor of childhood sexual abuse. I've done this for clarity, knowing that there is a risk of oversimplifying the multiple realities that converge at biological, social, and environmental levels when one assesses the full context in which a developing person or a developing system interacts. If the development-in-context model is ever to be empirically validated, those multiple realities must be taken into consideration in operationalizing research designs and in measuring processes and outcomes (see Cowan et al., 1996, for a correlational model that combines individual and systemic levels of analysis in adults to predict children's school outcomes). Equally important, assessment of presenting concerns in a clinical setting requires gathering information about system levels and their contexts in addition to individual dynamics. This type of assessment process goes beyond the more typical psychosocial history obtained in many settings and will be discussed further in the next section. To contribute to the complexity, families are unlikely to experience only one traumatic event. Recent research indicates that people are likely to experience many events that have the potential to be traumatic (Goodman, Corcoran, Turner, Yuan, & Green, 1998; Norris, 1992), with predictable consequences to family life.

Because the family is the primary unit of societies in collectivist cultures, and individuals are the primary unit in other cultures, families with different cultural identifications are likely to differ in their developmental processes as well. On the individual level of analysis, the transitions of adult life, whether these be traumatic or not, are accompanied by many developmental turning points (Graber & Brooks-Gunn, 1996) that influence life's progression even as they call for reinterpreting previous family narratives. When families are dealing with traumatic experiences of individual family members, their ability to metabolize the trauma as a family is impaired, as it is impaired on an individual level. Proximal processes for problem solving and resource building are taxed, and dysfunctional patterns become ingrained. This is the pattern noted above for the disengaged family. Rubin (1998) notes that any discussion of developmental pathways must incorporate multiple levels of analysis and that within-level factors (e.g., intrapersonal, intrarelational, etc.) may differentially affect measurement and outcomes.

Another potential oversimplification is that individuation, if it is indeed a parallel developmental strand to attachment (Franz & White, 1985; Gilligan, 1982), may interact with attachment in reciprocal ways that influence developmental outcomes. Note that high achievement and autonomy as developed by the individuals in the above scenarios are typically associated with individuation. To the extent that they contribute to healthy functioning, they build resources for the traumatized person, which may generalize to their attachments once traumatic material begins to be metabolized. This phenomenon may be the malleability of attachment style that has been reported as a result of new experiences, psychotherapy, or environmental changes (Diehl, Elnick, Bourbeau, & Labouvie-Vief, 1998).

PROMOTING RESILIENCE IN FAMILY SYSTEMS

Borrowing from Lewin's (1951) theories of person and environment fit, and his corollary that there is nothing so useful as a good theory, this section will describe definitions and strategies for assessing trauma, promoting trauma metabolism, and improving functional attachments from the development-in-context model. To keep the discussion at one level of analysis, let us assume that an individual with a history of CSA is the focus of our assessment and intervention, though the model can be applied to work with individuals, couples, or family groups. A second assumption is that the portion of treatment that is devoted to processing traumatic material follows a sequenced model (see Brown, Scheflin, & Hammond, 1998, for a comprehensive review of sequenced models of trauma therapy), beginning with safety and stabilization, titrating the processing of traumatic material, and integrating past material into current conditions.

Definitions

Assessment of the Environment

Assessment is required throughout the treatment period, whether the therapeutic approach focuses on short-term problems or long-term psychodynamic issues. In addition to the individual assessments that are usually conducted, assessment of the environment requires that data be gathered on potential environmental deficits, on lack of information within the environment, or on potential conflicts within the environment (Hurst & McKinley, 1988). An individual's lack of social support system is an environmental deficit as well as a personological one. Assessment of the deficit may entail eliciting geographical locations of potential and current social supports. Communities in which much of the population is older or in which there are many young families would exert pressure on a young adult with a need to develop attachments in his or her personal life. If an environment does not adequately publish its mental health delivery services, the environment lacks information. Such an environment would not facilitate an individual obtaining access to care. At the microsystem level, parents that provide sex education on a need-to-know basis could be considered as environmental systems that are lacking in information. A person with a history of CSA may not have had access to normal sexual education in such an environment.

Conflicts within the environment can include social promotion of alcohol or illegal drug use coupled with a denial of the effects of such substances on family systems and attachments. Similarly, widespread sexual imagery and public discourse about sex, in the absence of similar levels of discourse within families, is an environmental conflict. The potential for a mismatch between the person and her or his environment must also be assessed. As an example of mismatch, if a person presents with a family history of intergenerational sexual abuse and is working in a child advocacy system, there is a potential for continued reexperiencing of traumatic material. Assessment and intervention in the case of a mismatch might require incorporating career development issues as part of trauma treatment, either directly within the therapy context or by referral to qualified counselors adjunctively. If the microsystem history is that others in the family have worked in child advocacy systems, the clinical picture is very different from one where the person "fell into" her current job. Assessment of the environmental side of the helical model can itself be an intervention, because the individual begins to see the problem as potentially bigger than that which is "within the skin."

Trauma Metabolism

This term refers to information processing in which one examines material from past experiences that is disturbing or that impedes function in such a way that new meanings are created for use in the future. Because both person and environment are evolving, meaning making can take place whenever a life transition requires it. This definition of working through material in therapy implies managing material dynamically rather than resolving issues in a global, fixed manner. "Putting it all behind one" is not a goal of promoting healthy attachments between persons and their family systems. Incorporating the traumatic experience into family meaning systems is. When an individual has metabolized experiences contextually, a sense of safety is restored and the traumatic material is incorporated into personal schemata. The developing person owns the problem (I *have* a history of CSA) versus the problem owning the developing person (I *am* a survivor of CSA). Similar to a surgical scar or bony callus formation following a fracture, once healing

is attained through adequate processing, the traumatic material is incorporated as one of many other historically acquired experiences.

Improving Functional Attachments

In this model the term means making explicit the links between the person
and her or his environment such that available resources are acknowledged
and new resources can be developed. These links are bidirectional and require the passage of time.

Strategies for Building Resilence

Strategy 1. Widening the Lens

Clients often come in for treatment when their perspective has progressively
narrowed to the point that they can no longer see options for dealing with
their pain. Neither the family nor the broader social environment may be in
their frame of reference, except as sources of negative information.
Intergenerational genograms, with trauma and attachment variables defined
by the client, can provide a broader lens from which to view their families of
origin and their families of choice. These assessments also yield information
that can be used in treatment planning.

In the case of the preoccupied individual from an adaptive family system, the lens from which she views her environment is that of a damaged
self. The strengths that may be apparent to others are blocked from what has
become a tunnel of accumulated differences. The very adaptability of her
family may serve to reinforce her perceptions of a damaged self. Drawing
from macrosystemic assessment data, the therapist can explore with the client the social mores about sexual abuse that were likely to have existed at
the time when the abuse took place. Clearly, social constructions of CSA
and its reporting in the 1960s would provide a different perspective than
CSA reported in the 1990s. This addition of environmental cohort effects
diffuses the personal responsibility that the client may be taking as she realizes the contribution that a deficit social environment might have made to
her current dilemma.

For the avoidant individual from a disengaged family system, widening
the lens may involve exploring how Irish ethnic identifications, transplanted
many times in family moves, may have provided fertile ground for stifling
emotions and for suffering alone (McGoldrick, 1996). Further explorations
of personal values she would like to incorporate into her ethnic identifications may help to strengthen her attachments to family of origin and to
family of choice. Note that these explorations are as valuable for white fami-

lies as they are for families of color, particularly if we define ethnic identification as the basic human need to belong.

For the disorganized individual from a chaotic family system, the lens
will widen in very small increments, as a result of painstaking exploration
of how the person developed each defense in a family environment that was
basically uninhabitable for a child (parentification, blurring of boundaries,
and uncontrolled raw emotion). This process is joined with exploration of
how each defense served as a protection that now may be impeding personal
growth in an adult with adult-level resources. The therapeutic exploration
can include various family members, as the client is able to reconstruct her
perceptions of possible defenses she noted in others.

A thorough assessment of spirituality and religious practice with the
goal of reinforcing the individual's frame of reference as a member of a community will also require small incremental changes over time. Generally
speaking, the strategy here is to differentiate the intrinsic nature of spirituality in the developing person from institutional religion itself. Once that
differentiation has been accomplished, a shift toward determining to what
extent the religious practice is life-giving versus life-inhibiting occurs. Religious practices that may appear to be inhibiting on the surface may be productive of comfort and peace to the individual. They may also reinforce the
sense of belonging to a tradition that has evolved over many generations of
the family. Therapists from religious groups different from those of the client, or therapists who are areligious, will have to determine whether their
perceptions of inhibiting religious practices are stereotypical expectations
based on cross-cultural misconstruals. To widen the lens here, the therapist
need not know about many religious practices, but rather should invite the
conversation about religion and spirituality and its potential role in promoting trauma metabolism and improved family attachments.

Strategy 2. Normalizing the Disequilibrium of a Developing Ecology

This strategy can be applied to all three of the family systems in the case
material, because its purpose is to promote bonding through acknowledging similarities with other families. Borrowing again from biology, when the
human organism is faced with a stressor (Flach, 1989), its homeostatic set
point is disrupted and physiological distress follows until a new set point is
integrated. Applied to environments, this strategy predicts that as the system develops, its homeostatic balance *must* be disrupted for change to be
assimilated. Using systemic reframes, the therapist applies the individual
stress response as a metaphor for change in the family system. Clients usually experience relief when they realize that their particular family was in
crisis because it was changing and not because it was uniquely dysfunc-

tional. Thus, the family that was required to move every two years needed to rely on itself while it acculturated; the high conflict family did the best it could, given the many ways it was changing. Temporary chaos as a response to change is a normal.

Strategy 3. Generalizing Available Resources to Other Domains

In each of the three scenarios, the individuals achieved recognition and acceptance in educational and occupational roles. This success may have been at the cost of a growing internal chasm between how they experienced themselves and how the world saw them, however. Much psychological energy is expended in managing this incongruence with available resources. Sometimes the disparity between experiencing recognition for achievements during a day at work and a lonely, isolated, or fearful evening at home makes for an intolerable dualistic existence. Although on the surface professional achievements may appear to have little role to play in fostering healthy attachments, the resources that high achievers use to solidify their professional selves may be applicable in the personal social domain. To generalize these skills or characteristics from one domain to the other, clients must first acknowledge that they have them. For example, initiative is a characteristic that is valued in the workplace. It provides purpose and direction for the individual and furthers the mission of the organization of which he or she is a part. In traditional therapeutic frameworks, we explore triggers to dysfunctional behaviors. In this model, we also explore triggers to functional behaviors like taking initiative, in order to develop a context for applying each particular characteristic in the personal relationship sphere. What kinds of social environments might trigger initiative? What would it look like to take initiative in each environment? What would it look like to be successful in initiating a social relationship? Depending on the degree of traumatic interruptions in attachment, a hierarchy of progressively more safe social environments is generated for the person to practice generalizing the resources heretofore used most successfully only in professional roles. Once the person develops some mastery, the process creates a feedback loop that inspires motivation and restores psychological energy for building a social network. Although intimate adult attachments may not be an outcome of this therapeutic process, renewed energy and a wider social support network may be a sufficient outcome.

Strategy 4. Using Psychoeducation as a Bridge Between Individuals and Their Families of Origin

Experts from a variety of disciplines recently published their recommendations of practices for therapists who treat clients with posttraumatic stress disorders (Foa, Davidson, & Frances, 1999; Foa, Keane, & Friedman, 2000). These professionals recommended psychoeducational strategies as useful adjuncts to other types of treatment modalities. Although our focus here is not limited to posttraumatic stress disorder, the usefulness of psycho- education in helping clients generate systemic hypotheses to help them heal their relationships applies to these families. For example, where there is family chaos similar to the one described in the third scenario, information about the changing face of marriage may help to stabilize the individual's perception of parental dysfunction. Marriage contracts today have different meanings from contracts of 20 years ago, and radically different meanings from 50 and 100 years ago. Romantic attachments that lead to individual fulfillment are relative newcomers compared to marriages as religious obli- gation or marriages as civic responsibility. Such information can diffuse an individual's perceived inability to engage in intimate relationships because of poor role models. Adults who married 50 years ago cannot be compared to those who are marrying today. Social cohort effects provide interesting information for clients to assimilate in their meaning making, with a poten- tial by-product being hope that change for them is possible and that some form of relational bonding may ensue. Similarly, information about social cohort effects in religious practice, in sex education, and in immigration patterns can be effective in building bridges between clients and their rela- tional subsystems. Additionally, skills training can help clients replace mal- adaptive coping methods developed in disorganized families of origin. Although psychoeducation is not sufficient as a treatment modality by it- self, it can help to stabilize the foundation for deeper psychotherapeutic processing.

Strategy 5. Managing Anxiety

Functional anxiety is hardwired into individuals and environments as a safety mechanism and as a source of energy. When family systems become chroni- cally anxious, they subvert natural evolutionary adaptive processes (Fried- man, 1999) and promote regressive behaviors. Individuals, families, and societies can become mired in ineffective communication loops that impede social bonding and instead create an "us and them" mentality. Ironically, the more efficient media communications in U.S. society become, the more likely it becomes for emotional contagion to create barriers between individuals and family systems.

Child sexual abuse is one of those traumatic experiences that evokes primitive responses because it is both sexual and it involves children. In the face of such a climate, clients and their therapists must be able to contain their anxiety and channel it toward appropriate boundary formation. Trauma metabolism requires a safe holding environment. When material to be processed includes painful psychic, somatic, or spiritual factors, therapists must be able to juggle empathy with limit setting; anxiety is a natural consequence. Strategies for self-care for both clients and therapists must be intentionally structured into everyday life to prevent secondary traumatization. As developing human beings in dynamic environments, clients and their therapists are continually building resiliency.

CONCLUSION

The development-in-context model presented in this chapter may be a parsimonious way of conceptualizing the multiple complexities associated with integrating attachment and family systems theories. Its application to traumatic life experiences that disrupt attachments may provide a basis for generating hypotheses that can be tested in research and clinical settings. Perhaps the next 20 years will see an emphasis on developing resilient attachments by focusing on social contexts that are less likely to traumatize than those we have lived in up to this point.

REFERENCES

Ainsworth, M. D. S. (1989). Attachments beyond infancy. *American Psychologist, 44,* 709–716.

Alexander, P. C. (1992). Application of attachment theory to the study of sexual abuse. *Journal of Consulting and Clinical Psychology, 60,* 185–195.

American Psychiatric Association. (1994). *Diagnostic and statistical manual of mental disorders* (4th ed.). Washington, DC: Author.

Bowlby, J. (1988). *A secure base: Parent-child attachment and healthy human development.* New York: Basic Books.

Bronfenbrenner, U. (1979). *The ecology of human development: Experiments by nature and design.* Cambridge, MA: Harvard University Press.

Bronfenbrenner, U., & Ceci, S. J. (1994). Nature–nurture reconceptualized in developmental perspective: A bioecological model. *Psychological Review, 101,* 568–586.

Brown, D., Scheflin, A. W., & Hammond, D. C. (1998). *Memory, trauma, treatment, and the law.* New York: W. W. Norton.

Byng-Hall, J. (1999). Family and couple therapy. In J. Cassidy & P. Shaver (Eds.), *Handbook of attachment: Theory, research, and clinical applications.* New York: Guilford Press.

Courtois, C. A. (1988). *Healing the incest wound: Adult survivors in therapy.* New York: W. W. Norton.

Cowan, P. A., Cohn, D. A., Cowan, C. P., & Pearson, J. L. (1996). Parents' attachment histories and children's externalizing and internalizing behaviors: Exploring family systems models of linkage. *Journal of Consulting and Clinical Psychology, 64,* 53–63.

Diehl, M., Elnick, A. B., Bourbeau, L. S., & Labouvie-Vief, G. (1998). Adult attachment styles: Their relations to family context and personality. *Journal of Personality & Social Psychology, 74,* 1656–1669.

Elliott, D. M. (1994). Impaired object relations in professional women molested as children. *Psychotherapy 31,* 79–86.

Emery, R. E., & Laumann-Billings, L. (1998). An overview of the nature, causes, and consequences of abusive family relationships. *American Psychologist, 53,* 121–135.

Flach, F. (1989). *Stress and its management.* New York: W. W. Norton.

Foa, E. B., Davidson, J. R.T., & Frances, A. (1999). Expert consensus guideline series: Treatment of post-traumatic stress disorder. *The Journal of Clinical Psychiatry, 60,* 1–31.

Foa, E. B., Keane, T. M., & Friedman, M. J. (Eds.). (2000). *Effective treatments for PTSD.* New York: Guilford Press.

Franz, C. E. & White, K. M. (1985). Individuation and attachment in personality development: Extending Erikson's theory. *Journal of Personality, 53,* 224–255.

Freud, S. (1949). *An outline of psycho-analysis.* New York: W. W. Norton.

Friedman, E. H. (1999). *A failure of nerve: Leadership in the age of the quick fix.* Bethesda, MD: The Edwin Friedman Estate.

Gilligan, C. (1982). *In a different voice.* Cambridge, MA: Harvard University Press.

Goodman, L. A., Corcoran, C., Turner, K., Yuan, N., & Green, B. L. (1998). Assessing traumatic event exposure: General issues and preliminary findings for the stressful life events screening questionnaire. *Journal of Traumatic Stress, 11,* 521–542.

Graber, J. A., & Brooks-Gunn, J. (1996). Transitions and turning points: Navigating the passage from childhood through adolescence. *Developmental Psychology, 32,* 768–776.

Grand, S., & Alpert, J. L. (1993). The core trauma of incest: An object relations view. *Professional Psychology: Research and Practice, 24,* 330–334.

Gusman, F. D., Stewart, J., Young, B. H., Riney, S. J., Abueg, F. R., & Blake, D. D. (1996). A multicultural developmental approach for treating trauma. In A. J. Marsella, M. J. Friedman, E. T. Gerrity, & R. M. Scurfield (Eds.), *Ethnocultural aspects of posttraumatic stress disorder: Issues, research, and clinical applications.* Washington, DC: American Psychological Association.

Herman, J. L. (1992). *Trauma and recovery.* New York: Basic Books.

Hurst, J. C., & McKinley, D. L. (1988). An ecological diagnostic classification plan. *Journal of Counseling & Development, 66,* 228–232.

Kasambira, K. P., & Edwards, L. (2000). Counseling and human ecology: A conceptual framework for counselor educators. *Proceedings of the 8th International Counseling Conference, San Jose, Costa Rica,* 43–52.

Lewin, K. (1951). *Field theory in social science.* New York: Harper & Row.

Lopez, F. G., Melendez, M. C., & Rice, K. G. (2000). Parental divorce, parent-child bonds, and adult attachment orientations among college students: A comparison of three racial/ethnic groups. *Journal of Counseling Psychology, 47,* 177–186.

Marotta, S. A., & Asner, K. K. (1997). *Developmental tasks of a multicultural group of female incest survivors.* Paper presented at the American Counseling Association Annual Meeting, Orlando, FL.

McGoldrick, M. (1996). Irish families. In M. McGoldrick, J. Giordano, J. K. Pearce (Eds.), *Ethnicity and family therapy* (2nd ed.). New York: Guilford Press.

Moen, P. (1996). A life course perspective on retirement, gender, and well-being. *Journal of Occupational Health Psychology, 1,* 131–144.

Norris, F. H. (1992). Epidemiology of trauma: Frequency and impact of different potentially traumatic events on different demographic groups. *Journal of Consulting and Clinical Psychology, 60,* 409–418.

Rubin, K. H. (1998). Social and emotional development from a cultural perspective. *Developmental Psychology, 34,* 611–615.

Van der Kolk, B. A., & McFarlane, A. C. (1996). The black hole of trauma. In B. A. Van der Kolk, A. C. McFarlane, & L. Weisaeth (Eds.), *Traumatic stress: The effects of overwhelming experience on mind, body, and society.* New York: Guilford Press.

CHAPTER 11

Attachment Theory and Family Systems Theory as Frameworks for Understanding the Intergenerational Transmission of Family Violence

PAMELA C. ALEXANDER
STEPHANIE WARNER

Children who have been abused themselves or who have witnessed marital violence are at increased risk for abusing either their own children or their partners (Dutton, 1999; Egeland, Jacobvitz, & Sroufe, 1988; Hunter & Kilstrom, 1979; Oliver, 1993). Nevertheless, not all, or even the majority of, children who are abused become abusive themselves (Kaufman & Zigler, 1987). In fact, only one third of adults abused as children become abusive themselves, one third exhibit no subsequent aggressive behavior, and another one third are at increased risk for aggression given enough stress (Oliver). Given that childhood abuse thus increases the risk for subsequent aggression but by no means guarantees it, effective family violence prevention and treatment efforts require identifying those mechanisms that either potentiate the effects of family violence or that protect abused children from becoming abusive themselves.

Social learning theory is the most commonly cited perspective for explaining the intergenerational transmission of abuse; however, it is limited in many ways. For example, although modeling is used to explain how parental punishment leads to aggressiveness, it does not explain why so many abused children do *not* become abusive themselves. Furthermore, social learning theory does not explain the lack of specificity of behaviors seen in the cycle of violence. Oliver (1993) noted that "strong alternating intergenerational sequences" of abuse are the rule rather than the exception. For example, the experience of sexual abuse in one generation might lead to depression in the child (but not necessarily sexual abuse), which might lead to violence in the grandchild (but not necessarily sexual abuse). Similarly, neglectful parenting might lead to self-injurious behavior, which might lead to baby battering (but not necessarily neglect).

Therefore, given the limitations of social learning theory in explaining the intergenerational abuse cycle, it is important to entertain another perspective. In this chapter we propose that the intergenerational transmission of family violence can best be explained by the combination of attachment theory and family systems theory. Attachment theory, as a paradigm of family influence, provides the explanation for how the original parent–child relationship can lead to an "internal working model" and can provide the basis for the child's strategies for regulating affect (Bowlby, 1969/1982). Family systems theory posits that certain patterns of behavior (such as boundary intrusion, coercive control, triangulation, low cohesiveness, and parental unavailability) presumably learned in the family of origin may inadvertently be reproduced in the family of creation (Alexander, 1990). Attachment researchers have tended to focus on the parent–child dyad, whereas family systems researchers have tended to generalize about abusive families. Ideally, these two perspectives should be able to complement each other in any model of the intergenerational transmission of violence.

Following a brief overview of attachment theory, we will argue that the following mechanisms are relevant to understanding and predicting intergenerational transmission. First, attachment theory is a cognitive theory about the development of mental models of intimate relationships. Thus, a parent's internal working models (IWMs) of relationships developed from his or her own experience of family violence may directly increase the likelihood for engaging in aggressive behavior toward the child. These mental models may also influence the choice of a partner (i.e., assortative mating). The tendency of abused individuals to become involved in a violent relationship can thus also be a mechanism for the intergenerational transmission of violence. Conversely, a relationship with a supportive and securely attached partner can interrupt this cycle of violence. Thus, IWMs and the current family context have important reciprocal effects.

Second, attachment theory is also a theory of affect regulation. Thus, the experience of family violence and insecure attachment relationships may lead to deficiencies in self-soothing (e.g., depression), inadequate control of one's emotions in stressful situations (e.g., anger and impulsivity) and an excessive reliance on alcohol and drugs, all of which have been shown to increase the risk for abusive behavior toward others. Finally, one particular type of insecure attachment (disorganized attachment) not only is prevalent among abused children and among the children of traumatized adults (Ainsworth & Eichberg, 1991; Carlson, Cicchetti, Barnett, & Braunwald, 1989), but, through the mechanisms of role reversal, dissociation, and shame, may greatly increase the child's potential to engage in abusive behavior toward others.

Although most attachment research focuses on the parent–child dyad to explain these mechanisms, Bowlby emphasized that the attachment dyad could only be properly understood within the context of the family (Marvin & Stewart, 1990). Therefore, in the following review we will attempt to highlight the importance of considering this family context when inferring the effects of insecure attachment on the cycle of violence. Finally, after describing how each of the mechanisms proposed above can explain the transmission of violence from one generation to the next (or to the generation after that), we will explore the clinical implications of this research for the development of effective prevention and treatment interventions.

OVERVIEW OF ATTACHMENT THEORY

According to attachment theory, there is a biologically based bond between the child and the caregiver that assures the protection and survival of the child (Bowlby, 1969/1982, 1977). As a result of the child's experience with the primary caregiver, the child develops an internal working model of self as either deserving and worthy of attention or as undeserving. Relatedly, others are seen as either trustworthy and responsive or as untrustworthy, unresponsive, and rejecting. Moreover, when a child finds that his or her clear communication of negative affect to a caregiver is effective in eliciting a response, he or she will develop a secure "primary" strategy (Main, 1990). Conversely, when a child finds that this primary strategy of communicating negative affect leads to further rejection or conflict, he or she instead learns to either inhibit or exaggerate negative affects (Izard & Kobak, 1991). The internalization of whatever strategy the child thus develops "governs how incoming interpersonal information is attended to and perceived, determines which affects are experienced, selects the memories that are evoked, and mediates behavior with others in important relationship" (Zeanah & Zeanah, 1989, p. 182). Therefore, the IWM also represents a strategy of affect regulation that can impact intrapsychic processes, subsequent interpersonal interactions, and even the ability to reflect upon and alter behavior patterns that were learned in the past.

Through the use of the Strange Situation paradigm, a series of separations and reunions between the child and the caregiver (Ainsworth, Blehar, Waters, & Wall, 1978), Mary Ainsworth delineated the particular strategies developed by children to deal with the anxiety surrounding issues of attachment. She found that toddlers display one of the following: (a) *secure* behavior (i.e., seeking reunion with the parent upon her return and using the parent as a secure base to then explore the environment) associated with a history of responsive and nurturing parenting; (b) *avoidant* behavior (actively snubbing the parent upon her return) associated with a history of rejection by the parent; (c) *anxious–ambivalent* (clingy, angry, tense) behavior associated with a history of inconsistency by the parent; or (d) *disorganized* behavior (characterized by contradictory approach–avoidant behavior, dazed expressions, and apprehension on the parent's return) that was associated with frightened or frightening behavior by the parent, with the parent's history of unresolved trauma or loss, or with the parents' experience of relationship violence (Berman & Ogawa, 1993; Main & Cassidy, 1988; Main & Hesse, 1990; Main & Solomon, 1986, 1990).

Attachments in adulthood, although differing in some ways from those in childhood, still represent the need of adults under conditions of stress to seek proximity with the primary figure as a way of seeking comfort and security (Weiss, 1991). For example, secure adults (comparable to secure children) are coherent about their past, have access to both positive and negative emotions, and are self-confident, trusting, and comfortable with closeness (Collins & Read, 1990; Feeney & Noller, 1990; Hazan & Shaver, 1987; Main & Goldwyn, 1984). Dismissing adults (comparable to avoidant children) tend to idealize their past, have little access to specific memories, minimize the significance of early attachment relationships, and describe little overt distress while covertly exhibiting hostility, loneliness, and anxiety (Bartholomew & Horowitz, 1991; Kobak & Sceery, 1988; Main & Goldwyn, 1984; Mikulincer, Florian, & Tolmacz, 1990). Preoccupied adults (comparable to anxious–ambivalent children) tend to be confused, anxious, clinging, dependent, and jealous (Collins & Read, 1990; Hazan & Shaver; Kobak & Sceery). Finally, unresolved–fearful adults (comparable to disorganized children) tend to be socially inhibited and unassertive, lack a sense of personal agency, and are more likely to exhibit self-defeating and borderline tendencies (Alexander et al., 1998; Anderson & Alexander, 1996; Bartholomew & Horowitz, 1991).

THE INTERNAL WORKING MODELS OF TRAUMATIZED INDIVIDUALS

Alexander (1992) put forth the argument that abuse is not abuse is not abuse. In other words, even a particular type of child abuse (such as sexual abuse) of even a particular level of severity by even a particular family member is not necessarily experienced similarly by different children in either the same or different families. Instead, the attachment relationship preceding and following the abuse provides a better basis for predicting the child's experience. Thus, as noted by Zeanah and Zeanah (1989), abuse may be experienced as rejection, as inconsistency, or as trauma, depending upon the nature of the attachment relationship.

For example, abuse associated with rejection may occur to the extent that parents regard their children and partner coldly as property and subject to their needs. As a consequence, the avoidant children grown up (i.e., dismissing adults) deal with the experience of rejection by denying their own experience of abuse as well as the impact of their abuse on others. The distortion of memories and idealization of parents observed so frequently in dismissing adults (Main & Goldwyn, 1984) interferes with their ability to reflect on their own experience as children, to actually hear their children's distress and to consciously choose a different course of parenting behavior. Such a history of rejection also makes it difficult for nonabusing but dismissing parents to even see the need to intervene to prevent their partner from abusing their child, because they are well rehearsed in the process of failing to recognize negative affect.

Alternatively, abuse may be experienced by the anxious–ambivalent child as the parent's impulsive lashing out against the clingy, tense, demanding child followed by the parent's compensatory attentiveness and indulgence of the child (Crittenden, 1992). As a result of this pattern of attachment, the anxious–ambivalent child grown up (i.e., the preoccupied adult) develops a coy or coercive strategy of manipulative interaction with others, heightening negative affect as necessary to meet his or her overwhelming needs for reassurance. Needless to say, such adults are frequently at risk for marital violence as their jealousy and excessive dependency interfere with their ability to trust their partner (Green & Werner, 1996). However, they are also at risk for abusing their own children: Their own inconsistency with their child reinforces the child's manipulative or out-of-control behavior, thus eliciting the parent's frustrated impulsive response (Oldershaw, Walters, & Hall, 1986).

Finally, the disorganized child may experience abuse as chaos, fear, and trauma. The effects of this pattern of attachment will be described further in a following section because it is so prevalent in families with violence. The description of the disorganized child's IWMs was put forth most clearly by Liotti (1992), who speculated that the child of the parent with unresolved trauma triggers attachment-related anxieties in the parent. As a consequence, the parent looks to the child to help the parent control his or her anxiety, thus engaging in an emotionally dependent role-reversing interaction with the child. When the child necessarily fails to control the parent's anxiety, the parent may react with anger and abusive behavior or may react with inexplicable fear of the child or of some unseen threat. Attachment theory suggests that a child who is frightened (in this case, by the frightening or frightened behavior of the parent; Main & Hesse, 1990) will necessarily seek the attachment figure. However, what is a child to do when the attachment figure is, by definition, both the solution to the problem and the source of the problem (Main & Solomon, 1990). The child's response to this unsolvable paradox is to develop multiple incompatible models of the self and others (Liotti, 1992), seeing the self as unlovable and abandoned, as the rescuer of the parent, and as the source of fear of the parent—in other words, as all-powerful and as all-powerless. As a result of this confusing and contradictory set of IWMs, the disorganized child grown up (i.e., the unresolved adult) will exhibit approach–avoidant behavior toward his or her own emotions and memories (thus interfering with the resolution of past trauma) and toward significant others. This approach–avoidant behavior obviously may preclude the establishment of supportive relationships with other adults (Alexander & Anderson, 1994) and may result in increased risk for relationship violence (Lyons-Ruth & Jacobvitz, 1999). However, it may also lead to an excessive overdependence on one's child, thus perpetuating the cycle of abuse.

For any of the patterns of insecure attachment described above, IWMs may play a role in the selection of intimate partners—that is, in assortative mating. In one of the best illustrations of this process, Crittenden, Partridge, and Claussen (1991) found that meshed relationships (consisting of a preoccupied individual and a dismissing individual) were significantly more likely to result in marital violence and/or abuse of the children. No research has as yet been conducted on the assortative mating of unresolved individuals; however, their probable history of maltreatment suggests that the outcome may be even more problematic. Research has been conducted on the assortative mating of individuals with a history of family violence. Women with a history of abuse are at increased risk for marrying an abusive partner (Follette, Polusny, Bechtle, & Naugle, 1996), and men with a history of abuse or exposure to marital violence are more likely to be abusive to their partner (Dutton, 1999). Given the overlap between marital violence and child abuse (Appel & Holden, 1998), the effects are clear. A batterer is at increased risk for abusing his child, a battered woman is at increased risk for abusing her child, and the witnessing of marital violence by a child who may not even be abused him or herself has a significant impact on that child's internal working models of intimate relationships. Therefore, assortative mating by individuals abused in childhood is another mechanism for the intergenerational transmission of violence.

Although the selection of a partner can continue or even exacerbate the negative effects of an abuse history on one's family of creation, one's current marital relationship can also greatly reduce the negative effect of one's attachment on one's parenting. For example, one characteristic that has been found to differentiate women with a history of physical abuse who were *not* abusive to their own children from women with a history of abuse who *were* abusive was a supportive relationship with a spouse (Egeland et al., 1988). In other words, a currently secure attachment relationship may serve to overcome a presumably insecure attachment from childhood. Cohn, Cowan, Cowan, and Pearson (1992) similarly found that mothers with either a secure or insecure attachment were warmer and more structured in their interactions with their children depending on whether their spouse was securely attached. Moreover, Alexander, Teti, and Anderson (2000) found that only those sexually abused women who were dissatisfied with their current marital relationship exhibited emotional overdependence on their children (such as that described by Liotti). Therefore, although IWMs affect both the choice of one's partner and the interaction with one's family of creation, these cognitive models are also modified by one's partner and one's family of creation. Attachment theory and family systems theory are thus most valid when considered in conjunction.

AFFECT REGULATION IN TRAUMATIZED INDIVIDUALS

Given that early attachment relationships determine how strong emotions are processed and whether they are accessible in memory, the mechanism of affect regulation becomes an important mediator between abuse history and subsequent abusive behavior. As mentioned previously, dismissing adults have difficulty remembering their own experiences, thus hindering their ability to empathize with their child or partner. Furthermore, their lack of tolerance of negative affect in others interferes with their ability to deal with the frustrations inevitably encountered in parenting and in marriage.

Difficulty in self-soothing characterizes all insecure adults and may manifest in many forms, ranging from depression to anxiety to posttraumatic stress disorder (Crittenden, 1997). This poor affect regulation is a probable mediator in the intergenerational transmission of violence. For example, Alexander and Kretz (2001) interviewed a large sample of new mothers receiving home visitation services upon the birth of their child. When other kinds of childhood trauma (physical abuse, verbal abuse, neglect, witnessed marital violence, parental alcoholism) were controlled, sexual abuse history emerged as a unique predictor of child abuse potential, family conflict, and marital dissatisfaction (i.e., attachment-related concerns). However, this relationship was mediated by depression and parental stress. Other researchers have found substance abuse to be a common method for self-soothing among abuse survivors (Dhaliwal, Gauzas, Antonowicz, & Ross,

1996; Simmons, Sack, & Miller, 1996) and to also be an important predictor of family violence (Brown, Werk, Caplan, & Seraganian, 1999; English, Marshall, & Orme, 1999). Therefore, ineffective and even self-destructive mechanisms of affect regulation associated with different patterns of insecure attachment may mediate the transmission of violence.

DISORGANIZED ATTACHMENT AND THE INTERGENERATIONAL TRANSMISSION OF VIOLENCE

As described previously, Liotti (1992) has demonstrated how disorganized attachment can lead to parent–child role reversal and to multiple incompatible internal working models in the child. The connections among abuse, disorganized attachment, parent–child role reversal, dissociation, shame, and subsequent aggressiveness in the child suggest that this attachment dynamic is an important mechanism in the intergenerational transmission of violence.

Researchers and clinicians have noted the link between trauma (particularly sexual abuse) in the parent, disorganized attachment in the child (Ainsworth & Eichberg, 1991), and role reversal in their relationship (Alexander et al., 2000). For example, Sroufe, Jacobvitz, Mangelsdorf, DeAngelo, and Ward (1985) described a seductive role-reversing relationship between sexually abused mothers and their sons. Burkett (1991) similarly observed a pattern of role-reversal between incestuously abused women and their children. Cole and Woolger (1989) found that incest survivors were more likely to promote child-rearing attitudes of extreme autonomy in their children (including, for example, an item from the Parental Attitude Research Instrument [Schaefer & Bell, 1958] that states "The earlier a child is weaned from its emotional ties to its parents the better it will handle its problems"). Moreover, this autonomy promotion was more likely to occur when the woman described her own mother as negatively controlling or uninvolved. Finally, Cole, Woolger, Power, and Smith (1992) noted the importance of the current family context in that the parenting problems of incest survivors (as compared to adult children of alcoholics and a nonrisk control) were mediated both by their ability to regulate affect and by their relationship with their partners. Therefore, research on trauma and on disorganized attachment suggests that both are predictive of parent–child role reversal.

The connection between parent–child role reversal and dissociation in the child was demonstrated by Alexander and O'Grady (2001), who developed a reliable retrospective self-report measure of parent–child role reversal. Not only was parent–child role reversal predictive of elevated scores on a measure of dissociation and of unresolved attachment, but it was itself predicted by a variety of family dynamics. Namely, role reversal with one's mother was predicted by the parents' marital problems, physical abuse by mother (for daughters), mother's mental illness (for sons), and cross-generational alliances. Role reversal with one's father was predicted by physical abuse by mother (for daughters), absence of biological mother (for sons), and cross-generational alliance with father (for daughters). Therefore, parent-child role reversal is related to trauma and dissociation and is also affected by the broader family context.

Disorganized attachment and Liotti's multiple incompatible models have also been related to dissociative behavior. The behavior of the disorganized child in the Strange Situation (marked by dazed, disoriented expressions or by rapid shifts from an approach to an avoidant state) is phenotypically similar to a dissociative state. Liotti (1992) notes that some form of dissociative behavior can be observed even in the nonabused disorganized child of a traumatized parent (thus providing a possible bridge of the trauma from the first to the third generation even in the absence of abuse in the second generation). For example, in a longitudinal follow-up of Egeland's high-risk poverty sample, Ogawa, Sroufe, Weinfield, Carlson, and Egeland (1997) found that those children who had been classified as disorganized when toddlers were significantly more likely to exhibit elevated dissociation scores at age 19, even after controlling for intervening abuse.

When the child of the traumatized parent is also abused by the parent, however, the risk for a more severe dissociative disorder greatly increases. Anderson and Alexander (1996) interviewed 112 adult female incest survivors and found that those eight individuals who had been independently diagnosed with a dissociative disorder were not only significantly likely to have been abused more severely and at an earlier age, but were also more likely to describe themselves as closer to their perpetrator. That is, they were more likely to view their perpetrator as their primary attachment figure (i.e., disorganized attachment's "source of the problem and the source of the solution"; Main & Solomon, 1990). This finding can best be understood when the whole family context is considered. These women described chaotic, terrorizing households characterized by mutual marital violence (suggesting pervasive and extreme affect dysregulation) and were more likely to report having been physically abused, rejected, and/or neglected by their mother (the nonsexually abusive parent). It is, of course, not clear whether the abuse and neglect by the mother left the daughter with no alternative than to become attached to her abusive father or whether the father successfully orchestrated the estrangement between mother and daughter. In either case, the dynamic of disorganized attachment becomes much clearer within the frame of the larger family system.

Trauma and disorganized attachment have been associated not only with parent–child role reversal and with dissociation, but also with the concept of a bad self and an extreme sense of shame (Main & Hesse, 1992). Evidence for this connection comes from a study conducted by Loos (1999) in which college students who scored at a clinically elevated level on a measure of dissociation were compared with controls on a Stroop color-naming task and on a self-representation task. Subjects did not differ in processing either general anxiety-related words or neutral words in the Stroop task. However, dissociative individuals were significantly slower than controls in processing attachment-related words. Moreover, although dissociative individuals provided no more negative self-referential adjectives than did controls, they were more likely to characterize those negative descriptors as central to their sense of self. Finally, the degree of difficulty they exhibited in processing attachment-related words was directly predictive of their perception of the negative descriptors as core to their personality. Thus, although this study did not include a measure of disorganized attachment per se, it did demonstrate significant relationships between dissociation, attachment-related anxiety, and shame.

The next and essential part of the proof that disorganized attachment is an important mechanism in the intergenerational transmission of violence comes from evidence that disorganized attachment, parent–child role reversal, dissociation, and shame are all implicated in the development of aggressive behavior. First, longitudinal research demonstrates that disorganized attachment in toddlers is strongly predictive ($r = .55$) of controlling role-reversing behaviors directed toward parents in both middle-class and high-risk 6-year-old children (van Ijzendoorn, Schuengel, & Bakermans-Kranenburg, 1999). Disorganized attachment in toddlers predicts hostile behavior among preschoolers, externalizing behaviors by young girls, and disruptive behavior in boys (Holtzworth-Munroe, Stuart, & Hutchinson, 1997; Lyons-Ruth, 1996). Moreover, unresolved attachment (the adult counterpart of disorganized attachment) has been demonstrated to predominate among samples of male batterers (Dutton, 1999; Holtzworth-Munroe et al., 1997).

Second, parent–child role reversal has long been observed among abusive families (Macfie et al., 1999). The controlling role-reversing behavior observed in disorganized children (Main & Cassidy, 1988) has its counterpart in the boundary intrusive behavior observed in couples characterized by possessiveness, jealousy, and increased risk for domestic violence (Goodman & Fallon, 1995; Green & Werner, 1996).

Third, researchers and clinicians have begun to speculate on a link between dissociation and the disinhibition of aggression in males. For example, Putnam et al. (1996) have argued that, whereas dissociative females tend to internalize their aggression, as seen in suicide attempts and self-mutilation, dissociative males may tend instead to externalize their aggression. This suggestion was supported indirectly by Dutton, Fehr, and McEwen (1982), who noted that some batterers report an inability to recall the assaultive behavior, a tendency to black out during the incident, and altered states of consciousness, symptoms all characteristic of dissociation. Landsman (1999) found that 30% of a sample of male batterers exhibited clinically elevated levels of dissociation. In another sample of domestic violence offenders, Simoneti, Scott, and Murphy (2000) found that childhood trauma predicted dissociative symptoms, self-reported and interview-based assessments of dissociation were correlated with violence-specific dissociation, and both general dissociation and violence-specific dissociation were correlated with the frequency and severity of the violent behavior. Although more research is required to fully test the notion that dissociation leads to aggression, the demonstrated relationships between dissociation and other conditions known to predict aggressiveness (i.e., abuse history, disorganized attachment, role reversal, and shame) suggest that dissociation may be as much a disinhibitor of externally aggressive behavior as it is of internally aggressive behavior (e.g., self-mutilation; Putnam et al., 1996). It will be important for future research to assess whether dissociation also predicts abusive behavior toward children.

Finally, the concept of shame has been implicated in family violence. Recollections of public, random, or global punishment by parents significantly predicted self-reported anger, abusive behavior, and other personality variables associated with abusive behavior (Dutton, van Ginkel, & Starzomski, 1995). Other writers have noted the importance of men's experience of shaming as children as a determinant of their abuse of their wives (Browne, Saunders, & Staecker, 1997; Jennings & Murphy, 2000). Shame was also found to be a significant predictor of revictimization among sexual abuse survivors (Kessler & Bieschke, 1999).

In conclusion, abuse by parents and the dynamics of disorganized attachment may provide the impetus for aggressive behavior; role reversal may provide the child with early training in the mechanics and efficacy of controlling, coercive behavior; shame may allow the initial negative evaluation by the family of origin to be reenacted and reexperienced in the family of creation; and dissociation may impede the inhibition of aggressive behavior.

CLINICAL IMPLICATIONS FOR THE PREVENTION AND TREATMENT OF FAMILY VIOLENCE

Although a review of possible mechanisms of the intergenerational transmission of violence can make this cycle seem inevitable from one generation to the next, this research also suggests possible points of intervention. First, a supportive spouse can significantly modify the negative effects of a trauma history on parenting (Alexander et al., 2000; Cohn et al., 1992; Cole et al., 1992; Egeland et al., 1988). Although the individual's choice of a supportive partner is obviously outside the control of the clinician, it is possible for clinicians to enlist the involvement and facilitate the support of partners when working with survivors of childhood trauma (Kirschner, Kirschner, & Rappaport, 1993). It is also essential for clinicians to explore the parenting practice of trauma survivors in therapy. All too often, clinicians focus their attention on childhood abuse without either soliciting the involvement of the family of creation or monitoring the impact of the abuse history on the family of creation.

A second implication from attachment theory and family systems theory is that the development of a coherent narrative about one's past can have an important ameliorative effect on one's current behavior. Hunter and Kilstrom (1979) found that mothers with an abuse history who "repeated" this abuse on their own children were different from "nonrepeating" mothers with an abuse history in part by their inability to recognize and acknowledge their own history of abuse. Similarly, Egeland et al. (1988) found that an important factor preventing the cycle of violence (in addition to the effect of a supportive spouse) was the woman's coherent narrative, including both details and emotions, about her childhood experiences. A coherent narrative is the quintessential characteristic of secure attachment (Main, 1991), and thus, its impact on interrupting the cycle of abuse is clear. For many trauma survivors, the help of an individual therapist will be essential to provide the client with a secure base while he or she is slowly retrieving memories and making sense of his or her experience (Alexander & Anderson, 1994). However, following initial improvement, the use of a narrative therapy approach with the couple (cf., Freedman & Combs, 2000) may be especially useful in clarifying for the partner the basis for the trauma survivor's sometimes confusing and seemingly inexplicable behavior. Such an approach also provides the abused individual with an intimate witness and audience for his or her story. Given that both partners may have experienced violence in their families of origin, an approach such as that used by Virginia Goldner (1998) may be particularly helpful in deconstructing the impact of child abuse on both the current marital relationship and the parent–child relationships. The goal, of course, is the cocreation of a new template or internal working model of family relationships.

CONCLUSION

Attachment theory and family systems theory are logical complementary models in explaining the transmission of behaviors from one generation to the next. As such, they offer a comprehensive window into the inter-generational transmission of abuse. In this chapter, we have argued that at least three mechanisms are relevant to understanding this cycle of violence. First, IWMs influence interactions with the family of creation as well as the choice of a partner. Secondly, affect regulation associated with the primary attachment relationship determines one's propensity to engage in abusive behavior. Finally, disorganized attachment associated with abuse or unresolved trauma leads to several conditions known to contribute to aggression—parent-child role reversal, dissociation, and shame. By attending to the characteristics of individuals who have moved beyond their legacy of violence, it is possible to interrupt this cycle of violence.

REFERENCES

Ainsworth, M. D. S., Blehar, M., Waters, E., & Wall, S. (1978). *Patterns of attachment*. Hillsdale, NJ: Erlbaum.

Ainsworth, M. D. S., & Eichberg, C. G. (1991). Effects on infant–mother attachment of mother's unresolved loss of an attachment figure or other traumatic experience. In P. Marris, J. Stevenson-Hinde, & C. Parkes (Eds.), *Attachment across the life cycle* (pp. 160–183). New York: Routledge.

Alexander, P. C. (1990). Interventions with incestuous families. In S. W. Henggeler & C. M. Borduin (Eds.), *Family therapy and beyond* (pp. 324–344). Pacific Grove, CA: Brooks/Cole.

Alexander, P. C. (1992). Application of attachment theory to the study of sexual abuse. *Journal of Consulting and Clincial Psychology*, *60*, 185–195.

Alexander, P. C., & Anderson, C. L. (1994). An attachment approach to psychotherapy with the incest survivor. *Psychotherapy*, *31*, 665–675.

Alexander, P. C., Anderson, C. L., Brand, B., Schaeffer, C. M., Grelling, B. Z., & Kretz, L. (1998). Adult attachment and longterm effects in survivors of incest. *Child Abuse & Neglect*, *22*, 45–81.

Alexander, P. C., & Kretz, L. (2001). *Trauma history and the prediction of child abuse potential*. Unpublished manuscript.

Alexander, P. C., & O'Grady, K. (2001). *Parent–child role reversal: The development of a retrospective scale*. Unpublished manuscript.

Alexander, P. C., Teti, L., & Anderson, C. L. (2000). Child sexual abuse history and role reversal in parenting. *Child Abuse & Neglect*, *24*, 829–838.

Anderson, C., & Alexander, P. C. (1996). The relationship between attachment and dissociation in adult survivors of incest. *Psychiatry*, *59*, 240–254.

Appel, A. E., & Holden, G. W. (1998). The co-occurrence of spouse and physical child abuse: A review and appraisal. *Journal of Family Psychology*, *12*, 578–599.

Bartholomew, K., & Horowitz, L. M. (1991). Attachment styles among young adults: A test of a four-category model. *Journal of Personality and Social Psychology*, *61*, 226–244.

Berman, D., & Ogawa, J. R. (1993, April). *Seeing is believing: Observed trauma as an alternate route to unresolved status in the Adult Attachment Interview.* Poster presented at the meeting of the Society for Research in Child Development, New Orleans, LA.

Bowlby, J. (1969/1982). *Attachment and loss: Vol. 1. Attachment.* New York: Basic Books.

Bowlby, J. (1977). The making and breaking of affectional bonds: Part 1. Aetiology and psychopathology in the light of attachment theory. *British Journal of Psychiatry, 130,* 201–210.

Brown, T. G., Werk, A., Caplan, T., & Seraganian, P. (1999). Violent substance abusers in domestic violence treatment. *Violence and Victims, 14,* 179–190.

Browne, K. O., Saunders, D. G., & Staecker, K. M. (1997). Process-psychodynamic groups for men who batter: A brief treatment model. *Families in Society, 78,* 265–271.

Burkett, L. P. (1991). Parenting behaviors of women who were sexually abused as children in their families of origin. *Family Process, 30,* 421–434.

Carlson, V., Cicchetti, D., Barnett, D., & Braunwald, K. G. (1989). Finding order in disorganization. In D. Cicchetti & V. Carlson (Eds.), *Child maltreatment: Theory and research on the causes and consequences of child abuse and neglect* (pp. 484–528). New York: Cambridge University Press.

Cohn, D. A., Cowan, C. P., Cowan, P. A., & Pearson, J. (1992). Mothers' and fathers' working models of childhood attachment relationships, parenting styles, and child behavior. *Development and Psychopathology, 4,* 417–431.

Cole, P. M., & Woolger, C. (1989). Incest survivors: The relation of their perceptions of their parents and their own parenting attitudes. *Child Abuse & Neglect, 13,* 409–416.

Cole, P. M., Woolger, C., Power, T. G., & Smith, K. D. (1992). Parenting difficulties among adult survivors of father–daughter incest. *Child Abuse & Neglect, 16,* 239–249.

Collins, N. L., & Read, S. J. (1990). Adult attachment, working models, and relationship quality in dating couples. *Journal of Personality and Social Psychology, 58,* 644–663.

Crittenden, P. M. (1992). Quality of attachment in the preschool years. *Development and Psychopathology, 4,* 209–241.

Crittenden, P. M. (1997). Toward an integrative theory of trauma. In D. Cicchetti & S. L. Toth (Eds.), *Developmental perspectives on trauma: Theory, research, and intervention* (pp. 33–84). Rochester, NY: University of Rochester Press.

Crittenden, P. M., Partridge, M. F., & Claussen, A. H. (1991). Family patterns of relationship in normative and dysfunctional families. *Development and Psychopathology, 3,* 491–512.

Dhaliwal, G. K., Gauzas, L., Antonowicz, D. H., & Ross, R. R. (1996). Adult male survivors of childhood sexual abuse: Prevalence, sexual abuse characteristics, and long-term effects. *Clinical Psychology Review, 16,* 619–639.

Dutton, D. G. (1999). Traumatic origins of intimate rage. *Aggression and Violent Behavior, 4,* 431–447.

Dutton, D., Fehr, B., & McEwen, H. (1982). Severe wife battering as deindividuated violence. *Victimology, 7*, 13–23.

Dutton, D. G., van Ginkel, C., & Starzomski, A. (1995). The role of shame and guilt in the intergenerational transmission of abusiveness. *Violence and Victims, 10*, 121–131.

Egeland, B., Jacobvitz, D., & Sroufe, L. A. (1988). Breaking the cycle of abuse. *Child Development, 59*, 1080–1088.

English, D. J., Marshall, D. B., & Orme, M. (1999). Characteristics of repeated referrals to child protective services in Washington State. *Child Maltreatment, 4*, 297–307.

Feeney, J. A., & Noller, P. (1990). Attachment style as a predictor of adult romantic relationships. *Journal of Personality and Social Psychology, 58*, 281-291.

Follette, V. M., Polusny, M. A., Bechtle, A. E., & Naugle, A. E. (1996). Cumulative trauma: The impact of child sexual abuse, adult sexual assault, and spouse abuse. *Journal of Traumatic Stress, 9*, 25–35.

Freedman, J. H. & Combs, G. (2000). Narrative therapy with couples. In L. J. Bevilacqua (Ed.), *Comparative treatments for relationships dysfunction* (pp. 342–361). New York: Springer.

Goldner, V. (1998). The treatment of violence and victimization in intimate relationships. *Family Process, 37*, 263–286.

Goodman, M. S., & Fallon, B. C. (1995). *Pattern changing for abused women: An educational program.* Thousand Oaks, CA: Sage.

Green, R-J., & Werner, P. D. (1996). Intrusiveness and closeness-caregiving: Rethinking the concept of family "enmeshment." *Family Process, 35*, 115–136.

Hazan, C., & Shaver, P. (1987). Romantic love conceptualized as an attachment process. *Journal of Personality and Social Psychology, 52*, 511–524.

Holtzworth-Munroe, A., Stuart, G. L., & Hutchinson, G. (1997). Violent versus nonviolent husbands: Differences in attachment patterns, dependency, and jealousy. *Journal of Family Psychology, 11*, 314–331.

Hunter, R. S., & Kilstrom, N. (1979). Breaking the cycle in abusive families. *American Journal of Psychiatry, 136*, 1320–1322.

Izard, C., & Kobak, R. (1991). Emotion system functioning and emotion regulation. In J. Garber & K. Dodge (Eds.), *The development of affect regulation* (pp. 303–321). Cambridge, England: Cambridge University Press.

Jennings, J. L., & Murphy, C. M. (2000). Male–male dimensions of male–female battering: A new look at domestic violence. *Psychology of Men & Masculinity, 1*, 21–29.

Kaufman, J., & Zigler, E. (1987). Do abused children become abusive parents? *American Journal of Orthopsychiatry, 57*, 186–192.

Kessler, B. L., & Bieschke, K. J. (1999). A retrospective analysis of shame, dissociation, and adult victimization in survivors of childhood sexual abuse. *Journal of Counseling Psychology, 46*, 335–341.

Kirschner, S., Kirschner, D. A., & Rappaport, R. L. (1993). *Working with adult incest survivors.* New York: Brunner/Mazel.

Kobak, R., & Sceery, A. (1988). Attachment in late adolescence: Working models, affect regulation, and representations of self and others. *Child Development, 59,* 396–399.

Landsman, K. J. (1999). Personality, dissociation, and anger in male batterers. Unpublished manuscript.

Liotti, G. (1992). Disorganized/disoriented attachment in the etiology of the dissociative disorders. *Dissociation, 5,* 196–204.

Loos, M. E. (1999). Dissociation and the processing of threat related information: An attachment-theoretical perspective on maintenance factors in dissociative pathology. *Dissertation Abstracts International, 60,* 1306.

Lyons-Ruth, K. (1996). Attachment relationships among children with aggressive behavior problems: The role of disorganized early attachment patterns. *Journal of Consulting and Clinical Psychology, 64,* 64–73.

Lyons-Ruth, K., & Jacobvitz, D. (1999). Attachment disorganization: Unresolved loss, relational violence, and lapses in behavioral and attentional strategies. In J. Cassidy, P. R. & Shaver (Eds.), *Handbook of attachment: Theory, research, and clinical applications* (pp. 520–554). New York: Guilford Press.

Macfie, J., Toth, S. L., Rogosch, F. A., Robinson, J., Emde, R. N., & Cicchetti, D. (1999). Effect of maltreatment on preschoolers' narrative representations of responses to relieve distress and of role reversal. *Developmental Psychology, 35,* 460–465.

Main, M. (1990). Cross-cultural studies of attachment organization: Recent studies, changing methodologies, and the concept of conditional strategies. *Human Development, 33,* 48–61.

Main, M. (1991). Metacognitive knowledge, metacognitive monitoring, and singular (coherent) vs. multiple (incoherent) models of attachment. In C. M. Parkes, J. Stevenson-Hinde, & P. Marris (Eds.), *Attachment across the life-cycle* (pp. 127–159). London: Routledge.

Main, M., & Cassidy, J. (1988). Categories of response to reunion with the parent at age 6: Predictable from infant attachment classifications and stable over a 1-month period. *Developmental Psychology, 24,* 415–426.

Main, M., & Goldwyn, R. (1984). Predicting rejection of her infant from mother's representation of her own experience: Implications for the abused–abusing intergenerational cycle. *Child Abuse & Neglect, 8,* 203–217.

Main, M., & Hesse, E. (1990). Parents' unresolved traumatic experiences are related to infant disorganized attachment status: Is frightened and/or frightening parental behavior the linking mechanism? In M. T. Greenberg, D. Cicchetti, & E. M. Cummings (Eds.), *Attachment in the preschool years* (pp. 161–182). Chicago: University of Chicago Press.

Main, M., & Hesse, E. (1992). Disorganized/disoriented infant behavior in the Strange Situation, lapses in the monitoring of reasoning and discourse during the parent's Adult Attachment Interview, and dissociative states. In M. Ammaniti & D. Stern (Eds.), *Attachment and psychoanalysis.* Rome: Gius, Laterza and Figli.

Main, M., & Solomon, J. (1986). Discovery of a new, insecure-disorganized/disoriented attachment pattern. In T. B. Brazelton & M. W. Yogman (Eds.), *Affective development in infancy* (pp. 95–124). Norwood, NJ: Ablex.

Main, M., & Solomon, J. (1990). Procedures for identifying infants as disorganized/disoriented during the Ainsworth Strange Situation. In M. T. Greenberg, D. Cicchetti, & E. M. Cummings (Eds.), *Attachment in the preschool years* (pp. 121–160). Chicago: University of Chicago Press.

Marvin, R. S., & Stewart, R. B. (1990). A family systems framework for the study of attachment. In M. T. Greenberg, D. Cicchetti, & E. M. Cummings (Eds.), *Attachment in the preschool years* (pp. 51–86). Chicago: University of Chicago Press.

Mikulincer, M., Florian, V., & Tolmacz, R. (1990). Attachment styles and fear of personal death: A case study of affect regulation. *Journal of Personality and Social Psychology, 58,* 273-280.

Ogawa, J. R., Sroufe, L. A., Weinfield, N. A., Carlson, E. A., & Egeland, B. (1997). Development and the fragmented self: Longitudinal study of dissociative symptomatology in a nonclinical sample. *Development and Psychopathology, 9,* 855–879.

Oldershaw, L., Walters, G. C., & Hall, D. K. (1986). Control strategies and noncompliance in abusive mother–child dyads: An observational study. *Child Development, 57,* 722–732.

Oliver, J. E. (1993). Intergenerational transmission of child abuse: Rates, research, and clinical implications. *American Journal of Psychiatry, 150,* 1315–1324.

Putnam, F. W., Carlson, E. B., Ross, C. A., Anderson, G., Clark, P., Torem, M., Bowman, E. S., Coons, P. M., Chu, J. A., Dill, D. L., Loewenstein, R. J., & Braun, B. G. (1996). Patterns of dissociation in clinical and nonclinical samples. *Journal of Nervous and Mental Disease, 184,* 673–679.

Schaefer, E. S., & Bell, R. Q. (1958). Development of a parental attitude research instrument. *Child Development, 29,* 339–361.

Simmons, K. P., Sack, T., & Miller, G. (1996). Sexual abuse and chemical dependency: Implications for women in recovery. *Women & Therapy, 19,* 17–30.

Simoneti, S., Scott, E. C., & Murphy, C. M. (2000). Dissociative experiences in partner assaultive men. *Journal of Interpersonal Violence, 15,* 1262–1283.

Sroufe, L. A., Jacobvitz, D., Mangelsdorf, S., DeAngelo, E., & Ward, M. J. (1985). Generational boundary dissolution between mothers and their preschool children: A relationships systems approach. *Child Development, 56,* 317–325.

van Ijzendoorn, M., Schuengel, C., & Bakermans-Kranenburg, M. J. (1999). Disorganized attachment in early childhood: Meta-analysis of precursors, concomitants, and sequelae. *Development and Psychopathology, 11,* 225–249.

Weiss, R. S. (1991). The attachment bond in childhood and adulthood. In C. M. Parkes, J. Stevenson-Hinde, & P. Marris (Eds.), *Attachment across the life cycle* (pp. 66–76). New York: Tavistock/Routledge.

Zeanah, C. H., & Zeanah, P. D. (1989). Intergenerational transmission of maltreatment: Insights from attachment theory and research. *Psychiatry, 52,* 177–196.

Index

259